OFF THE BEATEN PATH™ SERIES

Wyoming

SECOND EDITION

Off the Beaten Path™

by Michael McCoy

The Globe Pequot Press

Old Saybrook, Connecticut

Cover and text design by Laura Augustine
Maps created by Equator Graphics © The Globe Pequot Press
Cover photo by Index Stock
Illustrations by Carole Drong

Library of Congress Cataloging-in-Publication Data
McCoy, Michael, 1951–
      Wyoming : off the beaten path / Michael McCoy ;
[illustrations by Carole Drong]. — 2nd ed.
    p. cm. —(Off the beaten path series)
    ISBN 0-7627-0425-X
    1. Wyoming—Guidebooks. I. Title. II. Series.
    F759.3.M37   1999
    917.8704´33—dc21   98-51174
                                                   CIP

Manufactured in the United States of America
Second Edition/First Printing

To Wyoming, "the way the West was ..."

Contents

Wyoming Brands

Introduction

The orginal edition of *Wyoming: Off the Beaten Path* was written by another team of authors, but when the offer to update the book came my way, I jumped at it. Wyoming, you see, is in my blood.

I was raised in Iowa where I always felt special because I was born in Wyoming. Among the wannabe cowpokes in my neighborhood—which included just about every boy under the age of eleven—saying you were from Wyoming was rather like saying Roy Rogers was your uncle. Don't ask me how or why, but for a while there, when I was three or four, I even believed I was the cowboy gracing the Wyoming license plate. Today, although my mailing address reads "Idaho," the first thing I see every morning when looking out my east-facing windows is the Wyoming Tetons.

My time actually residing in Wyoming doesn't add up to much—a grand total of six or seven years—but I've worked and/or lived in virtually every corner of the state. I was born in Wheatland, I graduated from the university in Laramie, and I got married in Grand Teton National Park. I've spent time as a National Park Ranger at Devils Tower, cooked shrimp and steaks at Grand Targhee Ski Resort, and worked archaeological projects out of Rock Springs, Worland, Rawlins, Casper, and other towns. I've hiked, bicycled, and/or cross-country skied in Yellowstone, the Great Divide Basin, the Wind Rivers, the Tetons, the Absarokas, the Wyoming and Salt River Ranges, the Medicine Bows, the Laramie Range, the Big Horns, the Gros Ventres, the Black Hills, and lesser known ranges like the Owl Creek and Green Mountains and the Rattlesnake Range. I've played pool or horseshoes and drunk beer with cowboys in places you've heard of and others you probably haven't, including lone-pony towns like Hyattville, Jeffrey City, Woods Landing, Hulett, Bondurant, Savery, and Manderson.

If I've learned one thing about Wyoming during my ramblings, it is this: The state-line greeting signs aren't stretching the truth when they tell you it's LIKE NO PLACE ON EARTH. Thanks to the sparsity of vegetation covering much of the state, passersby actually have opportunities to study the earth instead of a bunch of grass and trees. Wyoming reveals more about its inner self than just about any state of the Union, which explains why in the Tetons, the Big Horns, Wind River Canyon, and other locations you'll see camps and busses teeming with geology students from colleges throughout the United States. The long list of critters you can see afoot and on wing in Yellowstone and other parts of

Wyoming makes the state one of the great wildlife viewing areas of the world. Then there's the sky: endless, and unfathomly blue. Even the mindset of Wyoming's human residents is different. Difficult as it is to believe in this era of contracts, litigation, scams, and red tape, in Wyoming there really are folks who still seal business deals with a handshake. Those involved know—corny as it may sound—that a promise from a fellow honest man or woman is worth more than a bunch of words on a piece of paper, any day.

Wyomingites tend to be plainspoken, straightforward, and politically conservative, yet the first-time visitor might find the populace more complicated than expected. You might meet a rancher who adamantly opposes wolf reintroduction and despises grizzly bears, yet who has chosen to preserve his ranch lands in perpetuity under a conservation easement. He loves and respects that land more than anyone can understand, and he doesn't want subdivisions made of it; the man is a conservationist to his very soul. You may meet a one-time confirmed vegetarian from New York who now religiously hunts elk come fall because in Wyoming, living with nature is a fact of life and not something experienced only on television. He's learned that few food items in this world are tastier and less tainted than wild elk meat. You might participate in a whitewater float trip guided by a California-trained lawyer who, after a summer spent in the Tetons, couldn't bear the thought of returning to the bar and the smog, discovering instead that she prefers the outdoors, the oars, and the crisp high-country air.

Today's traveler can still capture a sense of the hardy individualism and its bipolar companion, spirit of community, which hand in hand built the West as we know it. In Wyoming you can ferret out and follow historic trails penetrating a countryside little changed in the last 150 years: the Oregon-Mormon, California, Bridger, Bozeman, Nez Perce, and Pony Express Trails, for starters. These pioneer Wyoming paths, some of which hosted tens of thousands of travelers in the 1800s, have largely reverted to "unbeaten" status, and by following them you will experience a wild sort of country visited by few pilgrims today.

Wyoming by its very nature is off the beaten path. That's obvious. Therefore, many of the attractions featured in this guide are *really* off the beaten path. Be aware when traveling through broad-shouldered Wyoming that services are often few and far between. Prepare accordingly, by always carrying plenty of food and water; by going equipped for minor emergencies, such as a flat tire, so that they don't become major problems; and by always topping off your gas tank before leaving a town for the wide-open spaces. Know, too, that the weather is unpredictable; it can be fierce in a dozen different ways and can change in less than a moment's notice. The climate can be extremely pleasant, too, but take precautions even then: Because of the intense, high-elevation sunshine, you should always apply a high-SPF sunscreen to your exposed skin and wear a hat and sunglasses to protect your head and eyes.

The Wyoming Division of Tourism has done a logical job of dividing the state into six travel regions, three of which I've borrowed for use in this book: Medicine Bow–Flaming Gorge Country (southern Wyoming), Devils Tower–Buffalo Bill Country (northern Wyoming), and Oregon Trail–Rendezvous Country (central Wyoming). The other three Division of Tourism regions—Jackson Hole–Jim Bridger Country, Grand Teton Country, and Yellowstone Country—I've combined into one region called Bridger-Yellowstone Country, which comprises most of western Wyoming.

After experiencing the grandeur and emptiness of Wyoming's landscapes and the forthright qualities of her people, don't be surprised to find yourself a little bit changed on returning home. And please, don't resist it: This old world would be a lot better off if everyone added even just a small piece of Wyoming to their character.

Wyoming at a Glance

Wyoming: Cowboy State, Equality State

Capital: Cheyenne

Motto: Equal Rights

Highest Elevation: 13,804' (Gannett Peak, Wind River Range)

Lowest Elevation: 3,125' (where the Belle Fourche River flows into South Dakota)

Land Area: 97,914 square miles (ranked 9th in U.S.)

Population: 453,588 (ranked 50th in U.S.)

Statehood: July 10, 1890 (44th state)

State Bird: Meadowlark

State Flower: Indian paintbrush

State Tree: Plains Cottonwood

State Mammal: Bison

INTRODUCTION

State Gemstone: Jade

State Fish: Cutthroat trout

State Reptile: Horned toad

State Dinosaur: Triceratops

Average Annual Precipitation: 14.5 inches

A Sampling of Radio Stations: Casper: KTWO-AM, 1030 kHz (the Voice of Wyoming); Cheyenne: KFBC-AM, 1240 kHz; Cody: KODI-AM, 1400 kHz; Evanston: KEVA-AM, 1240 kHz; Gillette: KIML-AM, 1270 kHz; Green River: KUGR-AM, 1490 kHz; Jackson: KMTN-FM, 96.9 MHz; Kemmerer: KMER-AM, 950 kHz; Laramie: KUWR-FM, 91.9 MHz (National Public Radio, available throughout the state); Rawlins: KRAL-AM, 1240 kHz; Riverton: KVOW-AM, 1450 kHz; Rock Springs: KRKK-AM, 1360 kHz; Sheridan: KWYO-AM, 1410 kHz; Worland: KWOR-AM, 1340 kHz

Major Newspapers: *Casper Star Tribune, Daily Boomerang* (Laramie), *Jackson Hole News, Northern Wyoming Daily News* (Worland), *Rocket-Miner* (Rock Springs), *Sheridan Press, Wyoming Tribune-Eagle* (Cheyenne)

Travel Information: The Wyoming Vacation Guide and the Wyoming Vacation Planner are both available through the Wyoming Division of Tourism, (307) 777–7777. On the Internet, information can be found at http://commerce.state.wy.us/west.

The area code for the state of Wyoming is 307.

The prices and rates listed in this guidebook were confirmed at press time. We recommend, however, that you call establishments before traveling to obtain current information.

Southern Wyoming: Medicine Bow— Flaming Gorge Country

S outhern Wyoming is the region responsible for the state's reputation as a windblown, God-forsaken desert. Even here, however,
impressive mountains occasionally jut out of the drylands, offering surprisingly verdant, protected havens, teeming with wildlife and forests of
aspen and pine. And the deserts themselves hold a host of surprises
that will delight those intrepid souls willing to spend the time and
effort required to earn a closer look.

Your journey begins in the southeastern corner of Big, Wonderful
Wyoming, then leads along the I–80 corridor, with plenty of side trips
taking you off that major thoroughfare. As you cross the state from east
to west, you'll visit cities and settlements with names and appearances
that bring to mind the Wild West: places like Cheyenne and Laramie,
Rock River and Medicine Bow, Green River City and Fort Bridger.
Finally, at Evanston, near the Utah border, you'll turn north to continue
on to Bridger-Yellowstone Country.

Laramie County

E ntering southeast Wyoming from the east, you'll intersect prehistoric Native American trails and newer trails, too, such as the
nineteenth-century Texas Cattle Trail. Consider forsaking I–80 and
crossing the Nebraska-Wyoming border on Highway 30, the old Lincoln
Highway (it's located just north of I–80). An abandoned wooden service station, like a symbol of the forgotten old highway itself, with

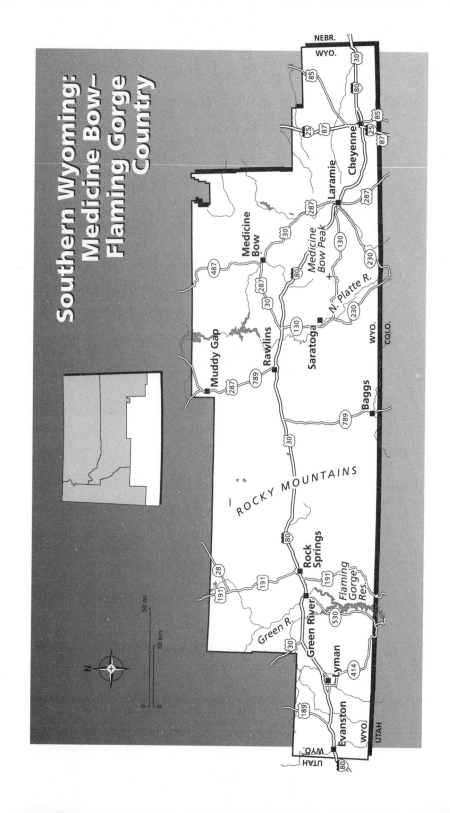

BEST ANNUAL EVENTS IN MEDICINE
BOW—FLAMING GORGE COUNTRY

"neb/wyo" painted in the middle of the dilapidated structure, will greet you.

The area around the border town of Pine Bluffs served as a crossroads for prehistoric peoples, pioneer sodbusters, and cattle drovers early on the scene. The nearby pine hills provided the Native American inhabitants excellent campsites with plentiful water, firewood, and small game. More than six hundred thousand cattle were driven through the Pine Bluffs crossroads area during the heyday of the Texas Cattle Trail in 1871, and the Pine Bluffs rail station served as an important cattle-shipping center for many years. The *Texas Trail Museum* (housed in Pine Bluffs' original 1915 power plant) at Third and Market Streets illustrates the important role played by the town in the development of the West, with its numerous displays on the area's cattle ranches and homesteads, early firefighting techniques, cowgirls of the West, Native American cultures, and the Lincoln Highway. The museum is located in the *Texas Trail Park,* where you can investigate a caboose, railroad boardinghouse, blacksmith shop, homesteader's log cabin, bunkhouse, and the first schoolhouse in Laramie County. The Texas Trail Park and Texas Trail Museum are open from 9:00 A.M. to 5:00 P.M., Monday through Saturday (closed Sunday) from Memorial Day through Labor Day, or by appointment. Call 245–3713 for information.

The *High Plains Archaeology Labs,* 217 West Third Street, and the nearby excavation sites are open to visitors during summer months. The archaeological dig is being conducted by the University of Wyoming. Crews of students under the direction of Charles Rehrer have uncovered nomadic Native American artifacts dating back nearly ten thousand years, some of which are on display at the archaeology labs. The dig site, a short walk away from the labs, is situated west of the Pine Bluffs rest area south of I–80, where you'll also find a tourist information center and a grouping of painted tipis and ancient tipi rings. Check at the archaeology labs for directions

*Desert Dust Winter
Stampede Rodeo,*
Rock Springs; February;
(307) 326–3771

*Sierra Madre Winter
Carnival,* Encampment;
February; (307) 327–5308

*Donald E. Erickson
Memorial Cutter Races and
Saratoga Draft Horse Pull,*
Saratoga; February;
(307) 326–8855

Medicine Bow Days,
Medicine Bow; June;
(307) 379–2571

*Woodchoppers Jamboree
and Rodeo,*
Saratoga/Encampment;
June; (307) 326–8855

*Stock Car Races and
Fireworks,* Rock Springs;
Fourth of July;
(307) 362–3771

Annual Fiesta Days,
Rawlins; July;
(800) 228–3547

Cheyenne Frontier Days,
Cheyenne; July;
(307) 778–7200

*Annual Cow Plop
and Steak Fry,* Rawlins;
August; (800) 228–3547

*Hams Fork River
Rendezvous,* Green River;
August; (307) 872–0511

and dig site access. For further information call the Pine Bluffs Chamber of Commerce at 245–3695.

The on-site tipis are painstakingly researched re-creations painted with the symbols and colors that were commonly employed by the Sioux Nation. Although many symbols were shared by the various tribes, the interpretations of some colors and symbols differed from tribe to tribe. Paints created from animals, minerals, and plants, were applied to a damp hide. After the hide dried, the coloring became permanent and was protected with a "varnish" made of the juice of the prickly pear cactus. Tools employed for painting included bones, yucca-plant spears, and willow branches.

Take time to enjoy a trail walk around the archaeological dig and rest area with the aid of a guidebook (available at the visitor center). Interpretive trail signs point out wildlife habitat areas, bird sites, and native grasses and other vegetation found in the *Pine Bluffs Nature Area.*

If you're in the area during the first weekend of August, check out the *Texas Trail Days,* replete with wagon trains, cowboy poetry readings, melodramas, parade, rodeo, street dance, and Western "bar-b-ques." For information call the Pine Bluffs Area Chamber of Commerce at 245–3695. Alternatively, on any Friday evening from early June through mid-August, you can take in the Summer Rodeo Series (632–3626),

The Lincoln Highway

*T*he idea for the Lincoln Highway originated at a dinner meeting of automobile industry tycoons in Indianapolis in 1912. At the time, the nation's two million miles of roads were largely unconnected, and railroads represented the only practical means of coast-to-coast travel. Within three years of the meeting, a patchwork made from existing roads wound its way across the country from Times Square in New York City to Lincoln Park in San Francisco, creating the first transcontinental highway. Wyoming residents lit bonfires along the route across the state on November 13, 1913, to signal the opening of the new Lincoln Highway.

Later improvements made the Lincoln Highway one of the premier roads of its day. The federal government took over the road system in the late 1920s; to mark the event, on September 1, 1928, the Boy Scouts of America installed more than three thousand Lincoln Highway markers along the route.

For the most part the Lincoln Highway ran parallel to the Union Pacific Railroad, which preceded the highway west. Today, fiber-optic cables transport modern-day telecommunications along this historic travel corridor.

with its full slate of bull riding, barrel racing, team roping, bareback riding, and more.

Forty-five miles west of Pine Bluffs, after passing through high plains that roll away in every direction from I-80, you will arrive at the capital city of Cheyenne and catch your first glimpse of the Rocky Mountains rising from the plains to the west. Cheyenne derives its name from the *Shey'an'-nah*, an Algonquin Indian tribe. The city's wild early days began with the arrival of the Union Pacific Railroad and the establishment of Fort D. A. Russell (now F. E. Warren Air Force Base), built for the protection of the railroaders in 1867. Maj. Gen. Grenville M. Dodge, a Union Pacific surveyor, plotted the city as a major rail terminus situated just east of the long pull over the Laramie Range.

In addition to the railroaders, early residents included mule skinners, soldiers, rustlers, stage-coach hands, outlaws, and other opportunists. The railhead made Cheyenne a natural base for numerous cattle barons, who established the elaborate Cheyenne Club, where they conducted cattle business and hosted lavish parties. A marker for the Cheyenne Club stands at the corner of Warren Avenue and Seventeenth Street.

BEST ATTRACTIONS IN MEDICINE BOW—FLAMING GORGE COUNTRY
(ALL AREA CODES 307)

Cheyenne Botanic Gardens,
Cheyenne; 637–6458

Vedauwoo,
outside Laramie; 745–8971

Snowy Range Scenic Byway,
outside Laramie; 745–8971

The Old Corral,
Centennial; 745–5918

Hobo Pool,
Saratoga; 326–8855

Rose's Lariat;
Rawlins; 324–5251

Aspen Alley,
south of Rawlins; 745–8971

Savery Museum, Savery;
383–7262

Natural History Museum at WWCC,
Rock Springs; 382–1666

Flaming Gorge National Recreation Area, south of
Green River; 875–2871

In the late 1800s, Cheyenne also became an important center for outfitting miners headed to the goldfields of the Black Hills, and a stagecoach line soon ran between the two areas. The Cheyenne–Fort Laramie–Deadwood Trail started at the corner of Capital Avenue and Sixteenth Street and ended in Deadwood, South Dakota. A trail marker can be visited at the corner of Capital Avenue and Twenty-second Street.

There's plenty to see and do around Cheyenne. The city is home to the rodeo known as the "Daddy of 'em All," *Cheyenne Frontier Days.* Although the majority of visitors flock in to see the world's oldest and largest outdoor rodeo—and you should too if it fits your schedule—be sure also to visit the excellent *Cheyenne Frontier Days Old West Museum,* located in Frontier Park at 4501 North Carey Avenue.

This fine museum is a must stop for those interested in capturing the essence of the Old West. An extensive collection of horse-drawn vehicles includes stagecoaches, a hearse, and a range chuck wagon. Native

American clothing, rodeo memorabilia dating back to the first Cheyenne rodeo in 1897, a rustic saloon, a Union Pacific exhibit, exhibits on Cheyenne history, and a wonderful collection of Western art make up additional displays. Among other tidbits, you'll learn about Will Pickett, the African-American cowboy who invented bulldogging by throwing a steer using only his teeth. In summer the museum is open weekdays from 9:00 A.M. to 5:00 P.M., and weekends from 10:00 A.M. to 5:00 P.M. During the winter, hours are 10:00 A.M. to 5:00 P.M. daily. Call 778–7290 for additional information.

Another fun diversion that's part of Cheyenne Frontier Days is **The Indian Village,** located near the entrance to Frontier Park at Eighth Street and Carey Avenue. Award-winning Native American dancers from tribes across the nation convene here to give free dance performances several times daily during week's celebration. Also, authentic Native American jewelry, clothing, and other items are available for sale. Frontier Days runs in late July for ten days. For information call (800) 227–6336 or visit the Web site: www.cfdrodeo.com.

Nearby the **Cheyenne Botanic Gardens** offer a pleasant contrast to the loud, dusty grounds of Frontier Park. Sit outside among the flowers, take a stroll along the garden pathways, or investigate the exotic plants in the 6,800-square-foot, three-sectioned greenhouse conservatory, which constitutes one of the West's most unusual solar energy demonstrations. See, smell, and touch; the inviting oasis is truly a feast of the senses—particularly during the often bleak windiness of a Wyoming

High-Tech Scratching Post

"*T*he first issue of N. A. Baker's Daily Leader *appeared [in Cheyenne] on September 16, 1867, and on October 25 the telegraph line came in from Laporte, Colorado. Difficulties encountered by the telegraph line crews have a place in Wyoming folklore. Indolent buffalo still roamed the treeless prairie between Omaha and the Laramie Mountains in great herds. They regarded the newly set poles as scratching posts, and several bison could rub a pole out of the ground in a few hours. The line boss decided to* spike the poles, points out, to discourage them. This, from the buffalo's point of view, added greatly to their value. Within a few hours, according to the legend, a waiting line of 30 buffalo had formed at every telegraph pole between Cheyenne and Omaha. And when a lone bison lumbered east from Cheyenne, oldsters allowed he had heard of a vacant pole 'somewhere this side of Omaha'." *(From* Wyoming: A Guide to Its Highways, History, and People, *published as part of the Federal Writers' Project in 1941.)*

winter. Not simply for show, the botanic garden offers social services, education, and therapy to seniors, youths at risk, and handicapped individuals, and also grows food the year around for distribution to gardens' volunteers and for low-income programs. The Cheyenne Botanic Gardens are located at 710 South Lions Park Drive. Hours are Monday through Friday from 8:00 A.M. to 4:30 P.M., and Saturday, Sunday, and holidays from 11:00 A.M. to 3:30 P.M. Admission is free, but donations are welcome. The phone number is 637–6458, and the E-mail address is botanicgardens@compuserve.com.

For such a sparsely populated state, Wyoming showcases a surprisingly grand *state capitol*. Its twenty-four-carat gold-leaf dome commands the skyline from all entrances to the city. Built from 1886 to 1890, the capitol features Corinthian columns and sandstone quarried at Rawlins and in Colorado. A statue commemorating Esther Hobart Morris, America's first woman justice of the peace, graces the entrance to the capitol. (A replica of the statue is also located in Statuary Hall in the U.S. Capitol in Washington, D.C.)

Wyoming has been designated the Equality State. Its first territorial legislature granted women the right to vote in 1869, and later the legislature required that women be allowed to vote in Wyoming as a condition of Wyoming's entrance into the Union in 1890. (The Nineteenth Amendment to the Constitution, giving all women citizens of the United States the right to vote, would not be passed for another twenty-nine years.) Wyoming also swore in the country's first all-female jury and elected the first female governor, Nellie Tayloe Ross, in a 1924 special election held to replace her husband, Governor William B. Ross, who had died in office. In 1933 Franklin D. Roosevelt appointed Nellie Tayloe Ross director of the U.S. Mint, a post she held until her retirement in 1953.

The Spirit of Wyoming, a bronze statue on the plaza between the capitol and the Herschler Building, stands over 18 feet high and depicts a cowboy and his horse seemingly at odds with the elements. The statue is the work of international award-winning sculptor Edward J. Fraughton.

Inside, note the eight large murals in the Senate and House of Representatives chambers. Illustrating early Wyoming life, they're titled *Chief Cheyenne, Frontier Cavalry Officers, Pony Express Rider, Railroad/Builders/Surveyors, Cattlemen, Trappers, Homesteaders,* and *Stagecoach.* The ceilings of both chambers are inlaid with striking Tiffany stained glass, crafted with the Wyoming state seal as the focal point. From there proceed to Room 302 where a 1982 mural, *Wyoming: the*

Land, the People, by Mike Kopriva depicts Wyoming's past and present culture and lifestyles. Before exiting the capitol, have a look at the mounted elk and bison to get an up-close perspective of the size of some of Wyoming's common wildlife. The capitol is open to the public Monday through Friday from 8:00 A.M. to 5:00 P.M. It is closed on weekends. Tours are available year-round. For information on access and in-session activities, call 777–7220. The capitol is located on Capitol Avenue and Twenty-second Street.

Now that you've seen where the legislature works, take a short walk over to the 1904 *Historic Governors' Mansion* at 300 East Twenty-first Street. The mansion housed nineteen Wyoming "first families" until being replaced by a new residence in 1976. Designed by an Omaha architect, Charles Mudrock, the building features Colonial Revival architecture, with a portico supported by four Corinthian columns flanking the main entrance. A tour video is available for viewing. The Historic Governors' Mansion is open year-round Tuesday through Saturday from 9:00 A.M. to 5:00 P.M., but it is closed at the noon hour during the winter months. Call 777–7878 for more information.

The *Wyoming State Museum,* which celebrated its centennial in 1995, houses major collections covering territorial days, Wyoming's first families, Native Americans, Western art, Hollywood Westerns featuring movie star Tim McCoy (once an adjutant general of the Wyoming National Guard), and Wyoming fossils and petroglyphs. One of the museum's treasures is the Historic Photographic Collection, comprising some 250,000 images dating back to the 1860s, from such legendary photographers as Joseph E. Stimson and W. H. Jackson. Photo subjects range from cattle brands to stagecoach robberies and from the Teapot Dome to Yellowstone National Park. The Wyoming State Museum is open Monday through Friday from 8:30 A.M. to 5:00 P.M. Saturday and Sunday hours vary with the season. For more information call 777–7022; E-mail: jallis@missc.state.wy.us.

A visit to Cheyenne would not be complete without a trip to *Lakeview Cemetery,* in operation for more than 115 years. Among the more interesting and unusual fatalities recorded in cemetery records are an 1887 death attributed to drinking ice water, an 1892 execution of a seventeen-year-old, and a 1902 death from flypaper poisoning. More common were deaths caused by railroad-related accidents, shootings, and flu epidemics. The first documented hanging by a mob occurred in 1883, the first streetcar death in 1903, the first automobile death in 1915, and the first airplane death in 1923. Wander among the tombstones to discover your own historical oddities. Lakeview Cemetery is an operational cemetery, so take care not interfere with funeral services. It is located at 2501 Seymour Avenue. The cemetery gates are always open, but the office is only open Monday through Friday from 8:00 A.M. to 5:00 P.M.

If you're a fan of unique architecture, take the *Historic Downtown Walking Tour,* featured on the city map available at the visitor's bureau (778–3133). Three popular favorites are the 1886 Union Pacific Depot, the Tivoli Building, and the Dineen automobile dealership, with its imposing lions hanging out near the roof. Cheyenne also boasts several wonderful art galleries and western clothing stores, which you'll pass on the walking tour.

By now the digestive juices should be flowing. You can't beat the *Cheyenne Cattle Company* for substantial evening fare, steaks, seafood, and other favorites. The Cheyenne Cattle Company, located at 1700 West Lincolnway, opens for evening meals at 5:30 P.M. Food prices are moderate to expensive. Call 638–3301 for further information.

The *Terry Bison Ranch* was formerly the southern headquarters of the huge land holdings of Wyoming's first governor, F. E. Warren. Presidents, generals, and senators found it a pleasant retreat. Earlier visitors to Warren's Terry Ranch included President Theodore Roosevelt and Gen. John "Blackjack" Pershing. Today you can bunk in a log cabin or

Tom Horn

Tom Horn, one of the last of his ultraindependent breed, was a free agent hired gun, a man who would do just about anything to earn his keep. Among other things, he was a highly skilled stock detective, working for the Wyoming Stock Growers Association. Raised by Apache Indians for part of his youth, Horn later served as an Indian scout, did a stint with Teddy Roosevelt's Rough Riders in the Spanish-American War, and worked for the Pinkerton Agency as an investigator. He was also a murderer . . . or was he?

After being found guilty of killing fourteen-year-old Willie Nickell,

Horn was hanged in Cheyenne on November 20, 1903. The debate regarding whether or not he was guilty of murder, however, continues to this day. A lot of folks believe that Nickell was actually shot and killed by a feuding neighbor, when he mistook young Nickell for his father. The pro-Horn faction maintains that Tom Horn never was the blood-thirsty murderer he was made out to be.

At a recent reenactment of Horn's trial in Cheyenne, using evidence that has surfaced since his execution, he was found not guilty of murder. And still, the debate continues.

park your RV and enjoy the summer Hell on Wheels rodeo action, chuck wagon dinners, horseback riding, fishing on a private lake, and motorized tours to view a bison herd of roughly two thousand head roaming thirty thousand acres—all within minutes of downtown Cheyenne. The Terry Bison Trailblazers croon the cowboy classics like "Cool Water" and "Red River Valley" as you dig into your fixins. Other facilities on the Terry Bison Ranch include the Senator's Steakhouse and Brass Buffalo Saloon and Terry Ranch Cellars, Wyoming's first winery. Take the Terry Ranch exit off I–25, 7 miles south of Cheyenne, and follow the signs. The season runs from Memorial Day to Labor Day, but the cabins and RV facilities are available year-round. The rodeo entrance fee is $8.00 for adults and $4.00 for children under twelve, and cabins rent in the $50 to $80 range, depending on the season. Food prices are moderate. For more information call 634–4171.

Another diversion in Cheyenne are guided tours of *F. E. Warren Air Force Base,* conducted by appointment.(You can make one by calling 773–3381.) To get there, at the west end of town take Randall Avenue to the F. E. Warren Air Force Base main entrance. The tour includes an excellent museum depicting the fort's early military history. Many of the older buildings, some dating back to 1885, are constructed in the Colonial style, red brick and imposing white columns. Also of interest is the new Archaeology Interpretive Center, which showcases Native American artifacts uncovered by the base's excavation program.

Originally a cavalry outpost, the base now commands some two hundred of the Strategic Air Command's Minute Man III intercontinental ballistic missiles over a three-state area. In 1930 President Hoover renamed Fort Russell in honor of Francis Emory Warren, Wyoming's first governor and a U.S. senator for thirty-seven years. Warren came to Wyoming in 1868 at age twenty-three, taking a job with A. R. Converse, owner of a mercantile store. The two became partners in the mercantile business and later in livestock operations. The Warren Mercantile Company grew into the largest supplier of furniture and hardware in Wyoming, and Warren's livestock holdings grew to three thousand cattle and more than sixty thousand sheep. By 1909 Warren was the richest person in Wyoming.

During Frontier Days, the base hosts Fort D. A. Russell Days, with a milk-can dinner (a meal usually consisting of sausage, potatoes, and corn) followed by a dance where you may—if you are able—do the Virginia reel under lantern light. Tickets are a modest $11 for a night of great fun. Guests are asked to come attired in Victorian period costumes or Western wear. Other activities include artillery demonstrations and infantry and cavalry horse drills of the 1800s.

For a delightful and nostalgic night's rest, step back in time and check in to the historically renovated **Rainsford Inn Bed and Breakfast,** listed on the National Register of Historic Places as part of the Rainsford Historic District. George D. Rainsford was a rancher who came to Wyoming in the late 1870s. One of the building's former owners was Willis Van De Vanter, the only Wyoming judge to sit on the U.S. Supreme Court. Your host today, Nancy Drege, purchased the property in 1991 and received a Certified Historic Restoration Award in 1992.

Many antiques, heirlooms, and works of local artists await your browsing. You have your choice of five spacious suites, one of which is handicapped accessible and four of which boast whirlpool tubs. The School Room reflects Nancy's earlier career, while the Cattle Baron Room features a Western flavor. For intimate occasions, it's hard to beat the Moonlight and Roses Room.

In the morning you have your choice of several delectable breakfasts. Rooms are between $61 and $95. There is a 10 percent discount for seniors, military personnel, AAA members, and business guests. The Rainsford Inn is located at 219 East Eighteenth Street. For reservations call 638–BEDS or E-mail: tobeds@aol.com.

> ## Southern Wyoming Trivia
>
> *The Great Divide Basin, an eastern extension of the Red Desert, is an immense and dry piece of Wyoming real estate approximately 50 by 100 miles in size. Water falling or melting there drains neither west to the Pacific nor east to the Atlantic; rather, it drains inward, to eventually soak into the ground or evaporate.*

From Cheyenne take Missile Drive to **Happy Jack Road** (Highway 210) headed west. This scenic back road to Laramie rises from Cheyenne's elevation of 6,062 feet to over 8,640 feet, before beginning the descent into Laramie. The terrain changes dramatically as rolling grasslands give way to the craggy outcroppings of the Laramie Range foothills, and the scent of pine supplants the smell of grass and sage. Keep alert for antelope, coyotes, deer, elk, and other critters.

Happy Jack Road derives its name from Happy Jack Hollinsworth, who started ranching in the foothills of the Laramie Range in 1884. Hollinsworth was always singing and whistling while working his ranch and hauling wood for sale in Cheyenne.

Twenty-six miles out of Cheyenne you'll come upon the entrance to 1,645-acre **Curt Gowdy State Park,** a great spot for camping, hiking, and fishing. The park encompasses Crystal and Granite Reservoirs, the water supply for Cheyenne. There's a $2.00 day-use fee per vehicle ($3.00 for out-of-state vehicles), or you can secure a campsite for $4.00

per night. The park is named after native son and world-renowned sportscaster Curt Gowdy. Long before radio and television and football, however, the area was a favorite campground for Native Americans, including the Comanche, Crow, Shoshone, Cheyenne, Arapahoe, and Sioux. Towering rock formations provide a beautiful backdrop for a relaxing stay.

Across Happy Jack Road to the north and less than a mile west is **Hynds Lodge,** built by Cheyenne business executive and philanthropist Harry P. Hynds and donated to the Boy Scouts of America. The building is open to groups large and small from June 1 through October 1 on a reservation-only basis. (The reservations office is open beginning the first work day of January, from 8:30 A.M. to 3:30 P.M.) The lodge includes sleeping accommodations for thirty; a large kitchen complete with appliances, pots and pans, and dishes; a dining area; and recreational facilities. Within walking distance, an amphitheater set amid a backdrop of gigantic boulders and rock formations hosts the **Happy Jack Mountain Music Festival** in June each year. For information on Hynds Lodge and the festival, call Curt Gowdy State Park headquarters at 632–7946.

You may want to stay and poke around this uncommonly beautiful area for a day or two. If you prefer relaxing in style to roughing it, for an outstanding base of operations check into **A. Drummond's Ranch Bed and Breakfast.** Your host is guaranteed to make memories. Meals are a celebration of living art, with fresh herbs garnishing delicious homemade food, served on china with fresh linen and pearl-handled silverware. The living room invites you to gaze at breathtaking mountain scenery and the enterprise's gardens of perennial flowers.

In the rooms terry-cloth robes await your use, as do Jacuzzi tubs adjacent to two of the four guest rooms. The Carriage House loft provides the ultimate getaway, with grand views, a gas fireplace, a private dining area complete with a miniature chandelier, and a deck with a gas cooking grill and a private Jacuzzi. You set your own pace and choose your favorite activity from among options that include hiking, horseback riding, mountain biking, cross-country skiing in winter, or simple quiet relaxation. The variety of resident animals, from llamas and horses to geese and goats, will bring out the "kid" in almost anyone.

Rates range from $60 to $175 per night and include a full breakfast. Personalized tour packages are also available, as is boarding for horses. For reservations call 634–6042 or E-mail: adrummon@juno.com. Drummond's is located at 399 Happy Jack Road, several miles east of the entrance to Curt Gowdy State Park.

Albany County

*C*ontinuing west on Happy Jack Road, you'll soon be greeted by the fantastic natural rock formations in the ***Vedauwoo*** (pronounced *VEE-dah-voo*) area. The name means "earthborn spirits" in Arapahoe, and Native Americans regard the area as a particularly sacred place. Using very little imagination, you can have a lot of fun transforming the rocks sculpted by eons of wind and weather into familiar objects. Seal Rock, for instance—just north of the highway and a few hundred yards before you reach the large Medicine Bow National Forest sign—quickly reveals the source of its name. A few hundred yards beyond the forest sign, turn left (south) to find other interesting rock formations and reach the Vedauwoo picnic area. (From there, Happy Jack Road continues on to the Lincoln Monument.)

Try to discover Bison, Loaf of Bread, Hawk, and Dinosaur Bone Rocks on your own. Be sure also to look to the west for the precariously balanced cube as you head south on the winding dirt road. Take your time or the often washboarded road will bounce you right out of your seat. The long-range vista encompasses Twin Mountain, Green Mountain to the east, and Pole Mountain to the west. Vedauwoo offers you a refuge in which simply to relax and contemplate your place in the universe (or something lighter if the mood dictates). If you are more active and adventuresome, you can scale Potato Chip Rock, located near the picnic area, with difficulty ratings ranging from an easy 5.00 to an experts-only 5.14. You can time your visit to Vedauwoo to join in on a ***Moonlight Interpretive Walk*** on the nights of the full moon. Each month focuses on a special theme, such as the Spirit Moon at Vedauwoo or the Pika Moon in the alpine mountains. (Some of these walks take place at locations other than Vedauwoo.) To confirm moonlight walk dates, times, and meeting places, call the Medicine Bow National Forest office at 745–8971 or stop in at the headquarters at 2468 Jackson Street in Laramie.

Continue on the Vedauwoo road until you encounter I–80, but before joining the rush of traffic westward, take

Vedauwoo

a brief detour to **Ames Monument**. Proceed through the underpass and bear left; a 2-mile trip beyond will take you to a 60-foot pyramid of native granite built in 1882 for $65,000 as a monument to Oliver and Oakes Ames, who helped finance the construction of the first transcontinental railroad.

Designed by noted architect Henry Hobson Richardson, the pyramid appears intentionally to have been placed smack in the middle of nowhere. The monument demonstrates the heavy stonework characteristic of the Romanesque-influenced architectural style made famous by Richardson. Originally the monument stood next to the Union Pacific tracks and the now-abandoned town site of Sherman, where the trains were safety inspected before they attempted the steep descent into Laramie from Sherman Hill. Around the turn of the century, the railroad moved the tracks a few miles to the south in order to follow a more desirable grade. As a result, Sherman died a ghost town's death.

U.S. Senator Oakes Ames did not fare much better. He was indicted for bribery in connection with the famous Credit Mobilier Scandal, dying before he could be brought to justice. The Ames brothers may have helped link the country by rail, but the next monument on the tour commemorates the man who kept the nation united and posthumously gave his name to the country's first transcontinental highway, Abraham Lincoln. Complete the loop back to I–80 and proceed to the summit of Sherman Hill, the highest spot on the coast-to-coast highway, with an elevation of 8,640 feet. Built in 1959 the **Lincoln Monument** originally stood alongside the Lincoln Highway route but was moved in 1969 to its present site. University of Wyoming art professor and sculptor Robert Russin crafted the 12^1/$_2$-foot bronze bust, which rises 42^1/$_2$ feet on a granite pedestal built with stone from the Vedauwoo area. There are a visitors center, rest area, and picnic sites at the summit. Happy Jack Road also completes its journey here, joining I–80 at the summit. (Backtracking about a mile on Happy Jack Road takes you to **Tie City**, where tie hackers once fashioned railroad ties out of logs. Today it is a trailhead for cross-country skiers in the winter and hikers the rest of the year.)

Prepare for a spectacular descent into the notoriously windy Laramie Basin, through a canyon lined on both sides by gloriously red rock. Ancient tipi rings, buffalo kill sites, and unearthed artifacts in the basin indicate that nomadic peoples frequented this area for at least ten thousand years, but it was not until the Union Pacific Railroad arrived in 1868 that a permanent settlement took hold. Named after Jacques LaRamie, a French Canadian fur trapper and the first white man thought to have visited the area (LaRamie shipped furs out from 1815 to 1827), the city was selected by the Wyoming Territorial Legislature as the site of the Wyoming Territorial Prison and the University of Wyoming.

The **Overland Trail** traversed the Laramie Basin, which was served by a large station complete with blacksmith shop, roadhouse, and toll bridge crossing the Laramie River.

In 1874 John C. Friend shipped a railcar load of pigment east from the "Rawlins Red" paint mines outside Rawlins. It was used to paint the Brooklyn Bridge.

Westbound travelers used the trail heavily between 1862 and 1868 before the Union Pacific Railroad made the journey more convenient and less treacherous. Overland Trail ruts can still be seen stretching out across the prairie along Highway 130 at a point approximately 11 miles west of Laramie.

An "end of the tracks" town, Laramie garnered a reputation as one rough place. In October 1868, for example, a fierce gun battle broke out in town between outlaws and vigilantes. The criminals fled, but not before four were caught and hanged: Asa Moore, Con Wager, "Big Ed," and "Big Steve," a foursome suspected of some fifty murders combined.

The first all-woman jury sat in Laramie in 1870, an event that moved King William of Prussia to send President Grant a congratulatory message. The breakthrough proved short lived, however, and women did not serve on juries again until 1950. On another suffrage front, Laramie's Grandma Louiza Swain went to the polls in 1871 and earned the distinction of being the first woman in the United States to vote in a general election.

Restored to its original 1890s condition, the Wyoming Territorial Prison lives on as a State Historical Site under the name of **Wyoming Territorial Prison and Old West Park.** Although only in operation for a few years, the park has earned the reputation as a class act. The prison when operational incarcerated such notables as Wild Bunch leader Butch Cassidy (Robert Leroy Parker), who did time for horse thievery. Gov. William A. Richards pardoned Cassidy in January 1896, before he'd served out his two-year sentence—but not before Butch gave his oath as a gentleman that he would do no more thievin' of horses or cattle or banks in Wyoming. (Butch kept his word, but unfortunately the governor forgot to include train robberies in the bargain.) Here you'll also learn about infamous prisoners, such as Clark "The Kid" Pelton, Minnie Snyder, and other evildoers of nearly every imaginable sort.

There's a re-created Wyoming Frontier Town on-site where you can grab a sarsaparilla and watch the Belle of the West Saloon Girls perform, or you can sit back and take a stagecoach ride. The park is also home to the National U.S. Marshals Service Museum, which covers more than two hundred years of law-enforcement history; the unique Tipi Campground; and the Happy Jack Gift Shop.

The performers at the Horse Barn Dinner Theater entertain with a top-quality, rip-roaring dinner shows, all for $24.95. Special events occur all season long, including the Laramie River Black Powder Shoot & Mountainman Rendezvous and U.S. Marshals' Day, which attracts mounted marshals from across the country. For park and dinner theater information, call (800) 845–2287. The *Wyoming Territorial Park* is located at the west end of Laramie at 975 Snowy Range Road.

Besides featuring a gorgeous, tree-lined campus, the *University of Wyoming* (founded in 1886, four years before Wyoming became a state) holds some real treasures tucked away in its buildings of native sandstone. Your first stop should be the visitors information center at 1408 Ivinson Avenue, where you can pick up a campus map and obtain a parking permit. Next find your way to the *Geological Museum* in the east wing of the S. H. Knight Geology Building. It is one of few such museums in the Rocky Mountains, and its fossils exhibit rivals the best found in any part of the country. In the 1960s Samuel H. Knight hand-hammered copper sheets into a lifesize *Tyrannosaurus rex* that now guards the entrance to the museum. Inside a 70-foot-long skeleton of the Jurassic-period brontosaurus (*Apatosaurus excelus*) is the only one of its kind residing west of the Mississippi River, and one of only five specimens on display worldwide. The 150-million-year-old fossil was discovered 70 miles north of Laramie in 1901. Overall fifty types of dinosaurs have been unearthed in Wyoming. The museum has dozens of interpretive displays that tell the dinosaur story and interpret the state's rich geology. You'll learn, for instance, that in prehistoric times Wyoming was covered by a sea and had a tropical climate. The museum is easy to recognize: Just look for the life-size statue of *Tyrannosaurus rex* guarding the entrance. It's open Monday through Friday from 8:00 A.M. to 5:00 P.M., Saturday and Sunday from 10:00 A.M. to 3:00 P.M. Call 766–4218 or visit the Web site at www.gm.uwyo.edu for information.

Moving from fauna to flora, the *Rocky Mountain Herbarium* on the UW campus represents one of the foremost plant collections in the nation. Located on the third floor of the Aven Nelson Memorial Building, the herbarium houses more than 540,000 dried plant specimens, including all of Wyoming's known flowering plants. It is the largest and most representative collection of Central Rocky Mountain plants existent. Although the herbarium is primarily a research facility, the public can visit during summer on Monday through Friday from 7:30 A.M. to 4:30 P.M., or by special arrangement. Fall, winter, and spring hours are from 8:00 A.M. to 5:00 P.M. weekdays. Call 766–2236 for more information or visit the Internet at www.rmh.uwyo.edu.

The University of Wyoming tour would not be complete without getting bugged at the *Insect Gallery* in Room 4018 of the Agriculture Building. The collection, started more than one hundred years ago, features live displays of such creatures as hermit crabs, Madagascar hissing cockroaches, and tarantulas, as well as thousands of mounted insects from all over the world. In all the collection includes more than a quarter of a million insect specimens. The gallery is open Monday through Friday from 9:00 A.M. to noon and 1:00 to 4:00 P.M. To schedule a visit call 766–5338. Other sites not to miss while on campus: the *Anthropology Museum* and the *University of Wyoming American Heritage Center & Art Museum.* One could spend hours at the latter, browsing through the center's extensive collections of printed materials and historic photographs depicting an earlier Yellowstone and other places in Wyoming. The Anthropology Museum (766–5136), open Monday through Friday from 7:30 A.M. to 4:30 P.M., is in the Anthropology Building (surprise!); the American Heritage Center (766–4114) is in the UW Centennial Complex at the far east end of campus. It's open Monday through Friday from 9:30 A.M. to 4:30 P.M., Saturday from 11:00 A.M. to 5:00 P.M.

Everybody's

I attended the University of Wyoming in the early 1970s, when Laramie had even more of a Wild West edge to it than it has today. One establishment I vividly recall from those days is a place they called "Everybody's."

Everybody's was housed in a dark old building on the rougher edge of downtown, just yards from the Union Pacific Railroad tracks. It opened its doors when the bars downtown closed, at 2:00 A.M. The proprietor kept the operation within the law, barely I think, by calling it a private club, so on entering you were handed a "membership card." Here's the really unexpected part: Most of the clientele

was Black. Every song on the juke box was by a Black performer—in those days, Aretha Franklin, the Supremes, Marvin Gaye, the Temptations, among them. Entering Everybody's was like walking off the streets of Laramie into a Twilight Zone version of New Orleans. Where all those Black folks came from in Laramie, Wyoming, I could never figure out.

I visited Everybody's on only two or three occasions during my days at the university; on one of those, I remember exiting after the sun had risen. Mixed drinks I recall, such as their high-octane screwdrivers—a glassful of vodka with a shot of orange juice—went for 50 cents.

Being a university town Laramie has its share of good restaurants and coffeehouses. One favorite is *The Overland Restaurant,* located near the railroad tracks at 100 Ivinson Avenue. Prices are moderate; if you're in town on a weekend, check out the wild game dinner special. The Overland also has a fine assortment of wines and beers. Call 721–2800 for information.

If you're looking for a private place to enjoy a quiet lunch during the warm weather months, try *Sara's Bakery and Jeffrey's Two* (742–0744), 116 South Second Street. It features baked goods and coffee in the mornings and lunch after noon, all served in an inner courtyard away from the street traffic and Wyoming breezes. *Jeffrey's Bistro* (742–7046), around the corner at 123 Ivinson Avenue, specializes in delicious desserts and fine dining. Prices are moderate.

For a bold jolt of java or mellow cup of hot chocolate, mosey over to the *Coal Creek Coffee Company* at 110 Grand Avenue. The folks there also serve great muffins, scones, and soup. On weekends the Coal Creek Coffee Company provides entertainment in the form of readings and coffeehouse singers. This is also the place to head for that early morning cup of coffee, as the enterprise opens at 6:00 A.M. weekdays and 6:30 A.M. weekends. Call 745–7737 for more information.

For a fine dining experience, pirouette over to *Cafe Jacques* and choose from a wide selection of innovative entrees served in an elegant atmosphere, with cozy dining nooks, linen tablecloths, and displayed artwork. Cafe Jacques is located at 216 Grand Avenue. For reservations call 742–5522.

For western-style nightlife downtown go to *The Buckhorn* or to *The Cowboy Saloon & Dance Hall.* Warning: Both taverns are elbow-to-elbow crowded when the university students are in town, but it's always fun to watch or participate in the partying.

By now you may have crisscrossed Ivinson Avenue a dozen times. The street's named for Edward and Jane Ivinson, founders of Laramie's most prominent pioneer family. Edward Ivinson was a banker who built an elaborate Queen Anne–style mansion in 1892 with the expectation of using the residence as the Governor's House once he became elected to that office. The gesture was a grand expression of self-confidence not matched by public sentiment. In 1973 the then-abandoned home, situated at 603 Ivinson Avenue, was converted into *The Laramie Plains Museum.* Years of renovation have brought the structure back to its previous level of elegance. Among its treasures are a well-outfitted kitchen with century-old appliances, a one-room schoolhouse located on the property, intricately hand-carved furniture made by prisoners at the Wyoming Territorial Prison, and period clothing ranging from wedding dresses to funeral wear. During the summer the museum periodically sponsors "Tea on Tuesday" fund-raisers. Volunteers prepare scrumptious desserts and finger foods to go with your tea or coffee, while you enjoy a program that illuminates the museum's collections and local history. The docent-guided tour, which lasts an hour, is priced at $4.00 for adults and $2.00 for students. Tours begin on the hour, with the hours of operation changing throughout the year. Call 742–4448 for an update.

Laramie Plains Museum

For the architecture buff Laramie shows off a variety of building styles. Tour **Historic Downtown Laramie** between First and Third Streets, extending from University Avenue to Garfield Street, to view landmark buildings dating from the 1800s. It's also a great opportunity to visit Laramie's several one-of-a-kind shops, both inside and out. A tour brochure may be procured by visiting the Laramie Area Chamber of Commerce office, 800 South Third Street.

Start at the 1910 **Elks Lodge Building** at 103 South Second Street, which illustrates the Italianate style, with a cornice supported by heavy brackets. **Saint Matthews Cathedral** at 104 South Fourth Street introduced a dignified old-English touch to the once rough-and-tumble town. Nearby, at Grand Avenue and Sixth Street, the **Albany County Courthouse** exhibits the Depression-era art deco style.

Two styles of houses were characteristic of railroad worker accommodations. In 1883 Theodore Bath constructed a row of seven small stone cottages, **Bath Row,** to rent to employees of the Union Pacific Railroad. They are among the oldest rental properties in Laramie. Several of the Bath Houses have been restored and are listed on the National Register of Historic Places. They are located in the 100 block of Sixth Street on the

Laramie, Fort Laramie, Laramie Peak, the Laramie Range, Laramie County, and the Laramie River all were named after Jacques LaRamie, a legendary free trapper of the 1820s who was reportedly killed by Indians along his namesake river.

east side. (The other style is the shotgun house, which we will visit later.)

Notice the mixture of masonry styles in the brickwork of the Tudor Revival residence at 156 North Eighth Street. For an example of a pre-1872 Gothic Revival house, with gables, decorated with verge boards and finials at the peaks of the roof gables, travel to 310 South Tenth Street. *The University of Wyoming Alumni House,* 214 South Fourteenth Street, is another fine example of Tudor Revival. The 1930s Art Moderne house, 1415 Custer Street, features rounded corners and contrasting yellow and mauve brickwork exhibiting a frieze effect.

The 1921 *Cooper Mansion,* now the home of the University of Wyoming's American Studies program, at the corner of Grand Avenue and Fifteenth Street, combines the Mission and Pueblo Revival styles popular in southern California. Rich decorations, such as tiled fireplaces, decorative hardwood flooring, a grand staircase with carved balustrade, and cypress beams imported from Europe highlight the interior. Wilbur Hitchcock, a noted Laramie architect and designer of many University of Wyoming buildings, designed the mansion for Arthur F. T. Cooper, a wealthy English rancher who settled in Albany County. The Cooper Mansion can be viewed Monday through Friday from 8:00 A.M. to 5:00 P.M.

Now travel to West Laramie for an example of the shotgun house, located at 154 Railroad Street. The shotgun style was originally one room wide, one story high, and usually two to four rooms deep. The entrance was on the gable end with the door and a window facing the street. Most Wyoming shotgun houses were built between the 1870s and 1920s as housing for Union Pacific workers. The name came about because it was said you could fire a shotgun through the front door and the shot would emerge through the back door.

Conclude your tour at 810 East University Avenue at *Annie Moore's Guest House,* a restored Victorian home that serves as a bed-and-breakfast. It was built in 1910 by an early Laramie rancher. Later it housed the Delta Phi Sigma sorority and operated as Annie Moore's Boarding House from 1937 to 1948. It has six antique-furnished guest rooms. Breakfast is delightful. Rooms run in the $50–$75 per night range. For information or reservations call 721–4177 or (800) 552–8992.

Before starting out on a driving tour of the nearby Snowy Range and historic Centennial, Saratoga, and Encampment, take a short ride to the remains of **Fort Sanders** on the southern outskirts of Laramie. In 1866 the federal government established Fort John Buford 3 miles south of present-day Laramie. The fort was later renamed Fort Sanders, after Brig. Gen. William P. Sanders, and enlarged to provide protection for travelers on the stage line that ran from Denver to Salt Lake City and on the Overland Trail, both of which passed nearby. The post was abandoned in 1882. In 1886 the Wyoming Territorial Legislature authorized the building of the first fish hatchery in Wyoming at old Fort Sanders. Unfortunately all that is left is a partial wall and some foundations of the old fort. There is a marker within the fenced area surrounding the shell of the Fort Sanders guardhouse. To view Fort Sanders take Third Street south out of town until it becomes Highway 287. Continue about 1¹/₂ miles and turn right onto South Kiowa Street. The structure is on your left a few hundred yards down the dirt road.

Fishing streams in the southeast portion of Wyoming are part of the Platte River drainage system. Lake Hattie, located off Highway 230, is one good place to find rainbow and brown trout. For information on other fishing spots, such as the Miracle Mile, visit the Wyoming Game and Fish office at 528 South Adams in Laramie, or call them at 745–4046.

For today's excursion consider packing a picnic lunch to enjoy along with the stunning scenery. Take the Snowy Range Road (Highway 130) headed west out of Laramie toward Centennial. En route you'll view windswept plains, pine- and aspen-forested foothills, lofty mountain basins holding pristine glacial lakes, and plenty of racing pronghorn antelope. Keep your eyes open also for coyote, foxes, and mule deer. The **Snowy Range Scenic Byway** was designated as the second National Forest Service Byway in the nation in 1988. Built as a wagon road in the 1870s, it was widened using horse-drawn equipment in the 1920s. (Note: The portion through the Snowy Range beginning a few miles past Centennial is open only from Memorial Day through October, weather permitting.)

Southern Wyoming Trivia

The Cheyenne Frontier Days Rodeo, the "Daddy of 'em All," was first held in 1897.

Ten miles out of Laramie, you'll see a marker for the Overland Trail on the north (right) side of the road. In another 11 miles, you'll reach the entrance to the **Vee Bar Guest Ranch** on the right. The original 1893 structure had its roof raised in 1912 when a second story was added. During its one-hundred-year history, this Centennial Valley landmark has served as a working cattle ranch, the Fillmore Stagecoach Stop, a boardinghouse, a buffalo ranch, and a year-round guest ranch.

Carla and Jim "Lefty" Cole and Sandy and C. L. Burton own the Vee Bar today, and they've worked long and hard to restore and preserve the Western gem. The showpiece barn is listed on the National Register of Historic Places. Activities include year-round horseback riding, hay wagon rides, skeet shooting, archery, overnight campouts, and river tubing. Great catch-and-release trout fishing is available on the ranch, too. Riders of all skill levels will enjoy the horse excursions to surrounding meadows and mountains, and several major cattle drives take place during the season; in addition, some cattle are moved on a weekly basis.

You choose the activities you want to participate in during your stay. Nighttime entertainment takes a variety of forms, from talks by historians and performing ventriloquists to cowboy poets and musicians leading a sing-along. The food is superb, varied, and served family style in the western tradition. There are always plenty of fresh fruits and vegetables and delicious homemade bread. You'll quickly understand why one guest is said to have remarked, "I've never been so cared for in my life."

For accommodations you can choose among a house in the meadow; cabins along the Little Laramie River, which meanders the entire length of the ranch; or the new duplex suites built from logs recycled from 1890s homestead buildings at Lefty and Carla's Centennial Valley Ranch. From early June to early September, the Vee Bar offers a variety of accommodation packages, including $1,495/person for a three-night stay and $2,895 for a full week. The rest of the year, guests can avail themselves of daily bed-and-breakfast rates (rooms go from $100 to $150 per night, depending on the month) and enjoy cross-country skiing, horseback riding, snowmobiling, or the nearby Snowy Range ski slopes. On Friday through Sunday in winter you can also take advantage of an evening candlelight meal with a choice of seven menu items. For information and reservations call 745–7036 or (800) 4–VEE–BAR, or visit the ranch's Web site: www.vee-bar.com.

Seven miles down Highway 130, at the base of the Snowy Range Mountains, you run into the quaint, historic mining town of Centennial (population 100). Founded in 1875, Centennial owes its name to America's centennial year, and its existence to the discovery of gold in the nearby hills. The promising vein soon played out, and only the stalwarts remained to populate what became a rest stop for travelers on their way to the Snowies. The town's annual **Grass Roots Day** attracts visitors from far and wide on the last Saturday in July. The **Country Junction** on the eastern edge of town (you can see the whole town from this vantage point) has a good selection of hard candy and ice cream, as well as unique and reasonably priced Western wear and gifts. It's open in summer from 10:00 A.M. to 5:30 P.M. seven days a week, and in winter on weekends only, same hours. The address is 2742 Highway 130; the telephone number is 745–3318.

Don't let the diminutive size of the 1907 railroad depot housing the *Nici Self Museum* discourage you from visiting. It's a great little museum within walking distance of the Country Junction. The structure is the oldest surviving depot of the Laramie, Hahn's Peak, and Pacific Railway Company, which originally was formed to haul the huge amounts of gold anticipated from the mountain mines. Historical collections include exhibits on blacksmithing, lumbering, mining, railroading, and ranching. Outside you'll find a beehive (wigwam) burner used to burn sawdust and a 1944 Union Pacific caboose. The museum is open Friday through Monday from mid-June through Labor Day from 1:00 to 4:00 P.M. or by special appointment; closed in winter because there is no heat! For information call 742–7158.

On up the hill, *The Old Corral* is actually relatively new, having been rebuilt after a recent fire. The restaurant specializes in steaks, and rooms let for $40 for a single and $59 for a double year-round. Check out the unique woodwork in the bar area. Food prices are moderate. For more information and reservations, call 745–5918 or (800) 678–2024.

The Forest Service Visitor Center a mile west of Centennial provides maps and information on the Snowies and the Medicine Bow National Forest, which you are now reentering. (You were also in part of the same forest near Vedauwoo, between Cheyenne and Laramie.) For information on Medicine Bow National Forest, call 745–2300.

Located about 32 miles west of Laramie, the *Snowy Range Ski Area* provides affordable skiing for the whole family beginning in mid-November and lasting through mid-April, depending on snow conditions. The facilities include four lifts, twenty-three downhill trails, a network of cross-country trails, certified ski instruction, and a cafe and lounge. For information call 745–5750 or (800) GO–2–SNOW.

Two miles farther up the road, a new restaurant/lodge occupies the historic S. H. Knight Science Camp Buildings of the former University of the Wilderness. The *Snowy Mountain Lodge,* which opened in 1995, is nestled under the trees at 9,800 feet. The 1920s-vintage restaurant area, crafted out of logs, is unusual in that it has a tree trunk rising through the floor and ceiling.

Thirteen restored rustic cabins await overnight guests; rates range from $45 to $130 per night. The restaurant is open from 8:00 A.M. to 9:00 P.M. daily with variations for hunting season and winter season.

Prices are moderate to expensive, and you can choose from a variety of steak, fish, and chicken dinner entrees. There are a number of hiking and cross-country ski trails on the property, which has several streams running through it. For added adventure, because the Wyoming Highway Department does not plow the road quite to the lodge in the winter, the lodge will bring you in from the main road via their tracked and heated Snow Rover. For information and reservations call 742–SNOW (7669).

The highest point on the Snowy Range Road is at Libby Flats, 10,000 feet above sea level. Medicine Bow Peak, elevation 12,013 feet, towers over the flats. The *Libby Observation Point* scenic outlook offers a stunning vista of alpine meadows and several mountain ranges in Wyoming and Colorado. The area abounds with trails, campgrounds, and lakes stocked with trout, and an incredible variety of wildflowers can be found on the Libby Flats Wildflower Trail. You can locate patches of snow in this area even during the peak temperatures of August. Bring a sweater to ward off the chilling winds at these lofty elevations.

Carbon County

The best is yet to come. Follow Snowy Ridge Road as it winds west from the summit at Libby Flats until you come to the mirrored surfaces of *Mirror Lake* and *Lake Marie.* Now is the time to bring out the picnic basket, sit on the rocks at the shore of Lake Marie, and meditate on its crystal-clear waters. The trailhead for Medicine Bow Peak— dramatic, glacier sculpted, reaching skyward—originates at Lake Marie.

Push on west until you come to North Brush Creek Road, then turn right. This will lead you to the top of Kennaday Peak (formerly called Bald Mountain or Old Baldy), named after an early homesteader and ranger. A flight of stairs gets you into the 14-foot-square glass observation room of the *Kennaday Peak Lookout.* From this vantage point far above the treeline, you earn a remarkable panorama. The lookout tower is in summer open Friday through Monday from 10:00 A.M. to 5:00 P.M., weather permitting. Slippery road conditions may prevail after a rain or snow. For information call the Brush Creek Visitors Center at 326–5562 or the Medicine Bow National Forest's Saratoga District Office at 326–5258.

Retrace your tracks back to Highway 130 and head west until you reach Highway 230, then go south 10 miles and turn onto Highway 70. Soon you'll arrive at Encampment, population 490. Native Americans gathered at Camp le Grand or Grand Encampment, situated at the base of the Sierra Madre Mountains, in order to hunt buffalo and other wild game. Later trappers rendezvoused in the area. In the late 1880s the area grew into a productive copper-mining district after Ed Haggarty made a big strike on the Continental Divide near Bridger Peak. When it held the title of "Copper Capital of the United States," Encampment also boasted the longest aerial tramway in the world. Built in 1902, it conveyed copper ore 16 miles from the famous Rudefeha Mine (named after the four original partners: Rumsey, Deal, Ferris, and Haggarty), or Ferris-Haggarty Mine, to the smelter at Encampment. Power was supplied by water through a 4-foot-wide wooden pipeline. The original partners were bought out by a Chicago promoter, and the name of the mining company changed to North American Copper Company. Millions of dollars worth of copper were shipped out of Encampment before the price of the metal collapsed in 1908. The mines closed and the owner was indicted for overcapitalization and fraudulent stock sales.

The excellent *Grand Encampment Museum,* operational for some thirty years, can keep you prowling around its intriguing displays for hours. The Doc Culleton Memorial Building and original pioneer town are at the heart of the museum. You'll also see a two-story outhouse that solved the problem of contending with the deep snows of winter. Then there's the folding oak bathtub and dozens of other odd finds The museum grounds feature numerous historic buildings, such as a tie hack's cabin, livery stable, false-front store, newspaper office, and stage station, and three original towers from the 16-mile aerial tramway. The museum also serves as a national repository of Forest Service memorabilia; among the related artifacts located on the grounds are the old Slash Ridge Guard Tower and the Webber Springs Guard Station. The Grand Encampment Museum is located at Seventh and Barnett Streets (although the museum is easier to find than are street signs in Encampment). Here you can also pick up a map for the tour of *Historic Homes and Business Buildings.* The museum is open daily from Memorial Day Weekend through Labor Day. Hours are 10:00 A.M. to 5:00 P.M., Monday through Saturday, and 1:00 to 5:00 P.M., Sunday. September through October it opens on weekends or by appointment. Call 327–5308 for information.

To take a look back at frontier life, time your visit for the annual *Woodchoppers Jamboree and Rodeo* held at Encampment on the third weekend in June. The event lasts two days and includes lumbering competitions, with lumberjacks arriving from as far away as California and Australia. You can also watch skilled ax throwers whiz axes through the air to their intended target, while you enjoy a delicious barbecue. Call Grand Encampment Museum at 327–5308 for information on the jamboree.

Side excursions out of Encampment include those leading to the nearby Sierra Madre copper-mining **Ghost Towns of Dillon and Rudefeha.** Both hold remnants of buildings and mining equipment in towns that once bustled with activity. Inquire locally about directions, road conditions, and whether a four-wheel-drive vehicle is required. Many roads passable in dry weather turn into quagmires after it rains.

If you're up to an hour-long hike, strike out on the **Indian Bathtubs Trail** to see the natural 4-foot-deep depressions in granite rock formations, which were used by Native Americans for bathing. You can obtain information and maps at the Encampment-Riverside Merchants Association or Riverside Visitors Center or by calling 321–5481 or (800) 592–4309. To reach the area from Riverside, take Highway 230 east 1 mile to Carbon County Road 200. Turn south on that road, also known as Blackhail Mountain Road, and proceed 1 mile to a parking area. Follow the trail, which travels in a southwesterly direction. It crosses a sagebrush flat and then proceeds up an incline to a bench at the halfway mark. It then crosses a rocky ridge before making a fairly steep descent to Cottonwood Creek. The round-trip should take about one hour, and good hiking boots are advisable. From the vantage point of the bathtubs, you'll earn good views of the entire Medicine Bow Mountain Range and the Encampment-Riverside Valley.

Eighteen miles north of Encampment, in Saratoga, you can relax your body in the hot mineral springs adjacent to the North Platte River. The town, originally called Warm Springs, was rechristened in 1884 after the famed Saratoga Springs resort area in New York State. The average temperature of the mineral waters here is a very hot 114 degrees Fahrenheit. The **Hobo Pool** is free and open twenty-four hours every day of the year; it's located at the east end of Walnut Street.

Stop in at the historic **Hotel Wolf,** built in 1893 and originally used as a stagecoach stop on the Encampment-to-Walcott stage line. The Victorian atmosphere and antique-decorated rooms transport visitors back a century. The food is excellent and moderate to expensive in price. The restaurant has earned a double-diamond rating from the American Automobile Association. Hotel Wolf is listed on the National Register of Historic Places. A room above the bar goes for $34 per night; for a better chance at peace and quiet, though, you'll have to pay a premium—$43 to $85 per night. The hotel is located at 101 East Bridge Street. Call 326–5525 for information.

For lighter fare stop in at **Lollypops** (326–5020), one door down at 107

East Bridge Street. The charming spot features great croissants, Belgian waffles, soups, sandwiches, ice cream, and nonfat yogurt.

You might also want to spend some time visiting Saratoga's art galleries and Whitney's Platte Valley Mercantile. The **Rustic Bar** at 124 East Bridge Street displays some impressive mounted wildlife, including two mountain lions above the back bar, two bucks with their antlers locked in a life-and-death struggle, and a whimsical scene of chipmunks and prairie dogs frequenting a bar.

The *Saratoga Museum* is located across from the airport at 104 Constitution Avenue in a vintage 1915 Union Pacific Railroad depot. Displays include Native American tools and weapons, railroad memorabilia, and Platte Valley artifacts. The museum is open seven days a week from Memorial Day to Labor Day from 1:00 to 5:00 P.M. For information call 326–5511. The Saratoga Historical and Cultural Association also sponsors guided tours to various local historical landmarks during the summer, which you can join by paying a nominal fee.

Saratoga is known as the town where "trout leap on Main Street." The North Platte River, which flows through town, is designated by the Wyoming Game and Fish Department as a blue-ribbon trout stream for approximately 65 miles—from where the river enters the state to the point at which Sage Creek flows into it. The fishing might not be so great in mid-February, but the *Donald E. Erickson Memorial Cutter Races* and *Saratoga Draft Horse Pull* make great excuses to visit Saratoga at that time of year. For information call Saratoga-Platte Valley Chamber of Commerce at 326–8855.

For unique accommodations while in the Saratoga area, consider *Far Out West* (326–5869). Here the cost of a room for two ranges from $60 to $95, and $15 more per additional person. Or, heading back toward Laramie on Highway 130, turn south on Carbon County Highway 203 for a stay at *Brush Creek Ranch.* The ranch entrance is 1 mile down the road on the left side. At Brush Creek, a working cattle ranch encompassing 6,000 acres, you can choose your accommodations from among the many rooms in the 7,000-square-foot main ranch house (built in the early 1900s and expanded in the 1930s). Or perhaps one of the renovated western-decor cabins would suit you better. Whichever you prefer, there's nothing quite like taking a load off on the peaceful veranda of the main house as the setting sun turns the sky tequila-sunset red behind the Sierra Madre Mountains.

You can find plenty to keep yourself occupied, such as horseback riding, hayrides, hiking, campfires and cookouts, cross-country skiing, and barn dances in the old loft. Kids eight and under can have a fun and educational time hanging out with the wranglers in the corrals. You're also invited to help out with the ranch chores, such as branding, mending fences, and rounding up cattle. "On Mondays," says ranch manager Dieter Greiner, "we meet with the guests to get them to think like a cow. It readies them for the real cattle moving." For those more interest in stalking trout than in steering steers, Brush Creek Ranch is an Orvis-endorsed lodge, one of only two in Wyoming. Weekly rates start at $1,025. For information call 327–5241 or (800) 726–2499 or write to Brush Creek Ranch, Star Route 10, Saratoga 82331.

The northerly road out of Laramie, Highway 30, is the original Lincoln Highway route to Medicine Bow. About 18 miles northwest of Laramie, Highway 34 angles off to the right (east) to the Wyoming Game and Fish Department's *Sybille Canyon Wildlife Research and Visitors Center* (about a 26-mile round-trip). It is home to a breeding and reintroduction program for black-footed ferrets, plus a short nature trail and picnic area. The center is open from April 1 through November 15 from 8:30 A.M. to 4:30 P.M., weekdays only.

The black-footed ferret, once prevalent on Wyoming's prairies, was thought to be virtually extinct until a number were captured in the mid-1980s. The ferrets were separated into three groups to prevent disease from wiping out the remaining population. Seven ferrets were sent to a branch of the National Zoo in Washington, D.C., eight journeyed to the Henry Doorly Zoo in Omaha, Nebraska, and the rest took up residence here at the Sybille Research Center. Since then several hundred ferrets have been bred in captivity, and a number have been reintroduced into the wild reaches of the nearby Shirley Basin. Other black-footed ferrets have been sent to captive breeding programs at zoos in Arizona, Colorado, Kentucky, Canada, and elsewhere.

Back along Highway 30 the next stop is Rock River, population 190, located 21 miles northwest of Bosler and a few miles outside Carbon County, in Albany County. Be sure to stop in at the *Rock River Museum* to have a look at the safe blown up in the infamous June 2, 1899, Wilcox train robbery pulled off by Butch Cassidy and his band of outlaws. As legend has it, four masked men stopped the Union Pacific train. They pounded on the door of the express car and demanded entrance, but the expressman refused to open the door. Being a bit impatient, the highwaymen stuck a stick of dynamite into the door and set it off. As depicted in the classic flick, *Butch Cassidy and the Sundance Kid,* the explosion demolished the railcar. More dynamite had to be used to open the safe before the Wild Bunch made off with $55,000.

The museum is located in the old First National Bank, which went out of business in 1927. Other interesting exhibits in and around the museum include dinosaur fossils, mineral displays, Rock River memorabilia, and photographs of the nearby Rock Creek ghost town, a major cattle shipping center before the railroad was rerouted. You can still find a few buildings, such as the Rock Creek pump house, standing at the ghost town site 8 miles north of Rock River. The Rock River Museum is located at 131 Avenue C. It is open Memorial Day through Labor Day on Tuesday through Sunday from 10:00 A.M. to 3:00 P.M. Call 378–2286 for more information.

After proceeding along Highway 30 for approximately 9 miles, you'll arrive at the *Como Bluffs Fossil Cabin*. The odd-looking structure, located on the right-hand side of the road, was constructed of dinosaur bones found in the area and was featured in "Ripley's Believe It or Not" as the oldest building in the world. Unfortunately the Fossil Cabin now is closed and in disrepair. Como Bluffs is the site of a major dinosaur discovery in 1877 and a supplier to major dinosaur exhibits in museums around the world. Yale scientist Othniel Charles Marsh and his rival Edward Drinker Cope of the Philadelphia Academy of Sciences fought over the bones, sabotaging one another's excavations and quarreling bitterly in the press for years. Although most of the quarry work was finished decades ago, a recent discovery of a previously unknown species of Brontosaurus around Como Bluffs has renewed paleontological interest in the area.

Reenter Carbon County as you approach Medicine Bow (population 389), located 18 miles northwest of Rock River. Along the banks of the river near here, Arapahoe and Cheyenne Indians discovered superb materials for fashioning their wooden bows. They called the wood "good medicine" and named the river Medicine Bow. In the early 1870s the town became a major supply point for forts in Wyoming, and the government established a military post in Medicine Bow to protect the railroad and freight wagons from Indian attack. The sleepy town today is one of the best-known names in all of the West, as it was the setting for Owen Wister's landmark Western novel, *The Virginian*. The classic phrase from the novel, "When you call me that, smile," reportedly originated in Medicine Bow during a poker game in which the Carbon County deputy sheriff was called a less than flattering name. Wister, gathering local color for his novel, overheard the deputy's retort, used it in the novel, and made Medicine Bow and the phrase famous.

Despite its small size Medicine Bow boasts two sites listed on the National Register of Historic Places: the *Virginian Hotel* (opened in 1911, nine years after publication of Wister's novel) and the 1913 Union Pacific Depot, which houses a fine museum: the *Medicine Bow Museum,* located across Highway 30 from the Virginian Hotel and open during the summer months from 10:00 A.M. to 4:00 P.M., Monday, Wednesday, and Saturday.

The museum contains plenty of interesting local and nonlocal western artifacts, including the blackjack table from the Medicine Bow Casino. The Owen Wister Cabin (used by Wister as a summer home and winter hunting lodge) and Owen Wister Monument (made of petrified wood) are located next to the museum. The Owen Wister General Store is the building where the author slept on the counter on arriving in Medicine Bow in 1885. Another interesting exhibit, *"The Brands That Tamed the West,"* is adjacent to the museum. Call 379– 2383 for additional information.

The Virginian Hotel boasted the first electric lights in Medicine Bow. At the time it was the largest hotel between Denver and Salt Lake City and the site of business dealings, romance, and shootings. A grand reopening in 1984 marked the restoration of the hotel's turn-of-the-century opulence. Inside there's a lunch counter where the locals gather, a grand old Western mural on the wall, and the Owen Wister Dining Room, which serves good food at moderate prices. The hotel's Shiloh Saloon is another favorite meeting spot for locals and travelers alike. Accommodations include rooms with a shared bath for $20 a night, small suites for $35 per night, and the spacious Owen Wister Suite,

Coyote, An Omnivore with Few Peers

*C*oyotes inhabit both the basin and range country throughout Wyoming. A diverse diet certainly is one thing that helps the crafty canid adapt to different environments. A biological study conducted in Yellowstone in the late 1930s documented the following "miscellaneous food and nonfood items" found in a sampling of more than 5,000 coyote droppings, in addition to the more common remains of large and small mammals, birds, cold-blooded vertebrates, invertebrates, and vegetable matter: horse manure, garbage, trash, muskmelon, corn refuse, paper, canvas-leather glove, rag, butter wrapper, twine, banana peel, orange peel, leather (one piece containing a rivet), cellophane, steak bone, grape seeds, mouse nest material, 7 inches of curtain, pear, prune seed, match, 2 square inches of rubber, tinfoil, shoestring, mud, paint-covered rag, 8 inches of rope, 3 square inches of towel, lemon rind, bacon rind, two pieces of shirt, canvas, gunny sack, isinglass, and botfly larvae.

with its two bedrooms, sitting room, and massive brass bed. The suite goes for $65 per night. For additional information call 379–2377.

Every July the town celebrates *Medicine Bow Days,* complete with a bull chip-throwing contest, dancing, melodrama, a rodeo, and the Hanging of Dutch Charlie at High Noon. Dutch Charlie and Big Nose George were suspected of killing two deputies in the area, and Dutch Charlie met his fate at Old Carbon, a ghost town 14 miles southwest of Medicine Bow. (You'll read more about the unusual fate of Big Nose George later.) For dates and information call 379–2571.

The *Dip Bar* in Saratoga—which takes its name not from its average clientele but from Diplodocus, one of the dinosaur species discovered nearby—houses what is purportedly the *world's largest jade bar.* The 40-foot bar was cut from a 4.5-ton jade boulder found outside Rock Springs. The house of libation also displays an eclectic collection of things western.

Speaking of the world's largest things, in 1982 the federal government attempted to harness the constant Medicine Bow winds with the construction of the *World's Largest Wind Turbine.* Rising high out of the plains, the 262-foot WTS-4 commands the skyline with unchallenged authority even though the feds abandoned the project in 1986, after spending millions of dollars on the experiment. In 1989 a modern-day Don Quixote purchased the broken wind turbine for $20,000 at a government garage sale. Over the next few years, retired engineer Don Young dared to dream the impossible dream, spending fifteen-hour days and a fair sum of money to get the wind turbine back in operation (the government had received bids of $1 million to replace the generator and $200,000 for removal and repair of the generator). A trial run in February/March 1992 proved a disappointment, and Young went back to the drawing board, with the help of an associate and $60,000 in capital. This time, hard work and patience paid off. By Thanksgiving 1992, Young got the wind turbine up and running. Over the next few months, the electricity it generated was sold to the Western Area Power Authority, allowing Young and his partner to recoup their investment. Unfortunately the pitch control system of the WTS-4 went awry in early 1994, causing the blade to hit the tower and shatter. The tower of the world's largest wind turbine can be seen on the southwest horizon from Medicine Bow.

Follow Highway 30 as it bends southwest. Nineteen miles later you'll find the entrance to Hanna, population 1,076, which has a long history of coal mining. The community was named after Marcus Hanna, the

Cleveland, Ohio, industrialist and U.S. senator. The area's vast coal deposits were discovered in 1886, and a **Miners Monument** memorializes the 228 miners who died during mine explosions in 1903 and 1908. To locate the monument follow the signs at the eastern edge of town.

If you're in the mood for a cool swim or a hot workout, the **Hanna Recreation Center,** 8000 Highway 72, is open to the public. The center has an inviting swimming pool and whirlpool for use at a modest fee. A newer Miners Monument and a Union Pacific snowplow engine are located near the center. For information and hours call 325–9402.

From this point, for a real treat follow take Highway 72 southeast 12 miles to Elk Mountain. The town of fewer than 200 residents takes its name from nearby Elk Mountain, elevation 11,167 feet. The **Elk Mountain Trading Company,** according to legend, once grubstaked a rancher who later amassed a fortune of $78 million. The trading post, part general store and part liquor store, is open Memorial Day through Labor Day from 9:00 A.M. to 10:00 P.M., during hunting season (September–October) from 5:00 A.M. to 10:00 P.M., and the rest of the year from 10:00 A.M. to 9:00 P.M. To check ahead to inquire if the Elk Mountain Trading Company and associated Wild Wonder Cafe are open, call 348–7478.

Exit I–80 about 25 miles west of Elk Mountain to view the site of **Fort Fred Steele.** After one look at the deserted, sagebrush-blanketed countryside, you might wonder how a soldier in his right mind could have accepted an assignment at this desolate outpost. In addition to the bleak surroundings, the fort sits smack in the middle of what is known as the "Wind Corridor"—a phrase you'll readily come to understand while driving between Laramie and Rawlins on I–80. Orders were orders, however, and there was little room for negotiation in the role of calvaryman. Not surprisingly, Fort Fred Steele gained the dubious distinction of posting the highest desertion rate of any fort in the West.

Named after a Union Civil War hero, Maj. Gen. Frederick Steele, the post was established in 1868 to protect Overland Trail and Union Pacific Railroad traffic. The 1881 brick powder magazine remains, as do the foundations of many buildings from the original fort. Civilians took over the buildings after the government abandoned the fort in 1886. The railroad tie business kept the fledgling town alive, and it even enjoyed a brief spurt of growth when the original Lincoln Highway route was built right through the town. By the 1930s, though, the town had pretty much dried up. The restored 1880s **Bridge Tender House** now serves as an interpretive center for the fort, which is administered by the state of Wyoming as a state historic site. Summer hours are May 1 to September 15 from

9:00 A.M. to 7:00 P.M. There are no overnight camping facilities, but there are picnic areas where you can watch the waters of the North Platte River roil past. For information call 328–0115.

Another 9 miles down the interstate, you'll come upon picturesque *Sinclair,* population 500. The Sinclair oil refinery at the edge of town reveals the derivation of the town's present name. During the oil boom of the 1920s, however, the company town that sprung up was known as Parco, built by and named after the Producers Oil and Refining Company. Designed in Spanish Mission style, Sinclair includes a town square with a large fountain fronting the *Parco Inn,* which has been closed for years. It once provided shelter to travelers on the bustling Lincoln Highway, which passed in front of the hotel. Amelia Earhart, President Franklin Roosevelt, and union leader John L. Lewis were among the notables who overnighted at the Parco. Every few years or so, some well-intentioned dreamer announces plans to renovate and reopen the Parco Inn, but so far it hasn't happened.

The Sinclair Oil Company purchased the refinery in 1934, and nine years later citizens voted to change the town's name to Sinclair. Although the Parco Inn's doors are closed, there's still plenty of interest to see in town. The First National Bank of Parco operated from 1924 to 1933 in a building that now houses the *Parco/Sinclair Museum,* with its rich collection of town and oil-refining artifacts. The museum is open year-round. If the museum door is locked, inquire about entrance at the Sinclair City Hall next door. Then, if you'd like to sample some of the tastiest Mexican food in the state, follow Lincoln Avenue west until you see the *Su Casa Cafe.* You'll be glad you did. (If you miss it, however, don't despair; there's another Mexican eatery just as good in Rawlins . . . read ahead.) Prices are inexpensive to moderate. For more information on Sinclair, call the City Hall at 324–3058.

> ### Southern Wyoming Trivia
>
> *The Jamaican National Bobsled Team, which made such a splash at the Winter Games in Calgary, Alberta, has chosen Evanston as their training site for the 2002 Winter Games in Salt Lake City.*

Twenty-seven miles north of Sinclair on Seminole Road (Road 351), you'll find *Seminole State Park,* so designated in 1965. The park's centerpiece is the reservoir that backed up after the 1939 construction of the Seminole Dam. The sprawling reservoir boasts 180 miles of shoreline, great trout and walleye fishing, and lakeside camping facilities. For park information call 328–0115.

Back in Sinclair, get on I–80 westbound for a couple of miles and exit at Rawlins, home of the *Wyoming Frontier Prison,* constructed in 1898 and active until 1982. A tour through the old cell blocks sends a chill up one's spine, as does a visit (round-trip, one hopes) to the gas chamber. Among the notable prisoners who served time at the Rawlins facility were Annie Bruce, who murdered her father with a poisoned plum pie; William Carlisle, one of the last great train robbers; Talton Taylor, the last man hanged by the state of Wyoming, in 1933; and Perry H. Carroll, the first man executed by gas in Wyoming, in 1937. The oldest man buried in the old prison cemetery was Jim Best, who died of natural causes at age eighty-nine. After serving his time, it's said, Best was released and given the standard new suit, $15 in cash, and a sack lunch. After enjoying his lunch on the lawn of the prison, he returned to the gate and asked to be readmitted. He was, then died shortly thereafter.

Guided tours of the prison are conducted May 1 through September 30, seven days a week from 8:30 A.M. to 4:30 P.M., off-season tours are given by appointment. The price for the tour is $4.25 for adults, $3.75 for children and seniors, or $15.00 per family. In the prison gift shop you can find, among other things, an interesting book written by an inmate of the prison, *The Sweet Smell of Sagebrush.* The native sandstone, castlesque Wyoming Frontier Prison is located at Fifth and Walnut Streets in Rawlins. For information call 324–4422 or E-mail: markset@trib.com.

Rawlins was named after Gen. John A. Rawlins, chief of staff of the U.S. Army, who discovered a spring at the base of the hills in 1867. The spot was first called Rawlins Springs, then later shortened to Rawlins. The town grew up centered around the point where the Union Pacific Railroad divided 20 miles east of the Continental Divide. The **Carbon County Museum** at Ninth and Walnut Streets contains a number of interesting exhibits, including the death mask and shoes made from the skin of notorious outlaw Big Nose George, sheep wagons, and a fine assortment of arrowheads and Native American pottery.

Speaking of which, while in downtown Rawlins slip into **Larson Hardware,** located on Cedar Street, where you'll find all the implements you'd expect to find in a hardware store, along with hundreds of prehistoric tools on display (but not for sale). Most of the arrowheads, spear points, hide scrapers, and other tools—which constitute one of the largest private artifact collections in the Rockies—were found by the store owner in the desert areas outside Rawlins.

Big Nose George was a robber and murderer. Asked why he had killed two deputies, Big Nose answered, "On the principle that dead men tell no tales." Sentenced to hang on April 2, 1881, Big Nose attempted an escape from his cell a week before his date with fate. After news of the escape attempt made the rounds in Rawlins, a swarm of armed men broke into the jail, hauled Big Nose George to a telegraph pole, and hanged him. No charges were ever brought against any members of the lynching party, who had worn masks to hide their faces. A doctor newly arrived in town, John Osborne (he was elected governor of Wyoming in 1892), took charge of Georges's body. Legend has it that the enterprising doctor removed the outlaw's skin, tanned it, and fashioned a pair of two-tone shoes. Doc Osborne put the rest of George's remains in a whiskey barrel and buried them behind his office on Cedar Street, where they were uncovered in 1950. In recent years his remains have been the subject of study by physical anthropologists at the University of Wyoming.

The Carbon County Museum is open May through September on Monday through Friday from 10:00 A.M. to 5:00 P.M. (closed for the lunch hour), and the rest of the year on Monday, Wednesday, and Friday from 1:00 to 5:00 P.M. Call 324–2740 for additional information.

Calamity

*B*ig Nose George was not the only well-known Western character to do time, both in and out of jail, in Rawlins. None is more famous—or infamous—than Martha Jane Canary, who whooped her way through the West working as a stagecoach driver, laundress, and at other, less-respectable professions. Calamity Jane, as she came to be called, even did a stint touring with Buffalo Bill's Wild West Show. Jane once spent a month in the Rawlins jailhouse after being arrested while on a drunken binge of legendary proportions, which she was enjoying with one of her many "husbands."

"Jane had a very affectionate nature," wrote Dora Dufran, a friend of Calamity's and a madam in Deadwood, South Dakota. "There were very few preachers around to bother her, so whenever she got tired of one man, she soon selected another." Apparently, she also possessed a prodigious thirst, one that beer wouldn't quench. Her standard barkeep order reportedly was, "Give me a shot of booze and slop her over the brim."

Orphaned as a youngster in Virginia City, Montana, Jane grew up as wild as the frontier surrounding her; DuFran wrote that she wasn't immoral, but simply amoral. And she owned a streak of compassion a country-mile wide: DuFran said that just about the only way to put a halt to one of Jane's big drunks was to tell her a friend needed her help. She would stop drinking at once, spend the night sobering up, and the next morning be ready—if not fresh as a daisy—for whatever was needed of her.

Try the scones smothered in honey butter served at the **Pantry Restaurant,** 221 West Cedar Street. Or, if you're wanting more substantial fare, you can order a full meal. Prices are moderate at the family-oriented restaurant, and the sandwiches and dinners are scrumptious. Hours are from 7:00 A.M. to 9:00 P.M. daily; for reservations call 324–7860. If it's tortillas, refritos, and chiles rellenos you've a hankering for, head to **Rose's Lariat** (324–5261), a minuscule eatery tucked along the way at 410 East Cedar. Here you'll be immersed in a south-of-the-border ambience rarely found this far north. Finally, for fine dining head to **The Aspen House,** where the management claims the only complaint they've ever received is that the portions are too large. It's open Monday through Friday from 11:00 A.M. to 2:00 P.M. for lunch, and Monday through Saturday from 5:00 to 9:00 P.M. for dinner. For reservations at the restaurant, located at 318 5th Street, call 324–4787.

A 55-mile side trip south from Rawlins on State Highway 71 and dirt county roads will take you into the Medicine Bow National Forest and the spectacular, timbered highlands of the Sierra Madre Range. The **Rawlins Uplift,** which you can't miss as you drive along, marks the eastern edge of the Great Divide Basin and the beginning of the state's southwestern desert basins. Precambrian rocks are exposed in the core of the uplift, while its flanks are composed of younger, outwardly dipping Paleozoic and Mesozoic strata. After driving through several miles of forest lands, prior to encountering State Highway 70, you'll drive beneath a mile-long canopy of aspen trees. Known locally as **Aspen Alley,** the groves put on a colorful show in autumn that attracts savvy Sunday-driving locals by the dozens.

A left turn onto State Highway 70 will take you back to Encampment, whereas a turn west (right) leads to Baggs, Wyoming, via Slater, Colorado, through the pastoral, little-visited valley of the Little Snake River. In microscopic Savery, Wyoming, don't miss the old ranch buildings and pioneer artifacts at the **Savery Museum** (383–7262), quite possibly the least-visited repository of things old in the entire Cowboy State.

Sweetwater County

I–80 leaving Rawlins penetrates a starkly beautiful red desert region, teeming with wild horses and steaming with their "stud piles"; the horses employ those poetically named mounds of manure to mark their territories. Take the Continental Divide exit west of Creston Junction and cross under I–80 to find the secluded **Henry B. Joy Monument.** Joy was president of the Packard Motor Company and a major force in the Lincoln Highway movement as the first president of the Lincoln Highway Association. The 1939 monument is surrounded by a fence anchored by four concrete Lincoln Highway markers.

Journey another 51 miles down the road, and you will find the *Point of Rocks Monument* and ruins of the *Almond Overland Stage Station* south of the highway. This station also served the South Pass City Route after gold was discovered in that area. The sandstone station was built in 1862 when "Stagecoach King" Ben Holladay moved his stage line south from the Oregon Trail to the Overland Trail because of Indian hostilities. For a time the infamous Jack Slade served as stationmaster. His violent temper resulted in the deaths of several men, and Slade eventually met his end at the end of a rope supplied by a Montana lynch mob. Ultimately the railroad replaced the stage line, and the station was abandoned in 1868.

From exit 122 take Highway 371 north 7 miles along the drainage of Horse Thief Creek to the living ghost town of *Superior*, population 273. At its peak, Superior boasted of 3,000 people, brought in by work in the subterranean coal mines. In forty years of mining activity, more than twenty-three million tons of coal were extracted from Superior area mines. The most intriguing site here is the *1921 Union Hall*, which once teemed with labor activity and social events. All that remains today is the shell of the building. Built in the shape of a trapezoid, the

Desert Beauty

*A*ny time I hear someone talking about how bleak the terrain surrounding Rock Springs is, I think back to the summer in the mid-1970s that Nancy and I spent working with an archaeological reconnaissance crew a few miles south of Point of Rocks. We became well acquainted with the Red Desert that summer, during which we camped in a canvas teepee that Nancy had sewn by hand.

Until then I, like countless others who make a practice of zipping through southern Wyoming on I–80 as fast as possible, believed the Red Desert country to be largely an empty wasteland, devoid of anything worthwhile other than oil and coal. But after walking and surveying some 16 square miles of that spacious land in preparation for proposed coal-mining activities, my outlook took a 180-degree turn. Our crew from Western Wyoming College eventually identified more than 200 prehistoric Native American campsites. Amid the stabilized sand dunes stretching south from Point of Rocks, we also encountered coyotes, pronghorn antelope, wild horses, golden eagles, and a host of other living things . . . but very few other humans. I came to realize that the desert is very much alive, but it often reveals it in subtle ways that can't be appreciated from the interstate.

remaining walls of the once-imposing hall stand as a stark monument to the boom-and-bust cycles of Wyoming's mining economy.

Return to I–80 and exit on Highway 191 North, then continue through Rock Springs 3 miles before turning right onto Reliance Road. Here you'll find another vivid reminder of the volatility of the coal-mining industry and of the hard life of coal miners: the abandoned **Reliance Tipple.** The Union Pacific Coal Company built the town of Reliance in the first decade of the twentieth century to house workers for the company's nearby mines. The Reliance Tipple, one of only a few historic coal tipples remaining in the state, was one of the largest and most mechanically advanced of its breed. Built in 1936 the steel-and-iron tipple—and the men, women, and children who worked there—sorted millions of tons of coal by size for loading into awaiting railroad cars. Interpretive signs around the tipple site provide a twenty-minute self-guided tour.

Don't miss the **Natural History Museum** at Western Wyoming Community College, which occupies a high blufftop within the city of Rock Springs. The museum's extensive collections include exhibits of Mayapan, Guatemalan, and Peruvian artifacts, such as water gourds, baskets, sling stones, blowguns, poison-dart quivers, and serpentine masks. The major attractions, however, are the full-size skeleton casts of dinosaurs that are located throughout the campus complex. A self-guided tour brochure obtained at the college information desk directs you to each dinosaur and gives a detailed description of the beast's natural history.

A triceratops greets you at the main campus entrance. Looking rather like a gigantic rhinoceros and weighing up to six tons, triceratops's nutrition came primarily from the giant palm fronds and leafy plants growing in then-tropical Wyoming. The original triceratops from which the cast was made was found in eastern Wyoming near Lance Creek in 1889.

Additional exhibits include a miner's coal car, cave art, a replica of a stone statue from Easter Island (where Charles Love, the staff archaeology and geology professor, has conducted research), and a Foucault pendulum. Located in the atrium of the student center, the pendulum continuously swings in the same plane. As the earth rotates, the room in which it resides rotates with it, but the pendulum swings free. Although it appears as if the pendulum moves with each motion, it is actually the room that has changed position. The pendulum swings over a polished slab of white Wind River Range granite that cooled down and solidified from its molten state more than two billion years ago. The green stone surrounding the granite was cut from a giant jade boulder discovered near Jeffrey City.

Western Wyoming Community College is located at 2500 College Drive. The museum is open from 9:00 A.M. to 10:00 P.M. during campus hours. School vacation periods may affect the schedule. For additional information call 382–1600.

You'll also want to take in the *Historic Downtown Rock Springs* tour, using the self-guiding pamphlet published by the Sweetwater County Joint Travel and Tourism Board. Copies are available at the Rock Springs Chamber of Commerce office, located at the intersection of Dewar and Firestone Roads, a few blocks from the Dewar Road exit off I–80. For information call 362–3771.

Southern Wyoming Trivia

The flooding of Flaming Gorge Reservoir eradicated most of Wyoming's populations of canyon mice, cliff chipmunks, and piñon mice.

The tour begins at the *Rock Springs Historic Museum,* situated at the corner of Broadway and B Streets. The building was constructed in 1894 as the Rock Springs City Hall and was used in that capacity until a new City Hall was constructed in 1978. The museum opened in 1988 as part of the Rock Springs centennial celebrations. The elaborate Richardson Romanesque stone structure, extensively renovated in 1992, is listed on the National Register of Historic Places and represents the only example of that style of architecture remaining in southwestern Wyoming. Museum collections detail Rock Springs history from the early 1880s through the present, and include exhibits on coal mining and the story behind this "City of Fifty-six Nationalities." The Rock Springs Historical Museum, located at 201 B Street, is open the year around, from 10:00 A.M. to 8:00 P.M. on Monday and Wednesday; 10:00 A.M. to 5:00 P.M. on Tuesday, Thursday, and Friday; and on Saturday from 11:00 A.M. to 4:00 P.M. Call 362–3138 for additional information.

Using the guide mentioned earlier, you can locate several additional historic Rock Springs buildings. The structure at 440 South Main Street, for example, is one of the most compelling in town, with its distinctive stonework and extraordinary roofline. The cut-sandstone exterior is just a facade; the building proper is composed of brick. See if you can find the disappearing 1892 date carved into the stone.

Rock Springs got its name from a spring discovered there in the early 1860s, which led to the establishment of an Overland Trail stage station at the site. The town boomed when the Union Pacific tapped the area's extensive coalfields for fuel to run its trains. (Ironically the spring disappeared with the onset of underground coal mining.) Despite modern residents' pride in the fact that Rock Springs was settled by a rich blend of ethnic groups, the town's history is marred by the 1885 Chinese Massacre, brought on when Union Pacific introduced Chinese workers to replace white workers. Some thirty Chinese workers were killed in the uprising, which ended only after federal troops were brought in to quell the violence.

For some local flavor go to **Grubs,** located at 415 Paulson Street. You may be obliged to stand in line several deep at the horseshoe counter before being served, but the hamburgers (called Shamrocks) and malts are worth the wait. **The Park Grill** (362–3701), at 19 Elk Street, specializes in Italian and American food. Located within the historic Park Hotel, the grill is appointed in art deco style, and its food prices are moderate. Finally a pair of supper clubs located west of Rock Springs are also worthy of a try for delicious steaks, seafood, and other entrees: the **Log Inn** (362–7166) and **White Mountain Mining Company** (382–5265). Prices at both restaurants are moderate to expensive.

If you're looking for a quiet place to stay—with a great breakfast to boot—Darlene Schertzer of the **Sha Hol Dee B&B,** at 1116 Pilot Butte Avenue in Rock Springs, is a gracious host and wonderful cook. Nightly rates are in the $50 range. The B&B lets only three bedrooms so make your reservations early.

Go several miles north of Rock Springs on Highway 191, then turn onto and follow Chilton Road (Road 17) as it winds amid an intriguing landscape of extinct volcanoes and immense sand dunes. Go prepared with food, water, and emergency gear; these roads penetrate backcountry with no services or human inhabitants. The **Killpecker Dune Field** is the largest group of sand dunes on the North American continent, second in size in the world only to the Sahara Desert. It features an off-road vehicle area for those equipped to take advantage of it. The Killpecker Dune Field is also home to a herd of rare desert elk.

The remains of volcanoes can be seen as flat-topped buttes, including Black Rock, Boars Tusk, and North and South Table Mountains. **White Mountain** to the west of Chilton Road contains petroglyphs dating from the seventeenth to early nineteenth centuries.

After an hour or two in the hot desert, you'll no doubt be craving some ice cream, so stop at the **Farson Mercantile,** located at the crossroads of Highways 191 and 28, for one of the best deals in the Cowboy State. For a more than reasonable price, you'll receive a mammoth scoop of ice cream; order two scoops and you may be compelled to share that which you can't eat with the neighboring wild horses and antelope.

The California and Oregon-Mormon Trails run through this open country. Just northeast of Farson on Highway 191 is the "Parting of the Ways," where pioneers opted for one of two alternatives on the Oregon Trail. The shorter Sublette Cutoff tackled a more treacherous territory, including the most difficult river crossing on the entire Oregon Trail. The cutoff took its name from a mountain man, William Sublette, who reportedly was the first white man to travel the route, which he did in 1826. The gentle descent from Steed Canyon on the east bank of the Green River allowed wagons a deceptively easy approach to the river. In June and early July, however, the time at which most emigrant wagons were faced with the crossing, they were met with high, swift water fed by mountain snowmelt. Sublette's fellow mountain man Jim Bridger took advantage of the dangerous situation, establishing a profitable fee-based ferry system. Mormon immigrants also operated a ferry system at nearby Names Hill, so-called because of the many early pioneers, including Bridger, who carved their names into the sandstone rock face.

A trail register kept by emigrant Winfield Scott Espy describes his arrival at the ferry camp in 1854:

> Found as the saying is "all sorts of people" American traders, Frenchmen, Mormons, Loafers, Dandies, Gamblers, Idlers, Grog shopkeepers, Half Breeds & whole Breed Snake Indians. . . . Boasting & bragging the order of the day as well as whiskey drinking & an occasional rowe.

The longer Oregon Trail alternative passed southwest to Fort Bridger before swinging northwest to meet the Sublette Cutoff near present-day Cokeville.

Take Highway 191 south out of Rock Springs to discover the scenic and recreational wonders of *Flaming Gorge National Recreation Area,* which reaches south into Utah. The reservoir, created by the damming the Green River, extends for 91 miles and provides ample activities, from camping and fishing to waterskiing and river floating in summer to cross-country skiing, snowmobiling, and ice fishing in winter. Don't miss taking in the gorgeous view from the Red Canyon Visitor Center at the north end of the dam. From Rock Springs you can travel completely around the reservoir for a 160-mile journey, following Highways 191, 260, 44, and 530, winding up at Green River. Be on the alert for bighorn sheep, elk, moose, mule deer, and pronghorn antelope. (And for the sometimes seemingly arbitrary speed limits, particularly in Utah.)

More than six hundred camping and picnic sites and hundreds of miles of hiking trails await you. The Firehole Canyon recreation site on the east side of the reservoir provides easy access to sublime high-desert vistas. There are also a number of Flaming Gorge interpretive programs; inquire about them at the visitor centers. Most facilities are open from mid-May to mid-September, while the route is open year-round, although travel at the higher elevations in winter can be hazardous. To reserve a camping site at any of the Flaming Gorge National Recreation Area locations, call (800) 280–CAMP.

The striking buttes on the northern outskirts of Green River, known as The Palisades, are the remains of a prehistoric sea bottom. The

Expedition Island

*B*y following Highway 530 from Flaming Gorge, you'll land in Green River, home to **Expedition Island,** where Maj. John Wesley Powell set out on his explorations of the Green and Colorado Rivers in 1869. A plaque in the center of Expedition Island (Green River Island Park) commemorates the spot where Powell embarked on his journey. Notes from the diaries kept by men on the Powell expeditions are as amusing today as on the day they were written:

Tried to drink all the whiskey there was in town. The result was a falure, as Jake Field persisted in making it faster than we could drink it.

—*Jack Sumner, 1869*

The present "City" [Green River] consisted of about thirteen houses, and some of these were of such complex construction that one hesitates whether to describe them as houses with canvas roofs, or tents with board sides.

—*Frederick Dellenbaugh, 1871*

The town, which started as a stage station, today ranks as the largest supplier of trona in the world. Trona contains the raw material for producing soda ash, which is used in the production of dozens of products, including baking soda, laundry detergent, glass, and paper. Ninety percent of domestic and 25 percent of global production of soda ash comes from the Green River area. An estimated one hundred billion tons of trona, laid down as sediments in an ancient landlocked lake, remain below the lands surrounding Green River.

individual buttes called Castle Rock, Teapot Dome, and Sugar Bowl were made famous by nineteenth-century artist Thomas Moran, in his painting of Native Americans and trappers fording the Green River. Moran is even better known for his memorable paintings of Yellowstone and the Tetons.

The **Sweetwater County Historical Museum** boasts an excellent collection of Native American clothing and artifacts, informative displays on trona mining, a large collection of historic photographs of Green River, and extensive research materials covering Sweetwater County topics. The museum is located on the ground floor of the County Courthouse, 80 West Flaming Gorge Way. Hours are from 9:00 A.M. to 5:00 P.M., Monday through Friday year-round; during July and August the museum is also open Saturday from 1:00 to 5:00 P.M. For information call 872–6435 or 352–6715.

One historic Green River building you should see is the **Green River Brewery** (875–5255), now occupied by a bar and lounge fittingly known as The Brewery. Snacks and more serious foods like pizza, sandwiches, and chicken wings are available at the enterprise. Adam Braum built the first brewery in the Wyoming Territory here in 1872, and it changed hands several times over the next several decades. In 1901 the new owner, Hugo Gaensslen, built a new brewery using locally quarried stone, modeling it after the Chicago Water Tower, a Windy City landmark. That brewery, now listed on the National Register of Historic Places, is located on West Railroad Street between North First West and Center Street. You'll also want to visit the **Old Post Office,** 3 East Flaming Gorge Way. The brick Greek Revival building appears an unlikely place to chow down on top-notch Mexican food, but that it is.

For a respite, maybe to enjoy a picnic or simply to take in nature, mosey down to **Scott's Bottom Nature Area.** Here you'll find a wide variety of plant species, from wild licorice to Russian olive; wildlife abounds at the site, too. A guidebook leads you on a ½-mile loop trail. For information visit the Green River Parks and Recreation Department at 50 East Second Street, or call them at 872–0511.

The Green River and its tributaries make southwest Wyoming a top destination for fishermen. To find cutthroat and lake trout (and probably inadvertently hook into a whitefish or two), go to the Green River Pioneer Trails at **Pioneer Trails Park.** Head west on I–80 to the LaBarge Road exit, then travel on Highway 372 for 10 miles, and, finally, go east on County Road 60. For licenses and more detailed fishing information, contact the Wyoming Fish and Game Department at 351 Astle Avenue, Green River 82935, or call 875–3223.

Jim Bridger

*I*n 1822 the Rocky Mountain Fur Company announced in the St. Louis Missouri Republican *that it was seeking "one-hundred young men to ascend the Missouri River to its source, there to be employed for one, two, or three years." Those unable to resist answering the intriguing want ad included an eighteen-year-old former blacksmith's apprentice named James Bridger. During the next forty-five years spent in the West, Jim Bridger evolved first into the king of the mountain men, and then into the greatest guide the region has known. Bridger was among the few beaver trappers who, after skill and luck allowed him to survive the countless perils of two decades in the wilderness, had the temerity and desire to remain in the West after beaver fur's role in the hat-making industry was supplanted by silk.*

After twenty years of negotiating streams flooded with runoff and traipsing through country thick with bears, Bridger "retired" to establish Fort Bridger, which was actually more of a mercantile and smithy than a fort. Out of his way station Bridger guided emigrants and explorers, including Capt. W. F. Raynolds. Bridger led Raynolds's party of thirty infantrymen and seven scientists into and through Jackson Hole and Pierre's Hole in 1859–60. The party's mission: to explore "the headwaters of the Yellowstone and Missouri rivers, and . . . the mountains in which they rise."

Raynolds employed Bridger because he wanted the best guide living. Ironically, and out of character, Bridger never did get the party to its destination. Some allow that it was on purpose and not by chance: Because he was getting paid by the day, Bridger, who by this time had reached the wise old age of fifty-six, probably was in no hurry to get anywhere (and least of all Yellowstone, which he undoubtedly recalled as a mosquito-infested morass in early summer). Rather than bearing north to Yellowstone from the Union Pass area, as had been the intention, the party entered Jackson Hole, where a Corp. Bradley drowned in the Snake River before the party crossed over Teton Pass.

Raynolds was quite impressed by Bridger's imagination and lively storytelling skills. Aubrey Haines, in The Yellowstone Story, *tells about one of Bridger's more famous tales, as related by Raynolds: "It was claimed that in some locality [thought to be Specimen Ridge in Yellowstone] . . . a large tract of sage is perfectly petrified, with all the leaves and branches in perfect condition, the general appearance of the plain being unlike that of the rest of the country, but all is stone, while the rabbits, sage hens, and other animals usually found in such localities are still there, perfectly petrified, and as natural as when they were living; and more wonderful still, these petrified bushes bear the most wonderful fruit—diamonds, rubies, sapphires, emeralds, etc. as large as black walnuts."*

Uinta County

Fort Bridger ranks as one of Wyoming's longest continuously settled sites. The first trappers' rendezvous took place at the location in 1825, years before the fort was constructed. In 1843 fur trapper, entrepreneur, and guide Jim Bridger built Fort Bridger with his partner Louis Vasquez. The Bridger-Vasquez partnership supplied emigrant wagon trains bound for Utah, Oregon, and California. The Mormon Church took over the property in 1855 after building its own Fort Supply in 1853, and the Saints burned Fort Bridger in 1857 after a skirmish with the federal government. Fort Bridger was subsequently rebuilt and used by the government until 1890.

Fort Bridger State Historic Site re-creates the post and associated activities of the pioneer days. The fort has many original and reconstructed buildings, including the commanding officer's quarters dating from 1884, the 1843 Bridger & Vasquez trading post, the first schoolhouse in Wyoming (1860), the 1867 commissary storehouse, and the guardhouse, built in 1887. The museum contains a wealth of information and displays on fur trappers, Native Americans, and the early military. You'll also find weapons, uniforms, Native American artifacts, and personal belongings of Jim Bridger. On Labor Day weekend hundreds of modern-day mountain men and their families rendezvous at Fort Bridger for a reenactment of the past, with authentic mountain man demonstrations, clothing, crafts, and encampment. At the celebration you can watch Native American dance contests, knife-throwing demonstrations, and muzzle-loader shoots the way they were practiced in the old days. Fort Bridger State Historic Site is located a few miles southeast of I–80 off exit 34. The site is open daily the year-round from 8:30 A.M. to 5:00 P.M. Guided tours are available June 1 through September 30 for a small fee. For information call 782–3842.

Take the Piedmont Road exit from I–80 to access the ghost town of Piedmont and the *Piedmont Kilns.* Back in 1869 Moses Byrne built five charcoal kilns north of Piedmont to provide charcoal for a smelter in Utah and coke that was used by the Union Pacific for its steam engines. Three of the 30-by-30-foot kilns remain standing in well-preserved states, as do several buildings at the town site, which was deserted after the railroad moved the track farther north in 1901. Hard to imagine it now, but there were once fifteen hundred people living in Piedmont. Treasure seekers still scour the area for gold that Butch Cassidy and his boys reportedly buried near here.

Evanston is the last major stop in southern Wyoming. Check out

Piedmont Kilns

Pete's Ruck 'N Rye, a funky old roadhouse located on the frontage road along I–80 (turn east after you take the Bear River Drive exit). It has a great jukebox and plenty of local flavor—of both the food and non-food varieties.

Like Rock Springs, Evanston emerged as a railroad and mining town. Also like its neighbor to the east, Evanston suffered racial strife when Chinese miners were hired as strikebreakers in 1869, and a riot ensued, forcing the evacuation of Chinatown. In 1922 a fire destroyed a sacred Chinese temple, called a *Joss House,* which when built in 1870 was one of only three such temples in the United States. A replica of the temple was completed in the early 1990s and stands on Depot Square, near Tenth and Front Streets. It contains artifacts salvaged from the 1922 fire. For information on this and other area attractions, stop at the Chamber of Commerce Office, located in the 1906 Carnegie Library Building in Depot Square at 36 Tenth Street, or call (800) 328–9708.

Conveniently the Old Carnegie Library also houses the *Uinta County Historical Museum.* Curators of the museum, which has been in operation only since 1987, have done an admirable job of collecting and displaying the heritage of southwestern Wyoming. The museum includes fine collections of artifacts and memorabilia of Native American and Chinese history, as well as materials on ranching, railroading, gambling, and bootlegging, all parts of Evanston's past and/or present. The museum is open 9:00 A.M. to 5:00 P.M. on weekdays the year-round, and additionally from 10:00 A.M. to 4:00 P.M. on Saturday and Sunday during the summer. The 1901 Gothic *Depot* in Evanston makes another interesting place to visit, as does Wyoming's lone remaining roundhouse. For information call the Chamber of Commerce at (800) 328–9708.

The Overthrust Belt near Evanston is part of a series of complex geological structures stretching from Alaska to Mexico that are rich in oil and gas deposits. The first major discovery near town occurred in 1975 at the Pineview Field, 25 miles southwest of Evanston. The *Bear River State Park* lies within the Evanston city limits. The park facilities are ideal for a picnic, hiking, wildlife viewing, cycling, cross-country skiing, and other summer and winter outdoor activities. Bear River State Park is located just south of exit 6, the Bear River Drive exit. The park headquarters telephone number is 789–6547.

Evanston features live parimutuel horse racing at *Wyoming Downs,* located 8 miles north on Highway 89. Thoroughbred and quarter horse racing takes place Memorial Day through Labor Day. For quality Italian food while in town to watch the horses run (or for whatever reason), try *Grazias* (789–8720), located at 123 Tenth Street. It's open for dinner from 5:00 to 10:00 P.M., Tuesday through Saturday. The *Pine Gables B&B* at 1049 Center Street was built in 1883 by Evanston's first merchant, A. V. Quinn. It operated as a European-style boardinghouse in the 1920s and 1930s. Victorian decor and plentiful antiques characterize the four guest rooms, each of which has a private bath. Rates range from $50 to $65 per night for a double. Call 789–2069 for information and reservations.

PLACES TO STAY IN MEDICINE BOW–FLAMING GORGE COUNTRY

BAGGS
Drifters Inn,
Highway 789;
(307) 383–2015

CHEYENNE
Days Inn,
2360 West Lincolnway;
(307) 778–8877 or
(800) 329–7466

Holding's Little America,
2800 West Lincolnway;
(307) 634–2771 or
(800) 445–6945

Motel 6,
1735 Westland Road;
(307) 635–6806

The Sands Motel,
1000 West 16th;
(307) 634–7771

Cheyenne Motel,
1601 East Lincolnway;
(307) 778–7664

ENCAMPMENT-RIVERSIDE
Vacher's Bighorn Lodge,
508 McCaffrey Avenue;
(307) 327–5110

Riverside Garage & Cabins,
downtown Riverside;
(307) 327–5361

Old Depot Bed & Breakfast,
201 1st Street in Riverside;
(307) 327–5230

EVANSTON
Best Western Dunmar Inn,
1601 Harrison Drive;
(307) 789–3770 or
(800) 654–6509

National 9 Inn,
1724 Harrison Drive;
(307) 789–9610 or
(800) 524–9999

Weston Super Budget Inn,
1936 Harrison Drive;
(307) 789–2810 or
(800) 255–9840

GREEN RIVER
Oak Tree Inn,
1170 West Flaming Gorge Way;
(307) 875–3500

Sweet Dreams Inn,
1410 Uinta Drive;
(307) 875–7554

LARAMIE
Comfort Inn,
3420 Grand Avenue;
(307) 721–8856 or
(800) 228–5150

1st Inn Gold,
421 Boswell Drive;
(307) 742–3721 or
(800) 642–4212

Motel 8,
501 Boswell Drive;
(307) 745–4856

University Inn,
1720 Grand Avenue;
(307) 721–8855

LITTLE AMERICA
Holding's Little America,
I-80 exit 68;
(307) 875-2400 or
(800) 634-2401

PINE BLUFFS
Sunset Motel,
316 West 3rd;
(307) 245-3591

Gator's Travelyn Motel,
515 West 7th;
(307) 245-3226

RAWLINS
Days Inn,
2222 East Cedar;
(307) 324-6615

Weston Inn,
1801 East Cedar;
(307) 324-2783 or
(800) 255-9840

ROCK SPRINGS
EconoLodge,
1635 North Elk Street;
(307) 382-4217 or
(800) 548-6621

Comfort Inn,
1670 Sunset Drive;
(307) 382-9490 or
(800) 221-2222

Holiday Inn,
1675 Sunset Drive;
(307) 382-9200 or
(800) HOLIDAY

Motel 8,
108 Gateway Boulevard;
(307) 362-8200

SARATOGA
Cary's Sage & Sand Motel,
311 South First;
(307) 326-8339

Hacienda Motel,
Highway 130 South;
(307) 326-5751

Saratoga Inn Golf &
Hot Springs Resort;
601 East Pic Pike,
(307) 326-5261

PLACES TO EAT IN
MEDICINE BOW-FLAMING
GORGE COUNTRY
(ALL AREA CODES 307)

BAGGS
Drifters Inn,
Highway 789;
383-2015

CHEYENNE
Lexie's,
216 East 17th Street;
638-8712

Little Philly,
1121 West Lincolnway;
632-6824

Avanti Restaurant,
4620 Grandview Avenue;
634-3432

Owl Inn,
3919 Central Avenue;
638-8578

ENCAMPMENT-RIVERSIDE
Bear Trap Bar and Cafe,
120 East Riverside;
327-5277

Sierra Madre Cookhouse ,
510 McCaffrey Avenue;
327-5878

EVANSTON
Michael's Bar & Grill,
1011 Front Street;
789-1088

Wally's Burgers,
1612 Harrison Drive;
789-1373

The Last Outpost,
205 Bear River Drive;
789-3322

JB's,
1969 Harrison Drive;
789-7537

GREEN RIVER
Embers Family Restaurant,
95 East Railroad Avenue;
875-9983

Green River Rendezvous,
950 West Flaming Gorge;
875-6455

LARAMIE
First Story Cafe,
101 East Ivinson;
745-5444

The Library Restaurant
& Brew Pub,
1626 East Grand Avenue;
742-0500

The Overland Fine Eatery,
100 Ivinson;
721-2800

Rose Cafe,
410 South 2nd;
745-4077

LITTLE AMERICA
Holding's Little America,
2800 West Lincolnway;
634-2771

PINE BLUFFS
Lickety-Split
(ice cream only),
10 Paintbrush;
245-3665

Uncle Fred's Place,
701 Parsons Street;
245-3443

RAWLINS
Rose's Lariat,
410 East Cedar;
324–5261

Square Shooter's
Eating House,
311 West Cedar;
324–4380

ROCK SPRINGS
Golden Corral,
1990 Dewar Drive;
362–7234

Wonderful House,
1676 Sunset Drive;
382–5462

Renegade Cafe,
1610 Elk Street;
362–3052

Santa Fe Trail,
1635 Elk Street;
362–5427

SARATOGA
Lazy River Cantina,
110 East Bridge Street;
326–8472

Saratoga Inn,
601 East Pic Pike Road;
326–5261

Old Mill Restaurant,
30 County Road;
789–4040

Hotel Wolf,
101 East Bridge Street;
326–5525

Western Wyoming: Bridger-Yellowstone Country

Bridger-Yellowstone Country is that portion of Wyoming primarily responsible for the state's well-deserved notoriety as a vacationer's paradise. Some three million visitors per year tour the greater Yellowstone-Teton region alone. Most of those millions, however, visit just the well-known and consequently most crowded sites. Little do they realize that wonderful places offering equal beauty and far more solitude typically lie hidden nearby.

From Kemmerer your trail leads north to Pinedale, a classic cowtown and gateway to the marvelous Wind River Range. An alternative route snakes along the Wyoming-Idaho border, through a largely bypassed, mountain-ringed agrarian corner of Wyoming, which was initially settled by Mormon pioneers dispatched from the Salt Lake Valley. From Pinedale and/or Star Valley, it is on to Jackson, Grand Teton National Park, and, finally, Yellowstone National Park—where even within one of the world's most popular natural areas, there are plenty of places that will startle and please those who are allergic to the well-worn path.

Lincoln County

A fossil of sorts—King Coal, that is—fueled the growth of Kemmerer, population 3,020. Mahlon S. Kemmerer, for whom the town was named, and his partner Patrick J. Quealy (as in Quealy Dome) opened the area's first coal mine in 1897, establishing the Kemmerer Coal Company. Other ventures proved less successful, as numerous mining ghost towns in the hills around Kemmerer attest. Nevertheless the world's largest operational open-pit mine, owned by Pittsburg-Midway, is found here today.

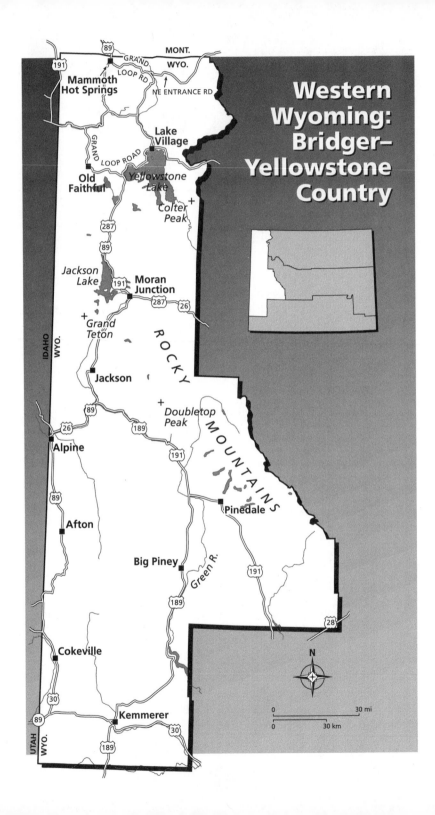

Western Wyoming: Bridger–Yellowstone Country

MONT.

WYO.

Mammoth Hot Springs

GRAND LOOP RD

NE ENTRANCE RD

Lake Village

GRAND LOOP ROAD

Old Faithful

Yellowstone Lake

+ Colter Peak

Jackson Lake

Moran Junction

+ Grand Teton

ROCKY

Jackson

+ Doubletop Peak

MOUNTAINS

Alpine

Pinedale

Afton

Big Piney

Green R.

Cokeville

Kemmerer

IDAHO WYO.

UTAH WYO.

N

0   30 mi

0   30 km

Kemmerer's other primary claim to fame was the opening of the J. C. Penney "Mother Store," under the name of Golden Rule Store by James Cash Penney in 1902. By 1912 Penney owned thirty-four stores, and he changed the chain's name to J. C. Penney. The Kemmerer store still operates, albeit at a new location. The restored *J. C. Penney Home* makes for an interesting visit. Located on J. C. Penney Drive across from the Triangle Park, it is open daily during the summer and in the winter by appointment. Inquire at the Chamber of Commerce or call 877–9761.

The *Fossil Country Frontier Museum* interprets the region's cultural history. A unique summer program involves local citizens presenting their Campfire Chats, centering the area's colorful past. The museum, located at 400 Pine Street, is open daily from 9:00 A.M. to 5:00 P.M. in summer, and 10:00 A.M. to 4:00 P.M., Monday through Friday, in winter. For more information call 877–6551.

The circa 1925 *Lincoln County Courthouse* has been restored and is worth touring to see the striking dome and its art deco and Native American features. The adjoining jail has been recycled to house a respectable collection of fossils. The courthouse and jail are located on Sage Avenue. (On the other side of the law, a woman named Madame Isabelle operated a house of ill repute that garnered enough money for her to build a grand house, which you can see at 301 Ruby Street.)

Kemmerer's sister city Diamondville is home to delicious Italian food served at *Luigi's Supper Club,* 819 Susie Avenue. Prices are moderate and the choices mouthwatering. It's open Wednesday through Saturday from 5:00 to 9:00 P.M. For information call 877–6221.

For $30 to $50 per night, you can stay at the *Kelly* or *Labarge Cabin* in the Bridger-Teton National Forest. Both are old ranger stations used when the forest had few serviceable roads, and the rangers made their rounds on horseback. The Kemmerer District

---

BEST ANNUAL EVENTS IN BRIDGER-YELLOWSTONE COUNTRY

Jackson Hole Powder 8's,
Jackson; January;
(307) 733–2292

All-America Cutter Races,
Afton-Thayne; January-February; (307) 883–4897

International Stage Stop Sled Dog Race, begins/ends in Jackson; February;
(307) 734–1134

Moose Chase Cross-Country Ski Race,
Teton Village; late January/February; (307) 733–6433

Annual Celebrity Ski Extravaganza,
Jackson Hole; March;
(307) 734–2878

Pole-Pedal-Paddle,
Jackson; April;
(307) 733–2351

Annual Mountain Days,
Alpine; June; (307) 654–7545

Green River Rendezvous,
Pinedale; (307) 367–4101

Grand Teton Music Festival, Teton Village;
July–August; (307) 733–1128

Rockin' the Tetons Rock & Microbrew Festival,
Grand Targhee; July;
(800) 827–4433

Targhee Bluegrass Festival,
Grand Targhee; August;
(800) 827–4433

Teton Science School Auction, Kelly; August
(307) 733–4765

Ranger Office handles reservations for the rustic cabins, both of which require a hike of about 12 miles to access. You can reach the Kelly cabin from Cokeville by driving 12 miles north on Highway 232 to a signed trailhead. The trail follows Coal Creek to the northeast before joining up with other trails and turning south to the cabin. You can find the LaBarge cabin from Afton by driving south on Highway 89 for 14 miles to a trailhead at Fish Creek, and then following the trail northeast to the Smith Fork and the headwaters of LaBarge Creek. Cabin facilities include bunk beds, a wood/gas cookstove, a woodstove for heat, a propane refrigerator, propane lights, and an outhouse. Reservations are required at both cabin locations. For reservations and maps contact the ranger station at 877–4415, or write P.O. Box 31, Kemmerer 83101.

Names Hill is one of the three well-known Oregon Trail registers in Wyoming, a place where emigrants carved their names for future travelers to see. Like Register Cliff near Guernsey and Independence Rock southwest of Casper, Names Hill evokes a haunting presence along the historic byway. It is located several miles south of LaBarge off Highway 189. Nearby Fontenelle Reservoir offers camping and picnicking facilities.

The Longest Graveyard in America

*T*ragedy along the Oregon Trail and other trails leading westward is etched into the Wyoming landscape. Historians estimate that between 6 and 10 percent of the 350,000 emigrants who traveled the Oregon Trail died along the way, approximately ten deaths for each mile of the route. The major danger was cholera, followed by accidents involving livestock, wagons, firearms, and river crossings. Contrary to popular myth, Indians were a minor hazard in terms of the numbers of deaths.

Still, Indian-related deaths weren't unheard of. Seventeen miles northwest of Kemmerer on Highway 233 are the graves of two who met their fate along the trail. In 1852 Nancy Jane Hill was traveling with a wagon train that was delayed for more than two weeks by Indian attacks. Although she survived the Indian threat itself, she succumbed to cholera and died on July 5 at the age of twenty. Her fiancé is said to have returned to her grave site three times over the next fifty-three years.

Alfred Corum and three brothers left Missouri in 1849 to seek their fortunes in the goldfields of California. Their wagon reached Hams Fork Plateau on July 3 and stopped because Alfred had been sick for over a week. As the brothers tended to his needs, more than two hundred wagons passed them on the dusty trail. Alfred died on Independence Day of unknown causes.

WESTERN WYOMING

**BEST ATTRACTIONS IN BRIDGER-
YELLOWSTONE COUNTRY**
(ALL AREA CODES 307)

*Fossil Butte National
Monument,*
west of Kemmerer; 877–4455

Star Valley Cheese Factory,
Thayne; 883–2510

*Museum of the
Mountain Man,*
Pinedale; 367–4101

Half Moon Lake, outside
Pinedale; 367–4326

*National Museum of
Wildlife Art,*
Jackson; 733–5771

*Otto Brothers Brewing
Company,*
Wilson; 733–9000

Lost Horizon Supper Club,
Alta; 353–8226

Darwin Ranch, miles from
nowhere; 733–5588

*Indian Arts Museum at
Colter Bay, Grand Teton*
National Park; 739–3300

*Museum of the National
Park Ranger, Yellowstone*
National Park; 344–7381

Ten miles west of Kemmerer on U.S. Highway 30, you'll see the entrance to *Fossil Butte National Monument.* The road here will take you 3¹/₂ miles north to the site where Fossil Butte rises 1,000 feet above Twin Creek Valley to an elevation of 7,500 feet. As its name alludes, the 8,180 acres of rugged topography yield one of the richest freshwater fossil fish deposits in the Western Hemisphere, preserved in limestone layers between 30 and 300 feet below the surface of the butte. The fossil deposits, laid down fifty million years ago in lake beds, were later thrust upward to become Fossil Butte. The base of Fossil Butte, whose specimens were investigated as early as 1877 and now are showcased in museums throughout the world, consists of the brightly colored beds of the Wasatch Formation.

The visitor center offers an orientation to the geologic story told in the rocks of Fossil Butte. You can also obtain hiking maps of the area; along the way, informative trail signs explain the exposed specimens. There are no camping facilities at Fossil Butte, but you can picnic in a small aspen grove about 4 miles from the visitors center. Fossil Butte is open daily from 8:00 A.M. to 7:00 P.M. year-round (closed on winter holidays). For information call 877–4455.

If simply looking at fossils isn't quite exciting enough, you can dig for your own at *Ulrich's Fossil Quarries.* Three-hour-long excavation outings take place from June through Labor Day, seven days a week, between 8:00 A.M. and 9:00 P.M., weather permitting. You'll be accompanied by an experienced staff member, and Ulrich's furnishes all tools and equipment needed for excavating. Bring your own snacks and liquid refreshments. The $55 fee allows you to collect and keep specimens other than those designated by the state of Wyoming as "rare and unusual." Winter hours for the associated gallery are 8:00 A.M. to 5:00 P.M., or by appointment. Ulrich's is located off the road to Fossil Butte. For advance reservations, which are required, or for further information call 877–6466. (No children under ten years of age are permitted.)

Continue on Highway 30/89 to Cokeville, established in 1874, the oldest town in Lincoln County. Keeping up Wyoming's tradition as the Equality

State, Cokeville elected a woman mayor and two women council members in 1922. Originally the town was known as Smith's Fork on the Bear River. The Oregon Trail runs right through town and on into Idaho. Many cutoffs converged near Cokeville at the ferry site on Smith's Fork, considered a primary hub of the Oregon Trail. You'll see an *Oregon Trail Monument* in Cokeville City Park at the corner of East Main Street and Park Street.

Western Wyoming Trivia

Cokeville, northwest of Kemmerer, once was a multimillion-dollar sheep-shipping site.

Star Valley and *Little Switzerland* are nicknames for a particularly isolated and fertile valley region of Lincoln County located north of Cokeville. Native Americans long valued the moderate climate and lush valley for grazing their horses and hunting for the abundant wildlife. Later emigrants using the Lander Trail between 1840 and 1870 stopped in Star Valley before continuing on toward Oregon. Mormon leader Brigham Young, realizing the potential of the rich farmlands, established the first settlement in the area. Star Valley today is known for its dairy products, notably cheese, and its large, redbrick Church of Jesus Christ of Latter-day Saints (LDS) buildings.

With a population of around 1500, Afton is the hub of Star Valley. Brigham Young disciple Moses Thatcher founded the town in 1885. Proclaimed the "World's Largest Elk Antler Arch," Afton's arch extends over Main Street at a height of 18 feet and contains more than three thousand antlers. In contrast the towering steeple of the original LDS "Church of the Valley" lends the town a distinct New England feel. An early Scottish resident named the community after Robert Burns's poem, "Flow Gently, Sweet Afton." On a more raucous note, Butch Cassidy and his gang, favoring the valley's isolation, once wintered here away from the pursuit of the law. Cassidy reportedly papered the local bar with banknotes from one of his gang's many robberies.

A small museum with a big name, the *Lincoln County Daughters of the Utah Pioneers Museum,* houses a number of pioneer homesteading items, such as a loom and spinning wheel. The museum is located at 46 East Fifth Street. It is open June through August, Monday through Friday from 1:00 to 5:00 P.M., or by appointment. Also erected by the Daughters of the Utah Pioneers is the *Star Valley Marker* at 347 Jefferson Street. The marker commemorates the settling of Star Valley in 1879. An interesting component of the monument is the bell, which originally was housed in an 1892 bell tower and was rung every Sunday morning at 9:30 and 9:50 to aid valley residents in adjusting their clocks.

Afton is home to Aviat Inc., a company that manufactures some of the finest in aerobatic planes. In late June the town hosts the *CallAir Fly-in,* with small craft pilots from throughout the West flying in for airplane-related fun, both on and above the ground. The *CallAir Museum* (886–9881) brims with aircraft and displays explaining Star Valley's surprisingly important role in the evolution of small-craft aviation.

Five miles east of Afton, you'll find the geologically intriguing *Intermittent Spring.* The natural oddity gushes for approximately eighteen minutes, expelling an extraordinary quantity of water; it then ceases to flow for about the same amount of time. It's one of only a handful of intermittent springs in the world, and the only one of its kind in the United States. Like Old Faithful, its cycles are fairly predictable; Intermittent Spring functions for nine months of the year. The best time to view it is during high-water runoff, from the middle of May through the middle of July. To find it take Second Avenue East to the dirt road leading to Swift Creek Canyon. You will need to walk a ³/₄-mile trail to reach the stream from the parking area, but it's a pleasant hike through a beautiful canyon.

Moving north on Highway 89 takes you to Thayne, population 267, where you can stock up on cheese at the *Star Valley Cheese Factory.* The bulk of the cheese produced here is shipped outside the region— some 60,000 pounds annually. You can also grab a bite to eat at the Star Valley Cheese Factory Restaurant. Good sandwiches and great pies. For information call 883–2510.

With the change in the seasons, Thayne and Afton turn to winter and snow to attract visitors, with their *Cutter and Chariot Races.* The All American Cutter Racing Association was organized in Thayne in 1948, but the tradition goes back to the 1920s, when local ranchers and farmers employed horse-drawn sleighs to deliver milk to the creamery, to pick up supplies, and to visit far-flung neighbors and relatives.

Western Wyoming Trivia

From the 1941 Wyoming: A Guide to Its Highways, History, and People: *"[Yellowstone] Park hotels are first-class; rates range from $2.75 a day without meals, to $9 a day with meals."*

Taking a cue from *Ben Hur,* perhaps, the chariot racers have added wheels to their sleighs. The world's first cutter race took place on Thayne's iced-over main drag when, reportedly, an LDS bishop bested a local rancher in the 1920s competition. Interest in the sport progressively grew over the years, and the first World Cutter and Chariot Racing Championship took place here in 1965. The horse-drawn chariots race a quarter mile on a straight, snow-covered track. The world record for a quarter-mile cutter race, 21.64 seconds, was set in 1994. Cutter and chariot racing is held in Star Valley from the first weekend in December through February. For information call 877–3984.

The **Auburn Rock Church,** one of the oldest buildings in Star Valley, played an important part in local Mormon history. Constructed of striking rough-cut stone in the late nineteenth century, like most LDS

Riding the Range—on Two Wheels

*I*n late July 1985 Nancy and I struck out on a backcountry bicycle tour of western Wyoming. Mountain biking was a fairly new sport at the time; touring on mountain bikes with camping gear in tow was almost unheard of. As we quickly discovered, however, there's no better way to become truly acquainted with Wyoming's backcountry than undertaking a tour such as this.

After a friend dropped us and our bikes off at the Tri-Basin Divide, a high saddle separating the Salt River and Wyoming ranges, we followed a gravel byway paralleling the sparkling Greys River. Other than one or two fishermen and a lone Forest Service timber cruiser, we saw no other humans for mile after mile of stunning countryside. A steep climb along Sheep Creek led us to McDougal Gap, then a quick downhill zip delivered us onto the high desert, where we pedaled up and over numerous rimrock ridges before reaching the campground in tiny Daniel.

The most memorable stretch of the five-day trip was that from Whiskey Grove Campground, nestled along the upper Green River, to the Horn Ranch, located at the upper, eastern end of the Gros Ventre River Road. After riding over the gnarly Kinky Creek Divide, we stopped in at the exceptionally isolated

Darwin Ranch for some route-finding advice. "You're going to try and ride what through where?" came the words from an angular, stooped cowboy who, incongruently, spoke with an Australian accent. His incredulous words were delivered as we reclined with him and three other ranch hands around the kitchen table of the rustic guest ranch, which sits amid stunning surroundings at the head of the Gros Ventre River drainage. Collectively they told us, in so many words, that the trail ahead was far too rough, and that trying to cover it on bicycles was a dumb idea.

But we pressed on anyway, soon learning that the cowboys were right. After already having spent eight hours on the bikes that day, the next 5 miles of trail took an additional four hours to cover. Together, up steep hills leading out of countless mud-filled draws, we pushed each bike, then held the bikes back on the equally steep downhills to keep them from turning into runaways. On finally busting out to the main road at the entrance to the Horn Ranch, we immediately set up camp and crashed, too tired even to cook supper.

The next day's trip to Moose in Grand Teton National Park, although long as measured in miles, was a lark compared to the previous day's odyssey.

Western Wyoming Trivia

In 1895 a minor skirmish between white settlers and Bannock Indians near Battle Mountain south of Jackson resulted in two casualties. However, by the time the news reached the East Coast, it had grown substantially in severity. A New York City newspaper reported: ALL RESIDENTS IN JACKSON HOLE, WYOMING, MASSACRED.

churches, in addition to serving a religious role it also operated as a community gathering place.

The tiny town of Freedom, straddling the Wyoming/Idaho border, is the headquarters of the prestigious *Freedom Arms* gun factory. Freedom Arms fashions collector handguns that command a hefty price. Freedom is the oldest settlement in the valley, established by Mormons in 1879. This area of lower Star Valley is also developing into quite a retirement and golfing mecca. Recommended: beautiful *Cedar Creek Golf Course* (883–2230). The associated Silo Lounge—which looks like . . . well, a silo—reveals the not-too-distant agrarian past of the present links.

Alpine Junction, population 200, is a haven for water sports enthusiasts, thanks to its proximity to the Grand Canyon of the Snake River and Idaho's Palisades Reservoir. Alpine Junction is auspiciously situated at the confluence of the Snake, Greys, and Salt Rivers. With an abundance of hotels and lodges, Alpine makes a great place to base out of as you explore the nearby river and mountain country. In mid-June the community hosts the *Good Ole Mountain Days* festival, with a country music jamboree, various games, a Native American jewelry show, a black powder shoot, a tomahawk throw, and a mustache contest. For information call 654–7545.

From Alpine, Highway 26/89 leads through the inspiring 3,000-foot-deep *Grand Canyon of the Snake River,* one of the scenic wonders of Wyoming.

Sublette County

Drive northwest out of LaBarge on Highway 189 to Big Piney (population 454) and stop at the *Green River Valley Museum* for an introduction to the valley's long and colorful history. The museum includes an interesting brand exhibit dating back to 1895, along with the original oil Wardell Buffalo Trap Mural that was featured on the 1995 Wyoming Archaeological Society poster. The museum is located on Highway 189 in Big Piney. It's open Tuesday through Saturday from noon to 4:00 P.M.

Just before you arrive at Daniel, note the historical marker telling about Father De Smet. It's located on the right side of Highway 189. The marker commemorates the one hundredth anniversary of the first Roman Catholic mass held in Wyoming, which occurred on July 5, 1840. To find the actual *De Smet Monument* and the spot where Father De Smet delivered the mass, follow the gravel road marked "Daniel Cemetery" for about 3 miles. An added dividend is the wonderful view of the valley and Green River you'll enjoy from this vantage. There's also a small chapel here built of native rock.

Nearby is the grave site of Pinckey Sublette, one of the brothers of William Sublette, the famous fur trader (and discoverer of the Sublette Cutoff), for whom Sublette County was named. Pinckey's extensive travels continued even after his death in 1865: He was exhumed in 1897 and shipped off to St. Louis, where he remained until 1935. Then a court ordered his body returned to Sublette County, Wyoming.

If you're interested in enjoying a week or more of top-notch fly fishing—along with horseback trail rides into the mountains, fantastic vistas in the shadow of the Gros Ventre Range, and gourmet meals—then let ranch manager Debbie Hansen and her staff at the *Flying A Ranch* pamper you. Built in 1929 the historic ranch has been completely refurbished, yet it retains its original character. Total comfort in a grand western atmosphere is the name of the game, and the Flying A provides it, with its six spacious handcrafted homestead log cabins, each of which provides a large sitting area, kitchenette, and private bath. Most

Early Day Trade Shows

*T*rappers and hunters used the Green River Valley for a number of their rendezvous, coming here to obtain supplies for the coming season and to sell or trade the bounty of their recent efforts. All told there were sixteen major Rocky Mountain rendezvous, with six of them held here in the "Valley of the Green." The first rendezvous occurred in 1825, within 20 miles of the confluence of Henry's Creek and the Green River, south of present-day Granger in Sweetwater County. The event lasted only one day, as trappers traded beaver and other pelts for needed supplies. Later gatherings carried on for more than a week and attracted all sorts of characters, who participated in the revelry of horse racing, skill contests, wrestling bouts, gambling, drinking and fighting, and yarn spinning. By the 1830s dwindling fur supplies and changes in fashion were signaling the end of the once-bustling beaver fur trade. The final rendezvous took place in 1840 along the Seedskeedee (Green River) near present-day Daniel in Sublette County. It had also been the site of the 1833, 1835, 1836, 1837, and 1839 rendezvous.

have a fireplace or wood-burning stove, and each cabin is named after an early valley settler.

For dinner the Flying A features a combination of western fare and continental cuisine, but before you feast on the shrimp scampi, Italian delicacies, or Mexican fare, cocktails are served at pondside at the Gilded Moose Saloon. The ranch caters to couples and not to families, so plan to use this as an escape from kids—whether your own or those of others. Rates run around $1,000 per week per person based on double occupancy, with a discounted schedule after September 1. The Flying A Ranch season runs from mid-June to late-September. For information during the season, call 367–2385, or write to them at Route 1, Box 7, Pinedale 82941. During the off-season call (605) 332–0946 or (800) 678–6543, or write 301 North Dakota Avenue, Sioux Falls, SD 57102. Call early because the ranch books up fast.

The Flying A is located 27 miles northwest of Pinedale and 16 miles southeast of Bondurant off Highway 191. Watch for the ranch sign on the right side of the road as you head northwest. (The gate to the entrance will probably be locked, but on making reservations the staff will give you the lock's combination.)

If it's a working cattle ranch experience you'd prefer, try the **Box "R" Ranch** near Cora. The ranch has been in the Lozier family for four generations—it was first homesteaded in 1898—and so it recently attained its "centennial ranch" designation. Once you've reached this secluded getaway, you'll immediately notice the Loziers' pride and joy, the huge horse barn with roofed saddling area.

The scenery is incredible on these deeded lands, bordering the sprawling Bridger Wilderness Area. You'll choose your personal mount for trail rides during your stay from some seventy-five head of horses and mules. Hearty meals are served ranch style, with the wranglers and guests dining side by side. You'll have the opportunity to help round up cattle (early, early in the morning) and move them to new grazing ground. If you've got the interest and are handy with tools, you can even dig in and help Irv Lozier and his son Levi mend fences or work on a guest cabin. All this for only $895 weekly per person, double occupancy. (Does the name Tom Sawyer come to mind?)

The Loziers offer seven ranch and mountain vacations to suit your fancy, ranging from a week of cattle drives to full-service wilderness pack trips. The Box "R" Ranch season runs from late May through mid-September. For complete rates and other information call 367–2291.

For reservations call (800) 822–8466 or write P.O. Box 100, Cora 82925. You can also check into the ranch Web site: www.boxr.com or E-mail them at: info@boxr.com.

Although the fur traders, emigrants, and mounted Indians and cavalry soldiers of yore are all long gone, the pioneer outlook and spirited wild-lands of Wyoming live on, little changed in many ways through the centuries. And nowhere does the pioneer spirit thrive as it does in and around Pinedale, situated near the site of the last mountain man rendezvous. Famously high in elevation and battered by long winters, Pinedale is the doorway to and chief outfitting center for the Wind River Mountains. The Winds encompass fifteen of Wyoming's highest peaks, with Gannett Peak, siting almost directly north of Pinedale, the crown jewel at 13,804 feet. In the Winds you can explore 400,000 acres of Bridger-Teton National Forest wilderness. The mountains hold twenty-seven active glaciers, more than 1,300 alpine lakes, and approximately

The Winds in Winter

*H*aving already spent a fair amount of time in the Wind Rivers backpacking in the summer months, when the high-country trout bite like crazy and so do the mountain mosquitoes, in the late 1970s I decided I'd like to visit the fabulous range during the quiet (and bug-free) white of winter. I was also interested in improving my skiing and general outdoor skills, so I signed on for a three-week winter-camping trip with the Lander-based National Outdoor Leadership School (NOLS).

It was late January 1977, midway through an unusually low-snowfall winter. Still, at the higher elevations our group of sixteen managed to find plenty of snow for practicing our telemark turns, for melting down to make drinking and cooking water, and for building snowcaves to provide cozy sleeping conditions. (Most of

the nights, though, we spent in tents, which weren't nearly as cozy—particularly when the mercury dipped to minus 20, as it did on more than one occasion.)

I was fortunate, because I was already quite practiced at downhill and cross-country skiing. Most of the group members hadn't yet earned their skiing legs, and I remember feeling extremely sorry for them—particularly when one of them would fall over backward while wearing a backpack crammed with eighty pounds of stuff. It was so much like a turtle stuck on his back that the rest of us always had to laugh before helping the hapless skier back to his or her feet.

For three weeks we didn't encounter another soul outside of our tight little group. Not surprisingly, very few folks venture into the Winds in the wild of winter.

600 miles of trails, branching out from nine major trailheads. For more information contact the Pinedale Area Chamber of Commerce at 367-·2242 or the Pinedale Ranger District of the Bridger-Teton National Forest at 367–4326.

Found 4 miles north of town on Fremont Lake Road, stunning *Fremont Lake* sits at the base of the Wind River Mountains. The lake, named after explorer John C. Fremont, is Wyoming's second-largest natural lake and one of the deepest and purest lakes in the nation. Famous for its large lake trout, Fremont Lake once gave up a record-breaking forty-pounder. Spend a day fishing, wading, or swimming at the sandy beach, or camp overnight at the Forest Service campground. Boat rentals and lake tours are also available.

Skyline Drive, beginning at the east end of Pine Street in Pinedale, takes you on a 26-mile, hour-long excursion amid a scenic collection of lakes, mountains, and valleys. Along the way you'll come to Elkhart Park, where you can detour on a hike to *Photographer's Point* in the Bridger Wilderness. The trail is well marked and delivers a fantastic view of Fremont Peak and the Continental Divide country across a deep glacial valley. The round-trip covers about 8 miles.

A longer drive takes you on a 100-mile trip that promises postcard images of wildlife, mountain walls, and alpine lakes. The highlight of the trip, a gigantic glacier-sculpted monolith known as *Square Top Mountain,* towers over the headwaters of the Green River at 11,679 feet. As an added bonus you'll visit the beautiful *Green River Lakes.* Take Highway 191 west 6 miles, and then head north on Highway 352. After the road turns to gravel, travel another 20 miles to reach Green River Lakes and Square Top Mountain. Along the way you'll pass Kendall Warm Springs, home to the rare Kendall dace, a 2-inch-long fish. The remains of Wyoming's first dude ranch, the Billy Wells Ranch, are also along this stretch of road. Be alert for moose, elk, and deer. The Green River Lakes parking area marks the jumping-off spot for day hikes and longer trips. You can camp overnight at the Green River Lakes Campground or nearby Whiskey Grove.

A number of Pinedale area outfitters can lead you on a wide variety of adventures in the Winds. *Bridger Wilderness Outfitters* for instance (367–2268) offers summer and winter wilderness survival courses; youth camps teaching first aid, horseback riding, and leadership skills; fly-fishing pack trips; guided big-game hunts; and stays at the DC Bar Guest Ranch, one of the oldest guest ranches in the area.

Western Wyoming Trivia

Make a point spending a few hours in Pinedale's *Museum of the Mountain Man.* It's located on the east edge of town just off Highway 191 at the top of the hill as you head north on Fremont Lake Road. You'll be treated to an excellent presentation on the fur-trading era and the life of the mountain men. Look for Jim Bridger's own rifle. The kids will especially enjoy the hands-on exhibits, such as the beaver fur that invites you to PLEASE TOUCH ME. Special programs and living-history demonstrations are scheduled during the summer season, and there are additional exhibits on the Plains Indians, tie hacking, and pioneer ranching life. The museum is lively and spacious, a delightful start or end to any day. It's guaranteed to leave a mark on the landscape of your imagination. The museum is open May 1 through October 1 daily from 10:00 A.M. to 6:00 P.M., and in winter from 10:00 A.M. to 4:00 P.M., Monday through Friday. The entrance fee is $4.00 for adults and $2.00 for children. Call 367–4101 for additional information.

In early July, Pinedale hosts the *Green River Rendezvous,* with a reenactment of the 1830s rendezvous, when trappers, traders, and Native Americans gathered at the Green River. Events include a two-hour award-winning pageant (Wyoming's oldest), rodeos, concerts, historic demonstrations, a discussion of Plains Indian culture, and a pit-roasted buffalo feed. For information call 367–4101.

The 1929 *Log Cabin Hotel,* a National Historic Landmark, rents nine cabins and two rooms in the main building. Many have cooking facilities. It's said that ownership of the motel once changed hands in a poker game, but it's no gamble staying at the Log Cabin today. Rates are $70–$85; for more information call 367–4579. Another Pinedale-area overnighting option: *Window on the Winds B&B,* which dishes up a great breakfast (like blueberry dumplings and baked eggs, if you're lucky!) after a night in your rustic room's comfy lodgepole-pine bed. The bed-and-breakfast is located at 10151 Highway 191 in Pinedale; rates range from $45 to $95. For reservations call (888) 367–1345. Even more off the beaten track is *Half Moon Lake Resort* (367–6373), located a few miles northeast of town, 2 miles off the Fremont Lake Road. Cabins, dining, and boat and mountain-bike rentals are among the options at this beautifully situated getaway.

McGregor's Pub, at 21 North Franklin Avenue in Pinedale, serves a variety of excellent dishes, from prime rib to fresh fish at moderate to expensive prices. It's considered *the* place in town for a special dinner out. For reservations call 367–4443.

Teton County

From Pinedale travel northwest on U.S. Highway 189/191, soon crossing the Hoback Rim. Sort of a minicontinental divide, the rim marks the watershed divide separating the Columbia and Colorado River systems. After reaching Hoback Junction, where the Hoback River joins the Snake, you'll notice the traffic beginning to pick up. By the time you reach *Jackson*, it's nearly bumper to bumper.

That's because there's lots to see and do in Jackson, the southern jumping-off point for Grand Teton and Yellowstone National Parks. In keeping with Wyoming's reputation as the Equality State, in 1920 the town of Jackson became the first town in the United States to be governed entirely by women, when voters elected Grace Miller as mayor and chose other women for the four council positions, as well for city clerk, treasurer, and town marshal. The women remained in office until 1923.

Stop in at the historic Wort Hotel at the corner of Glenwood and Broadway and belly up to the *Silver Dollar Bar*, which is inlaid with 2,032 silver dollars. Also check out the display of cattle brands in the lobby near the big old fireplace. JJ's Silverdollar Bar and Grill serves (arguably) the best prime rib in town, as well as other great entrees. Prices are moderate to expensive. For information call 733–2190.

At the *Sweetwater Restaurant* (733–3553), located at the corner of King and Pearl Streets, you can eat indoors or dine on the deck. The lamb and trout are real crowd pleasers. Prices are moderate to expensive. For Asian fare try the *Lame Duck,* hidden away at 680 East Broadway. *Jedediah's Original House of Sourdough* (733–5671) at 135 East Broadway has great pancakes and other sourdough specialties. It's a good choice for breakfast, as is *Nora's Fish Creek Inn* (733–8288), located west of Jackson in the little town of Wilson. For exotic supper fare, including wild game, venture over to the *Gun Barrel Steak & Game House* (733–3287). Compared with the rest of Wyoming, Jackson restaurant prices run moderate to expensive . . . to *very* expensive at gourmet treats like *The Range* (733–5481) and the *Snake River Grill* (733–0557).

> ## Western Wyoming Trivia
>
> *Jackson Hole is the broad, flat expanse of land enclosed by the Teton Mountains on the west; the Yellowstone Plateau on the north; and the Gros Ventre, Hoback, and Snake River Ranges on the east and south. Jackson—without the "Hole"—is the town occupying the southern end of Jackson Hole.*

Behind the Wort Hotel at the corner of Glenwood and Deloney is the *Jackson Hole Historical Society & Museum,* with its extensive collection

Western Wyoming Trivia

James Stevenson and Nathaniel P. Langford, members of the 1872 Hayden Survey, reported that they reached the summit of the Grand Teton on July 29 of that summer. William O. Owen, who climbed the Grand in 1898 with three others, went to his grave claiming that his was the first ascent.

of early Jackson-area photographs, Native American beaded items, fur trade artifacts, and an interesting exhibit of lodgepole furniture from the old Moosehead Ranch. The museum is open summers only when the historical society also offers walking tours of Jackson on Tuesday, Thursday, and Saturday, beginning at 10:00 A.M. For more information call 733–2414.

Jackson Hole, as the greater valley stretching away northward from the town of Jackson is known, hosts a number of exceptional events during the year. The **Grand Teton Music Festival** takes place in Teton Village from late June or early July through mid- or late August. Musicians from the leading orchestras, symphonies, and conservatories across the nation journey to Jackson to perform in more than thirty orchestral and chamber music concerts, all conducted at the acoustically acclaimed Walk Festival Hall. For a schedule of performance dates and information, call 733–1128, or write P.O. Box 490, Teton Village 83025.

Later in the year the **Fall Arts Festival** showcases the area's rich artistic traditions and talents with a variety of exhibits, workshops, and demonstrations. The festival continues for three weeks, during which Jackson galleries exhibit the works of regionally and nationally acclaimed artists. Special events include quilting demonstrations, a western art symposium, a dance festival, and a miniature art show and sale. For dates and a complete list of activities, contact the Jackson Hole Chamber of Commerce by calling 733–3316 or (800) 443–6931, or via the Internet at: www.jackson-holechamber.com.

Don't miss the photo ops offered by the four-cornered, elk-antler entrance-ways to the **Town Square,** which is especially beautiful when adorned with Christmas lights during the holiday season. And, speaking of antlers, the **National Elk Refuge** sprawls away beginning at the north edge of Jackson. Several thou-

Abandoned cabin in the Tetons

sand elk migrate here for the winter and linger until spring, when they gradually head back to their mountain territory. Boy Scout troops of the

Jackson area gather the shed antlers each spring and sell them at an auction in the Jackson Town Square in May, usually raising more than a hundred thousand dollars. Eighty percent of the funds raised goes back to purchasing pelletized alfalfa feed for the wintering elk. For information on winter sleigh-drawn tours of the National Elk Refuge, call 733–9212.

Western Wyoming Trivia

A pair of employees at the National Elk Refuge in Jackson Hole recently built the refuge's new 6,400-square-foot headquarters. They completed the job for an estimated one-third of what it would have cost had the refuge employed a private contracting firm.

The sleigh rides begin just across the highway from the heralded, hillside, 51,000-square-foot ***National Museum of Wildlife Art,*** open since 1994. Its architecture, consisting of native rock, mirrors the surrounding countryside, helping the immense building blend into its setting so completely that some passersby fail to notice it. The museum's collection comprises hundreds of artworks in a variety of media, including painting, sculpture, and photography. More than one hundred artists are featured, including John James Audubon, Antoine-Louise Barye, Albert Bierstadt, Carl Runguis, Charlie Russell, and Thomas Moran. Indoor exhibits span more than two hundred years of wildlife art, and there's also a wonderful outdoor sculpture garden. The facilities include an auditorium, meeting rooms, and the Rising Sage Cafe (operated by the people who bring you the high-end Spring Creek Resort). The National Museum of Wildlife Art is located off Highway 26/89/191 about 3 miles north of the Jackson Town Square. For information call 733–5771.

Western Wyoming Trivia

Effie Jane Wilson, born 1891, was the first white child born in Jackson Hole. Rose Park Marshall, who preceded Effie Jane by ten years, was the first white baby born in Yellowstone National Park.

Before heading north into Grand Teton National Park, consider taking a detour "over the hill"— the hill being 8,429-foot Teton Pass—to Teton Valley, Idaho. Why mention Idaho in a book about Wyoming? Because traveling via Idaho is the only way to drive into the western reaches of Teton County, Wyoming.

From Driggs, Idaho, go west on Ski Hill Road. In about 6 miles you'll cross State Line Road and roll into beautiful downtown Alta, Wyoming. A superb place to stay in Alta, particularly for families, and in winter or summer, is the ***Teton Tepee Lodge*** (353–8176). For a multicourse, Oriental-style dinner that will remain among your most memorable dining experiences (let's just say it's unique), make reservations for a weekend evening at the ***Lost Horizon Dinner Club*** (353– 8226). From Alta it's another 5 steep uphill miles to ***Grand Targhee Ski & Summer Resort***

(353–2300), widely recognized by downhill skiers as one of the country's premier deep-powder ski areas. In summer chairlift rides to the top of the mountain provide unmatched views of the high Teton peaks, and the resort's two or three summer music festivals are well on their way to becoming legendary.

As you drive back to Jackson, swing into the tasting room of the **Otto Brothers Brewing Company.** It's located in Wilson, at the eastern foot of Teton Pass, in a tiny old log cabin near the hardware store. Whether you sample the Moose Juice Stout or another of Otto Brothers' foamy concoctions, you can't go wrong. And if it's winter and you happen to have your ice skates along, don't miss the lighted rink at nearby **Owen Bircher Park.** With laughing kids of all ages decked out in their most colorful winter garb, and snow piled high on the sides of the rink, the scene is a Currier & Ives card come to life.

Now, back in Jackson, head north from town on U.S. Highway 191. (Alternatively, from back in Wilson, you could choose to sneak along the back gravel route, known as the Moose-Wilson Road.) The **Gros Ventre River Ranch,** on the eastern edge of the Bridger-Teton National Forest along the Gros Ventre (pronounced *grow vahnt*) River Road, offers luxurious accommodations with far-ranging views of the Tetons. The ranch can house thirty-four guests in its heated log cabins and additional guests in the log lodge and old homestead house. A short drive takes you to the site of the giant 1925 Gros Ventre Slide, which swept down Sheep Mountain and across the Gros Ventre River, creating the mile-long lake you see today. The waters burst through their natural earthen dam in 1927 and demolished ranches downstream, as well as the town of Kelly (since rebuilt in another location).

The Gros Ventre River Ranch takes guests by the week or for a three-day minimum. Rates vary by season and type of accommodations. Summer season runs from May 1 through October 31. Winter season runs from December 1 through January 8 for housekeeping cabins only and January 9 through March 31 for accommodations, meals, and use of ranch facilities. For information call 733–4138, or write P.O. Box 151, Moose 83012.

If you're looking for a unique Western experience while in the Tetons or surrounding areas, consider joining up with one of several operations that provide summer wagon train rides or, in winter, sled-dog tours. Contact the **Bar-T-Five Covered Wagon Cookout and Wild West Show** in Jackson at 733–5386 or **Grand Teton Covered Wagon Cookouts** in the Buffalo Valley at 543–2407. If there's snow on the ground, and you'd like to give mushing a try, call **Jackson Hole Iditarod Sled Dog Tours** at 733–7388.

Back on the main highway heading north, you'll drive through the heart of *Grand Teton National Park,* established on a smaller scale in 1929 and now encompassing almost 500 square miles. One of the youngest mountain ranges on the North American continent, the Tetons rise to over 13,000 feet and tower 7,000 feet over the valley meadows below. The absence of foothills makes the Tetons' lofty peaks appear all the more impressive.

Like Yellowstone National Park to the north, Grand Teton offers plenty of hiking opportunities, with more than 250 miles of trails winding through mellow meadows and up steep mountain drainages. Several trails start at picturesque glacial Jenny Lake, with the pack of peaks known as the Cathedral Group providing an awesome backdrop. For trail conditions, backcountry permits, and information on how to remain bear aware, call 739–3300. (Entrance fees to GTNP are $20 per car for a seven-day pass, which will also get you into Yellowstone.)

Young Mountains

*G*eologically speaking, the jagged, abrupt Tetons are in their infancy. Look across Jackson Hole to the east, and you'll see rising, in dramatic contrast to the faulted, bereft-of-foothills Tetons, the Gros Ventre Mountains, a classic—and much older—folded range, embraced by rolling foothills.

Why are the Tetons so strikingly steep and composed of bare rock? At less than ten million years old, they are the youngest and least eroded of all the Rocky Mountains. Most of the activity along the young Teton Fault, which follows the eastern base of the mountains, has happened within the last five million years. The Tetons and Jackson Hole are both tilted blocks of the earth's crust. As the Teton block moves upward along the fault line, the Jackson Hole block moves down. This explains why the highest peaks of the relatively small range rise immediately along the east front

rather than in the middle of the range, as is common with older, more eroded mountains.

The Tetons surely would be a magnificent sight to see even if they hadn't undergone a final sculpting. But "finish work" did occur here and throughout the region in very recent geologic times. Periodically during the last two million years, glaciers covered Yellowstone and much of Grand Teton National Park and Jackson Hole, then retreated. In the mountains the ice-fields left behind ragged horns, shimmering lakes, and steep cirques at the head of deep U-shaped valleys. On the slopes and in the valleys below, they deposited boulders and laid down the gravels and rock debris of terminal moraines and lateral moraines. They also dug out future lake bottoms, fashioned the depressions called kettles, and dammed rivers with the soils and rocks they deposited.

Be sure to stop at the **Chapel of the Transfiguration** near Moose. The log chapel was constructed in 1925 and is still in use for church services and weddings. The plate glass window behind the altar frames a most inspiring view of Grand Teton, the tallest peak in the park at 13,772 feet, and the second highest in all of Wyoming. (Only Gannett Peak in the Wind Rivers is higher, by just 32 feet.) The park offers a number of ranger-led activities, such as a "fire-and-ice cruise" that includes a discussion of how forest fires and glaciers have shaped the area landscape; Native American art and culture discussions; and wildflower hikes and programs for budding naturalists. Inquire at the visitors centers for dates and times of programs. By all means don't miss the **Indian Arts Museum** at the Colter Bay Visitors Center, with its extensive, one-man collection of Native American clothing and art. Exhibits include an 1850s Crow shield, ceremonial pipes, dozens of beaded moccasins, and fine examples of prehistoric basketry. Under lock and key here and viewable on request is the controversial Colter Stone (see "John Colter," p. 72). The visitor centers in the park are typically open from mid-May through Labor Day. For more detailed information call Grand Teton National Park at 739–3300.

Yellowstone National Park

The world's first national park, Yellowstone was created on March 1, 1872, with President Ulysses S. Grant signing the "Organic Act" legislation. The park encompasses some 2.2 million acres, less than 5 percent of which is roaded or otherwise developed. The balance remains wilderness, containing more than sixty species of mammals, two hundred types of birds, and a half-dozen species of game fish. In addition the park has twelve tree species and dozens of types of wildflowers. The lowest elevation is 5,314 feet at the north entrance, and the highest spot is Eagle Peak Summit at 11,358 feet. The park's regular season is from early May through the beginning of November; the winter season is from early December through early March. For information call 344–7381, or visit the Web site: www.nps.gov.

Western Wyoming Trivia

Probably due to underlying heat and magma, the ground beneath LeHardy Rapids, located in Yellowstone National Park about 3 miles north of Fishing Bridge, has bulged upward 3 feet in the last seventy-five years.

Staying off the beaten path in Yellowstone National Park can be quite a trick because there are only a few designated roads to get you through. One tactic is to completely avoid the peak tourist season and visit in spring or fall when the beaten track becomes less traveled, or postpone your Yellowstone adventure until the

Fishing Cone

Yellowstone's bubbling, aromatic West Thumb Geyser Basin is the site of Fishing Cone, a geyser with a most peculiar history. The cone rises from the shallow, near-to-shore waters of Yellowstone Lake, looking rather like a crater on the surface of the moon. A member of 1870s Washburn Expedition, whose members visited the site, told folks back home about his experience of catching a fish in the lake then inadvertently dropping it into this cone-shaped geyser. On pulling it out, the fish was well done!

Word spread, and by 1903 prospective visitors were reading in national publications that a trip to Yellowstone was incomplete without the hook-and-cook experience. The practice became so popular—practically a "must," rather like witnessing the great falls of the upper Yellowstone River—that National Park Service personnel eventually banned fishing in the area in order to protect overly enthusiastic bait-and-boilers from cooking themselves.

winter season. The park takes on an altogether different appearance under a deep mantle of snow, so even if you've been there dozens of times during the summer, Yellowstone will seem like a new place.

In winter Yellowstone's heartland is accessible by ten-passenger enclosed and heated snowcoaches, snowmobiles, cross-country skis, and showshoes only. Warming huts throughout the park provide shelter for a brief rest (or possibly for a bivouac in serious weather conditions). Overnight accommodations are available at Old Faithful and also at Mammoth Hot Springs at the north edge of the park. Room rates range from $80 to $140 at the Old Faithful Snow Lodge; and $80 to $120 at the Snow Lodge Cabins. At Mammoth, which can be reached by car in winter, there is a variety of accommodations, ranging from $62 to $265. The park offers snowcoach tours, guided ski tours, ski lessons, and snowmobile and cross-country rentals.

No matter what activities and modes of travel you engage in, you'll have an unforgettable experience, for the phrase "winter wonderland" might well have been coined to describe Yellowstone. The geysers that are so spectacular in summer are perhaps even more so in winter; with snow-covered branches and glistening ice surrounding newly erupted geysers, the landscape takes on a fairy tale appearance. Buffalo and elk plowing through the deep snows are likewise a awesome sight. For snowmobilers the newly completed 370-mile Continental Divide Snowmobile Trail from West Yellowstone to the Lander area offers a host of loop and point-to-point possibilities. (For a copy of the snowmobile trail map, call the Bureau of Land Management at 347–5100.) For winter activities, rates, and lodging reservations in Yellowstone, contact TW Recreational Services at 344–7901.

If traveling Yellowstone during the peak season is your only option, don't despair. Some of the following sights and strategies will keep you away from the major crowds and provide Yellowstone experiences relatively few have shared.

To earn an up-close view of the aftermath of the 1988 fires, walk the 1-mile Duck Lake Trail, which begins near the large mudpot in the parking lot of the West Thumb Geyser Basin. Not from here locals in the know stay at the *Lake Yellowstone Hotel,* with its grand pillared entryway and rocking chair views of Yellowstone Lake. It's a gorgeous structure that's

John Colter

*D*uring the winter of 1807–08 John Colter, lately of the Lewis and Clark Expedition, made a roundabout, 500-mile trek through the primeval heart of northwest Wyoming. Employed by Manuel Lisa, a young Spaniard from New Orleans who'd established a trading post at the confluence of the Yellowstone and Big Horn Rivers, Colter was surveying the country for its trapping potential, while also trying to convince Indians to travel to and trade at Lisa's Fort Remon.

Colter left no known maps, but it's believed that from Fort Remon he crested the Pryor Mountains, then followed the Clark's Fork River into the rugged Absaroka Range. From Dead Indian Hill he traveled down to the Shoshone River, near present Cody, where he encountered the stinking springs that became known as "Colter's Hell." From Togwotee (TOE-guh-tee) Pass he dropped into the northern end of Jackson Hole. At the opposite end of the uninhabited valley, he's thought to

have forded the Snake River before pressing over Teton Pass into Teton Valley. This portion of the trek is supported by the only known physical evidence remaining of Colter's adventure: The controversial "Colter Stone," a rhyolite slab etched on one side with the year "1808" and on the opposite side with the name "John Colter." The rock was discovered in 1931 by Teton Valley resident William Beard. (The Colter Stone can be seen today, on request at the Indian Arts Museum at Colter Bay in Grand Teton National Park.)

After returning to Jackson Hole, Colter traveled north along the west bank of the Snake until wading the river above Jackson Lake. Finally, in what must have been the dead of snow-smothered winter, he traversed the future Yellowstone National Park en route back to Lisa's fort. There he made little of his remarkable journey, leaving much, including the exact route taken, to speculation. Still, there's no disputing that John Colter accomplished one of the greatest backpacking trips ever.

listed on the National Register of Historic Places. Rooms rates range from $138 to $152. For information on and reservations at these and other accommodations in the park, call 344–7311 or 242–3708, or visit the Web site: www.ynp-lodges.com.

Another intriguing stop is the **Fishing Bridge Visitor Center** on the north end of Yellowstone Lake. The exhibits here center on Yellowstone's birds and mammals, and they will help you more readily identify the wildlife you see during your subsequent park travels. The center, open from 8:00 A.M. to 7:00 P.M. in summer, also covers lake geology within Yellowstone. A National Historic Landmark, the center was built in 1929–30. For information call 242–2450.

The best way to avoid the crowds during the summer months is to take off on your choice of more than 1,200 miles of **hiking trails** within Yellowstone. It's said that nearly 95 percent of park visitors wander no farther than 400 feet from their cars; so, even when the traffic between Old Faithful and Madison Junction is backed up bumper to bumper, most of Yellowstone's backcountry goes untrod by hiking boots. Pick up a guide to Yellowstone's hiking trails at one of the park's visitor centers or at one of the Hamilton Stores located throughout the park. (Check out the burled lodgepole pine logs used in the porch construction and the sign above the entrance of the original **Hamilton Store** near the Old Faithful Inn.)

All overnight hikes and some day hikes into restricted areas require backcountry use permits. Apply at a park ranger station or visitor center up to forty-eight hours before beginning your hike. Know your hiking capabilities and limitations: As a general rule plan on one hour for every 2 miles and add an hour for every 1,000 feet you ascend. Check out the topography on a map in advance so you know the difficulty of your proposed hike. Be prepared: Carry a trail map, compass, matches, insect repellent, first-aid kit, knife, bear spray, and rain gear as a minimum.

For starters in the Canyon-Tower area, try the relatively tame **Tower Falls Trail,** which comes out at the base of the falls. Or Uncle Tom's Trail, a strenuous walk dropping some 500 feet in a series of 300 stairs and paved inclines to the base of the Lower Falls. The **North Rim Trail** offers several views along its route, including that of the Artist Point Road Bridge, Crystal Falls, and Upper and Lower Falls. All of these are listed in the pamphlet, *Canyon,* that is available at park visitor centers.

To get even farther away from the crowds, you can expand your hiking ventures beyond the Yellowstone backcountry into the Greater Yellowstone area—to the nearby Absaroka-Beartooth Wilderness, one of the highest alpine areas in the nation, or into the Shoshone National Forest east of the park.

Yellowstone's volcanic past and present are evidenced by its geysers and hot springs, mudpots, and fumaroles. The park contains the largest and most varied concentration of geothermal features in the world. Overall there are some ten thousand known thermal features here, including nearly two hundred geysers. Some geyers erupt almost continually, while others may lie dormant for months or years. The world's largest geyser, **Steamboat Geyser,** shoots water and steam more than 300 feet in the air, and its eruptions can last up to twelve hours. Steamboat Geyser is located in the Norris Geyser Basin in the Back Basin segment.

The Wolf

*T*he mid-1990s reintroduction of wolves to Yellowstone's Lamar Valley has resulted in additional thousands of people flocking to the park to have a look. The wolf has, in many ways, supplanted the bear as the animal to see while in Yellowstone. This is largely because, since park rangers began discouraging the human feeding of bears in the 1970s, seeing one has become a much less common occurrence. Winter is the opportune time to see these controversial canids without the disturbance of crowds.*

The endangered Canadian wolf hadn't been seen in Yellowstone for more than sixty years until their reintroduction during the winter of 1994–95. For the most part the wolves kept to the Lamar Valley during the summer of 1995 and caused considerable "wolf jams," as tourists strained their necks to get a peek. The wolves have since moved out into Pelican Valley and other park— and nonpark—locations, breaking into several identifiable packs.

The mature gray wolf (Canis lupus) is approximately three times larger than

the coyote (Canis latrans). To determine whether it's a wolf or a coyote you're looking at, consider the following facts. The wolf is full-bodied, while the coyote is more slender or delicate in stature. The wolf will reach an average height of 26–34 inches versus only 16–22 inches for the coyote. This adds up to a weight of 70–120 pounds for a mature wolf and just 27–33 pounds for a coyote. The ears of the wolf are rounded and relatively short, and its muzzle is large and broad. In comparison the coyote's ears are long and pointed, and its muzzle is long and narrow. Incidentally, by no means are all gray wolves are gray; their coats can range from snow white to coal black.

The sight of a wolf shadowing through the woods or trotting through a snowy meadow or the sound of Canis lupus howling at the winter moon can stir primeval feelings within even the most "civilized" man or woman. Check with the park about recent wolf sightings, and take a pair of binoculars or a zoom lens to get a close-up view in case you do encounter a wolf.

The *Museum of the National Park Ranger* at Norris is bypassed by the majority of park visitors. It's particularly interesting, however, with its displays tracing the history of the park ranger profession from soldiers to today's specialists. And the porch fronting the shimmering Gibbon River is an unusually enticing spot to relax on a warm summer afternoon. At Mammoth Hot Springs, stop at the U.S. Engineer's Office for a glimpse at an unusual piece of architecture. Designed by the Minneapolis firm of Reed and Stem in 1906, the building is known affectionately as The Pagoda, owing to its Asian appearance.

Petrified tree, Yellowstone

To leave the park head out the northeast corner via the Lamar Valley, aiming for Cody via *Chief Joseph Scenic Highway.* The highway was officially dedicated on September 12, 1995, celebrating the completion of a twenty-seven-year, multiagency effort to build and improve one of the most spectacular alpine highways of the West. The finishing of the Chief Joseph closed the last pavement gap in Wyoming's state highway system.

PLACES TO STAY IN BRIDGER-YELLOWSTONE COUNTRY

AFTON
Mountain Inn,
83542 Highway 89,
Route 1;
(307) 886-3156

Silver Stream Lodge
(seasonal),
95329 Highway 89;
(307) 883-2440

ALPINE
Alpen Haus,
junction of Highways 89 & 26;
(307) 654-7545 or
(800) 343-6755

Best Western Flying Saddle Lodge,
Highway 89 & 26;
(307) 654-7561

COKEVILLE
Valley Hi Motel,
Highway 30 North;
(307) 279-3251

JACKSON
Elk Refuge Inn,
U.S. Highway 89 North;
(307) 733-3582 or
(800) 544-3582

Motel 6,
600 South U.S. Highway 89;
(307) 733-1620

Painted Buffalo Inn,
400 West Broadway;
(307) 733-4340 or
(800) 288-3866

Rusty Parrot Lodge,
175 North Jackson;
(307) 733-2000 or
(800) 458-2004

Super 8 Motel,
750 U.S. Highway 89 South;
(307) 733-6833 or
(800) 800-8000

KEMMERER
Antler Motel,
419 Coral Street;
(307) 877-4461

Lake Viva Naughton
Marina Motel,
Highway 233,
15 miles north of town;
(307) 877-9669

PINEDALE
Lakeside Lodge Resort
Marina (seasonal),
on Fremont Lake;
(307) 367-2221

Pine Creek Inn,
650 West Pine;
(307) 367-2191

Wagon Wheel Motel,
407 South Pine;
(307) 367-2871

TETON VILLAGE
Crystal Springs Inn,
3285 West McCollister Drive;
(307) 733-4423

Best Western Inn
at Jackson Hole;
(307) 733-2311 or
(800) 842-7666

**PLACES TO EAT IN
BRIDGER-YELLOWSTONE
COUNTRY
(ALL AREA CODES 307)**

AFTON
Elkhorn Restaurant,
465 Washington;
886-3080

Barron Drive Inn,
838 Washington;
886-3745

Colter's Bar (Old West
atmosphere),
355 Washington;
886-9891

ALPINE
Bette's Coffee Shop;
654-7536

Brentoven's Restaurant,
1 Colonial Lane;
654-7556

COKEVILLE
A & W;
279-3271

JACKSON
Billy's Burgers,
adjacent to Cadillac Grille
across from Town Square;
733-3279

Bubba's Bar-B-Que,
515 West Broadway;
733-2288

The Gun Barrel Steak
and Game House,
862 West Broadway;
733-EATS (3287)

Million Dollar
Cowboy Steakhouse,
across from Town Square
on Cache;
733-4790

Snake River Grill
(fine dining),
across from Town Square
on Broadway;
733-0557

Jackson Hole Pub
& Brewery,
265 South Millward;
739-BEER (2337)

KEMMERER
Busy B Cafe,
919 Pine;
877-6820

Little Mexico,
801 South Main;
877-9969

PINEDALE
Corral Bar
& Calamity Jane's,
30 West Pine;
367-2469

Sue's Bread Box,
423 West Pine;
367-2150

McGregor's Pub,
21 North Franklin;
367-4443

TETON VILLAGE
Mangy Moose Saloon
& Restaurant,
south end of Teton Village;
733-4913

The Alpenhof Lodge
Dining Room,
north end of Teton Village;
733-3462

WILSON
Nora's Fish Creek Inn,
5600 West Highway 22;
733-8288

Pearl Street Bagels,
5400 West Highway 22;
739-1261

Northern Wyoming: Devils Tower— Buffalo Bill Country

Northern Wyoming is a land of jarring contrasts. Verdant, storm-attracting mountains like the Absarokas (*Ab-SORE-uh-kuhs*) and Big Horns rim dry valleys such as the Big Horn Basin, a baked expanse of badlands and irrigated farmlands, where fewer than seven inches of precipitation fall in a typical year. The extreme northeast corner, best known as home to Devils Tower National Monument, actually includes a western extension of South Dakota's alluring Black Hills. This area holds a terrain unlike that found anywhere else in the state, where numerous plant and animal species common to the Midwest and the West rarely found together comingle.

From Cody, the eastern gateway to Yellowstone National Park and one of many Wyoming namesakes of William F. "Buffalo Bill" Cody, this route takes you to the warm-water wonders of Thermopolis. From there you'll travel north through Big Horn Basin towns like Worland and Greybull, then over the high Big Horns to Sheridan and Buffalo. Finally, from Gillette you'll head to Devils Tower before turning south toward Sundance and Newcastle.

Park County

One way to travel to Cody from Yellowstone is through the spectacular Wapiti Valley, as the canyon of the North Fork of the Shoshone River is called. President Theodore Roosevelt called the Wapiti

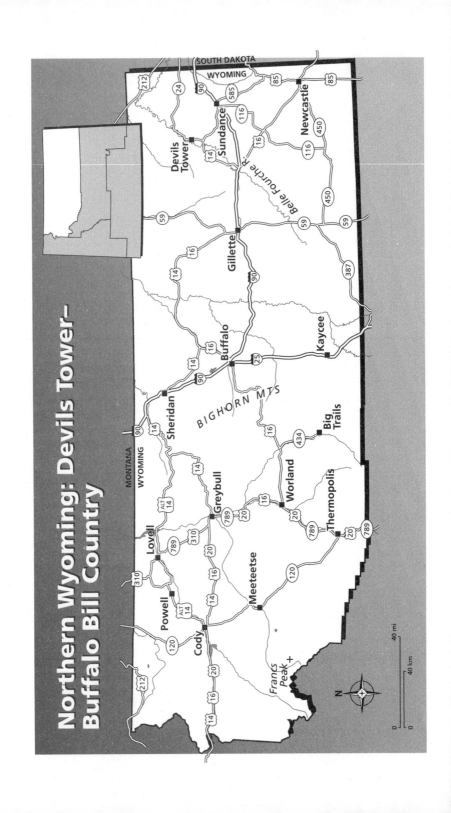

Northern Wyoming: Devils Tower–Buffalo Bill Country

BEST ANNUAL EVENTS IN DEVILS TOWER—BUFFALO BILL COUNTRY
(ALL AREA CODES 307)

Plains Indian Powwow,
Cody; June; 587–4771

Wildflower Festival and
Craft Fair, Buffalo; June;
684-5544

Cody Stampede Rodeo,
Cody; Fourth of July;
587-5155

Sheepherder Rodeo & Dog
Trails, Kaycee; Fourth of
July; 738–2381

Annual Frontier Festival,
Cody; July; 578–4014

Gift of the Waters Pageant,
Thermopolis; August;
864-3192

Buffalo Bill Festival,
Cody;, August; 587–2297

Deke Latham Memorial
PRCA Rodeo, Kaycee; Labor
Day Weekend; 738–2381

Valley between Cody and Yellowstone "the most scenic 50 miles in America" (or "in the world," depending on which account one reads). The road drops through the Shoshone National Forest, the first national forest in the country, created by President Benjamin Harrison on March 30, 1891. Wapiti Valley holds fast-moving rivers and lazy streams, sheer desert cliffs of colorful rock formations and heavily timbered north-facing slopes, and large populations of wildlife, from airborne eagles and peregrine falcons to grounded bear and elk.

To see this rough-hewn stretch of the West as it was meant to be seen—aboard the back of a horse, that is—stop in at one of several resorts and dude ranches lining the way. ***Absaroka Mountain Lodge*** (587–3963), for instance, which you'll find situated about 12 miles east of the entrance to Yellowstone.

William F. Cody was an early promoter of building a dam to impound waters that would be used to irrigate the potentially fertile lands around Cody. The ***Buffalo Bill Dam*** was completed in 1910 at a cost of nearly one million dollars. The view of the Shoshone Canyon is tremendous from the glass-walled visitor center or from the open walkway on top of the dam. The dam is located 6 miles west of Cody on the Yellowstone Highway (U.S. Highway 14/16/20). The visitor center is open from approximately May 1 through the end of September from 8:00 A.M. to 8:00 P.M. daily. For information call 527–6076.

The reservoir created by the dam and the shorelines surrounding the lake are within the boundaries of ***Buffalo Bill State Park,*** with its excellent trout fishing, camping, hiking, and water sports. Aided by the Wyoming winds that are so common, the spot is growing in popularity as a destination for savvy wind surfers. The park entrance fee is $3.00, and camping is an additional $4.00 per vehicle. For information call 587–9227.

The Shoshone River Canyon offers ample opportunity for thrilling rafting excursions. ***Wyoming River Trips*** is Cody's oldest and most experienced river-rafting company, with a number of trip options to choose from through the boating season. For rates and schedules call 587–6661 or (800) 586–6661, or write to Box 1541–V, Cody 82414.

Alternatively, as beautiful as the Wapiti Valley is, you may opt to take a different route from Yellowstone to Cody: the *Chief Joseph Scenic Highway* (mentioned at the end of the previous chapter), which leads through country even more majestic than the Wapiti Valley, if the majesty of mountains and valleys such as these can be ranked. The road has been widened and turnouts have been constructed, allowing visitors to sightsee and take advantage of the many photo opportunities along the way. On parts of the scenic highway, you'll trace the route taken by Chief Joseph and his 800 fellow Nez Perce Indians as they fled the U.S. Army in 1877. If it happens to be late September when you're traveling the route, the displays of oranges, yellows, and reds put on by autumn-burnt aspen and smaller shrubs are out of this world, providing explosions of color that contrast magnificently with the drab brown hillsides. At Sunlight Creek the highway crosses the highest bridge in Wyoming, standing 280 feet above the creek. Stop at the side of the road after crossing the bridge and walk back to enjoy the heart-stopping view of the canyon below.

Farther up the road pull off at Dead Indian Summit for a panoramic view that encompasses the North Absaroka Wilderness, Sunlight Basin, the lofty Precambrian heights of the Beartooth Plateau to the north, and Yellowstone National Park to the west. Look down on the road you followed to get to this point: It seems to disappear, consumed by the medley of lush valley lands, colorful rock upthrusts, and snow-topped mountains. The Chief Joseph Scenic Highway meets State Highway 120 at a point approximately 17 miles northwest of Cody.

There's a lot to see in Cody in addition to the world-class attraction known the *Buffalo Bill Historical Center* (307–587–5714). More than one full day is required to really do the town justice. With that in mind, consider bunking at the *Cody Guest Houses.* Here you'll find a variety of accommodations to choose from, including the charming Annie Oakley and Buffalo Bill western cottages; luxurious three-bedroom homes (the 1906 Victorian House and the Mayor's Inn), and the four-bedroom Western Lodge.

A three-year restoration transformed the Victorian House into a real showpiece. The home's original front door, with its leaded stained glass, opens into another era. Artistic hand stenciling graces walls framed by renovated woodwork, and the works of local artists are featured in the gallery. Other rooms and amenities include a formal parlor and living room, dining room, den with television and stereo, spa, patio and barbecue, fireplace, and laundry facilities.

Next door, in the Western Lodge, you can experience a different way of life. Abundant windows surround the living room, and Western-theme paintings and crafts abound throughout the spacious home, which can accommodate as many as eight people. After days on the road, you and the kids will enjoy getting your own separate quarters, and the billiards room will keep both kids and adults occupied for hours.

Each guest house has a kitchen, and all can be rented by the day or by the week. Peak season rates (June 1 through September 30) run from $95 to $195 nightly for the cottages; $300 for the Western Lodge; and $450 for the Victorian House. The Cody Guest Houses office is located at 1401 Rumsey Avenue. For information on weekly rates or for reservations, call 587–6000 or (800) 587–6560.

Start your exploration of Cody at *The Irma,* the historic hotel built of native wood and limestone by Buffalo Bill Cody in 1902 and named after the famous westerner's youngest daughter, Irma Louise. The dark old dining room, which originally served as the hotel bar and billiards room, retains its turn-of-the-century western feel: A fancy antique cash register sits at the check-out counter; the walls are covered with wildlife paintings and big-game mounts; an elk-antler chandelier hangs from the tin-covered ceiling; and small molded bison heads decorate the sides of the dining-booth benches. The ornate, French-produced cherrywood back bar that leans against one wall was shipped in 1900 to Buffalo Bill from Queen Victoria of England, as a gift of thanks for Cody and his Wild West Show's royal performance. The Irma, listed on the National Register of Historic Places, still operates as a hotel, with renovated rooms furnished in turn-of-the-century motif. Each room is named after a Cody-area settler and goes for $71 to $98 nightly. The Irma is located at 1192 Sheridan Avenue. For information call 587–4221 or (800) 745–IRMA.

The original Buffalo Bill Museum opened in 1927 in the log structure that now houses the *Cody Chamber of Commerce.* The rudiments of the museum go back even farther, to 1917, when, shortly after Buffalo

---

BEST ATTRACTIONS IN DEVILS TOWER—BUFFALO BILL COUNTRY
(ALL AREA CODES 307)

Buffalo Bill Historical Center, Cody; 587–5714

Old Trail Town, Cody; 587–5302

Charles J. Belden Museum, Meeteetse; 868–2264

Hot Springs State Park, Thermopolis; 864–3765.

Wind River Canyon, south of Thermopolis

Tensleep Preserve, outside Tensleep; 366–2671

Medicine Lodge Creek State Archaeological Site, outside Hyattville; 469–2234

The Medicine Wheel, outside Lovell; 548–6541

King's Ropes and Saddlery, Sheridan; 672–2702

Bradford Brinton Museum, Big Horn; 672–3173

Fort Phil Kearney, outside Story; 684–7629

Bill's death, some Cody residents created the Buffalo Bill Memorial Association. Its mission: To "build, construct, and maintain an historical monument of memorial stature in honor of and to perpetuate the memory of our late lamented fellow townsman Hon. William F. Cody." The impressive **Cody Mural,** found in the LDS Church at Seventeenth Street and Wyoming Avenue, covers the entire domed ceiling of the chapel foyer and depicts significant events of the period between 1827 and 1893. Summer tours are offered Monday through Saturday, 9:00 A.M. to 9:00 P.M. For information call 587–3290.

Serious carnivores won't want to leave Cody without sampling a mouth-watering steak at **Cassie's Supper Club,** a historic landmark that was originally opened in the 1920s and operated as a house of ill repute by its owner, Cassie Waters. In addition to the quality steaks, a variety of chicken, seafood, and pasta dishes await your taste buds. Prices are moderate to expensive. After you eat, you can stomp your feet to live country music in the saloon on Tuesday through Saturday, join the dip-and-twirl dance lessons on Wednesday evening, or participate in a Sunday evening open-mike session, where anyone can get up to play or sing. Cassie's is located at 214 Yellowstone Avenue. For reservations or information call 527–5500.

Old Trail Town, on the western outskirts of Cody, takes you right back to the frontier days, with the reconstruction/relocation of more than twenty historic buildings of the late 1800s. Check out the bullet holes in the door of the Rivers Saloon from Meeteetse, then stop in at the cabin that was used by Butch Cassidy and gang in the Hole in the Wall country, south-west of Kaycee. Before you git out of town, visit the adjacent cemetery and final resting place for the likes of mountain man John "Liver-Eatin'" Johnston and buffalo hunter Jim White. Old Trail Town, located at 1831 DeMaris Drive, is open daily from 8:00 A.M. to 8:00 P.M., mid-May through mid-September. The cost of admission is $3.00 for those twelve and older, free for those under. For additional information call 587–5302.

Northern Wyoming Trivia

The town of Powell was planned in the late 1890s by the Department of Interior, as headquarters for the Shoshone River Reclamation Project, an effort designed to deliver water to the thirsty Big Horn Basin that was initiated by William F. "Buffalo Bill" Cody.

Before heading south toward Meeteetse and leaving Park County, consider swinging up to Powell, population 5,292. Take Highway 14A northeast from Cody to get there. Named after the legendary Colorado River explorer Maj. John Wesley Powell, the town is home to the **Homesteader's Museum,** which honors the folks who settled the surrounding valley. Located at the corner of Clark

Old Trail Town, Cody

and First Streets in a historic log building built in 1932 by local American Legionnaires, the museum preserves the heritage of the area via photographs, artifacts, early tools, and farm machinery. The museum is open May 1 through September 30, Tuesday through Friday, 1:00 to 5:00 P.M., and the rest of the year on Friday and Saturday, 10:00 A.M. to noon and 1:00 to 5:00 P.M. For information call 754–9481.

On the return trip to Cody, stop at the *Heart Mountain Relocation Center Monument,* located about 12 miles northeast of Cody on Highway 14A. On-site information explains the relocation camp, where some 11,000 American citizens of Japanese ancestry—two-thirds of them American born—were confined for nearly three years during World War II, making it the third-largest "city" in Wyoming at the time. The Heart Mountain Relocation Center was one of ten camps built to house collectively more than 100,000 Japanese Americans. People were held in detention here even if they had family members serving in the U.S. armed forces. This camp was closed in November 1945, and all that remains today are a few foundations. A portion of the center is listed on the National Register of Historic Places.

En route to Meeteetse, at a point approximately 12 miles outside Cody, pull over to the *Halfway House Stage Stop.* Located halfway between Corbett Crossing and Stinking Water Creek, the stage stop was in use as late as 1908 before automobiles made it obsolete.

For a settlement supporting a population of fewer than 400, Meeteetse offers a variety of interesting sites. The town's curious name derives from the Crow Indian word for "meeting place of the chiefs." Stop in at the more than one hundred-year-old *Cowboy Bar* (868–2585), located at 1936 State Street, for a cool one, and take a gander at the hand-carved Italian rose and cherrywood bar. The Meeteetse Social Club meets regularly at the saloon on weekends for an old-fashioned gathering, with card playing and socializing. Then wander next door to the venerable **Meeteetse Mercantile Company** to enjoy the aura of an Old west general store. The enterprise stocks a wide array of products, from yard goods to home furnishings. For the tourist, there's a good selection of books on the West and on western clothing. It's open 8:00 A.M. to 8:00 P.M., Monday through Saturday, and 9:00 A.M. to 5:00 P.M. on Sunday. For more information call 868–2561.

Three free museums also compete for your attention: the **Meeteetse Museum,** 952 Mondell Street, with its collection of historical artifacts and town displays; the **Meeteetse Bank Museum,** 1033 Park Avenue in an old bank building; and the **Charles J. Belden Museum,** at 1947 State Street. The last features Charles Belden's world-famous Western and ranch photographs, which have appeared in numerous magazines, including the prestigious likes of *National Geographic.* The first two museums are open May 15 through September 30 on Monday through Saturday from 10:00 A.M. to 5:00 P.M., and on Sunday from 1:00 to 4:00 P.M. For information call 868–2323. The Belden Museum is open daily May 15 through September 30 from 9:00 A.M. to 5:00 P.M. For information on this museum, call 868–2264.

Charles Belden was comanager of the famous Pitchfork Ranch, founded 18 miles southwest of Meeteetse in 1878. Many of his photographs of the ranch, which was only recently sold and left the Belden family, and of other places in the West are classics that bring back to life the spirit of the western way. As Belden used to say, "If the picture doesn't tell a story, it's not worth taking." His definitely were worth taking.

Northern Wyoming Trivia

The Wyoming Bicycle Guidance Map, *produced by the Wyoming Department of Transportation, can be obtained by contacting the Bicycle Coordinator, P.O. Box 1708, Cheyenne 82003–1708. The map rates roads as to their suitability for safe cycling, featuring information such as pavement widths, traffic volumes, and prevailing winds.*

Meeteetse goes all out for its three-day Labor Day weekend celebrations. Activities include a rodeo, a street dance, an old-time parade, a western barbecue, 5K and 10K foot races (they honor a local resident, the black-footed ferret), and an arts and crafts fair. Meeteetse may no longer have six stage lines running through, or seven bars and eleven brothels, but it still knows how to have a good time, Wild West style. For information call the Meeteetse Tourist Information Center at 868–2603 or write to them at Box 509, Meeteetse 82433.

For good grub and a delightful overnight, try the **Broken Spoke Cafe and Bed & Breakfast,** located next door to the Charles J. Belden Museum. The building was built in 1894 and renovated a century later, in 1994. The cafe features specials and delicious homemade pies every day. Servings are plentiful, and the prices are inexpensive to moderate. The bed-and-breakfast, located in an upper loft section of the building, is appointed in a western motif. There are two separate rooms; the larger one includes two bunk beds and a queen-size bed. Room rates are extremely reasonable: $25 for one person, $35 for two, or $40 for three. A hearty, all-you-can-eat breakfast goes for an additional $5.00 per person. For information or reservations call 868–2362.

On the outskirts of Meeteetse, the *Amelia Earhart Monument* marks the famous aviator's fondness for this area. Earhart was in the process of having a log cabin built on the nearby upper Wood River when she disappeared over the Pacific Ocean in 1937. The partially completed walls of the structure can still be seen near the site of the abandoned Double D Dude Ranch, located approximately 2 miles beyond the Brown Mountain Campground (25 miles southwest of town on the Wood River Road). Beyond the campground a four-wheel-drive vehicle or travel on foot is required. To inquire about road conditions and for more specific directions, stop in at the USDA Forest Service offices at 1002 Park Avenue in Meeteetse, or call 868–2461. Here you can also learn about the area's many other campgrounds and trailheads for staging hiking and horseback-riding adventures.

Hot Springs County

The turn onto the back road leading to some of Wyoming's best-preserved petroglyphs lies about 30 miles outside Meeteetse on the way to Thermopolis. For precise directions to and entrance information regarding the *Legend Rock Petroglyph Site,* contact the Hot Springs State Park Headquarters on Park Street in Thermopolis, or call 864–2176. Legend Rock is a lengthy expanse of sandstone cliffs whose face is embellished with dozens of unique petroglyphs. The oldest works date back some two thousand years. You can drive to within about 100 yards of the cliff face at the site, where there also are a rest room and picnic tables. A caveat, please: Do your part to help to preserve the petroglyphs for the enjoyment and education of future generations by refraining from touching or otherwise disturbing them.

Most visitors' favorite is the petroglyph depicting a rabbit with big ears, drawn in a style reminiscent of the figures created by the Mimbres culture, which thrived in New Mexico about a thousand years ago. It's reportedly the only known rabbit rock art in Wyoming. Other intriguing figures include that of Kokopelli, the well-known hump-backed flute player of the American Southwest. Unlike the rabbit and Kokopelli, the bird petroglyph you'll see here is a figure common in Wyoming rock art and is typically termed the *Ghost Dance Style Bird.*

According to an Arapahoe elder, Paul Moss, the turtle petroglyph is the "Creation Panel." In Arapahoe legend the turtle went down to the bottom of the ocean and brought up on his back the mud with which the continents were formed. In Native American teachings the turtle represents the oldest symbol for earth.

Also nearby: a unique working cattle ranch known as the ***High Island Ranch & Cattle Company.*** The ranch comprises a lower lodge situated on the high plains at 6,000 feet above sea level and an upper lodge in the Owl Creek Mountains at an elevation of around 9,000 feet. In all forty-five thousand acres await investigation, so don't worry about running into crowds out here. Located approximately 35 miles from the main camp, the mountain lodge at Rock Creek offers excellent trout fishing within a stonefly's throw of the front porch. After bunking at the lower ranch on Sunday, on Monday you'll join other guests in riding to the upper camp, then come back down on Friday. As you ride between prairie rangelands and the high elevations of the Owl Creek Mountains, you'll witness the not-soon-to-be-forgotten sights of the Washakie Needles and a 75-foot-high waterfall. Also keep your eyes open for wild elk and ancient tipi rings.

In addition to personalized individual outings, riding options at the ranch include an honest-to-goodness 1800s-style cattle drive in late August and cattle roundup weeks held periodically throughout the summer. Get ready for high adventure as you move those dogies along, then sleep beneath the stars to the chilling sound of a coyote serenade. Whether you choose to relax or to work the ranch from presunup to sundown, pick your week and grab a saddle. You'll need to bring an assortment of gear to participate in the trail rides (call for information), as well as your appetite for adventure. Weekly rates run from $1,000 to $1,500, with 25 guests staying Sunday through Saturday. For information, reservations, and directions, call 867-2374. The regular ranch season runs from mid-May through mid-September. (If hunting is your bag, inquire about the ranch's guided big-game hunts, which take place generally from September through November.)

Both Hot Springs County and Thermopolis, population 3,247, take their names from the world's largest natural hot springs, located at Thermopolis. The Thermopolis *anticline*—a fold in the earth's surface, with rock strata sloping downward on both sides of a common crest—is the largest of several folds along the southern shoulder of the Big Horn Basin. Fractured rock within the anticline provides an avenue for rainwater and snowmelt to seep down into the hotter rocks underground before it rises again to the surface as hot springs.

Driving into **Hot Springs State Park** in summer is a feast for the senses—a rainbow of aromatic flower gardens line the way. The entrance is embellished with a large calcified monolith called Tepee Fountain. An 1896 treaty signed by the Shoshone chief Washakie and the Arapahoe chief Sharp Nose gave the healing waters of the hot springs to the white man, with the condition that the Native people would always have free access to a portion of the springs. Thus the State Bath House is open to anyone at no charge. And if you neglected to bring your own towel or swimsuit, the items can be rented for a small fee.

Submerge yourself into the soothing hot mineral waters, maintained at a steady temperature of 104 degrees Fahrenheit. Facilities include private lockers, showers, and inside and outdoor hot mineral pools. As you soak in the hot waters outside, you can often watch the park's bison herd wander along roads that wind to the top of the colorful bluffs embracing Thermopolis. The bathhouse is open Monday through Saturday from 8:00 A.M. to 5:30 P.M., and on Sunday from noon to 5:30 P.M. It's closed holidays during the winter, but it is open on holidays during the summer, noon to 5:30 P.M. The park is located at 220 Park Street. For more information call 864–3765.

Privately owned hot springs in the vicinity offer a few more niceties, such as water slides, large outdoor swimming pools, saunas, Jacuzzis, and game arcades. The **Star Plunge** is open daily from 9:00 A.M. to 9:00 P.M., except from December 1–20. An all-day pass goes for $7.00. For information call 864–3771. You can also contact **Hot Springs Water Park,** which offers similar facilities at like prices, by calling 864–9250.

Don't miss enjoying other activities in the state park, such as strolling across the replica of a 1916 swinging bridge, which spans the Big Horn River and offers a great view of Mineral Terrace; taking advantage of the pleasantly shaded picnic facilities; and motoring along the high-climbing Buffalo Pasture Road to get a look at the park's primary buffalo herd. For a map outlining the buffalo grazing areas, pick up a Hot Springs State Park brochure at the headquarters near the park's entrance.

Every summer in early August, Hot Springs State Park, in conjunction with local Native Americans, hosts the **Gift of the Waters Pageant,** commemorating the signing of the treaty that transferred ownership of the hot springs. The pageant offers outstanding opportunities to see Indians in the full splendor of their ceremonial clothing, watch and hear their all-consuming dancing and drumming, and learn about tribal legends. For information on the pageant, call the Thermopolis Chamber of Commerce at 864–3192.

A relatively new Thermopolis attraction with ties to ancient history is *The Wyoming Dinosaur Center.* To find the museum simply follow the green dinosaur tracks painted on the town streets. You can watch dinosaur bone preparation in the laboratory and at nearby excavation locations. The 16,000-square-foot center is dedicated to keeping Wyoming's dinosaurs in Wyoming (previously, many of them went to Montana and elsewhere). Since the early 1990s, paleontologist Ed Cole has made a number of discoveries in the mountains east of Thermopolis, one of which appears to be among the largest dinosaur finds in the Rocky Mountains. Some of Cole's findings are displayed at the center. The entrance fee for adults is $6.00 and for children $3.50; the museum and excavation site tour package costs $12.00 for adults and $8.00 for kids. Hours at the center are 8:00 A.M. to 8:00 P.M. daily in summer, and 9:00 A.M. to 5:00 P.M. the rest of the year. For more information call 864–2997, visit the Web site: www.wyodino.org, or E-mail the museum at: wdinoc@wyodino.org.

The *Hot Springs Historical Museum,* at 700 Broadway, has rightfully earned its reputation as one of the best small-town museums in the state. Among its exhibits of western and local lore are stagecoaches, a cherrywood bar from the famous Hole in the Wall Saloon, a display on the coal industry, Native American artifacts, and a frontier town replete with newspaper office, dentist's office, and general store. The $2.00 entrance fee ($1.00 for kids) is a deal. The museum is open year-round Tuesday through Saturday from 8:00 A.M. to 5:00 P.M., except for Thanksgiving, Christmas, and New Year's Day. For information call 864–5183.

For winter travelers Thermopolis sponsors *Cutting Horse Competitions* from November through March. For information on these horse-drawn sleigh races, call the Chamber of Commerce at 864–3192.

Getting hungry? *Pumpernick's,* at 512 Broadway, serves great muffins, sandwiches, and dinners in a cozy setting. Prices are inexpensive to moderate. For information call 864–5151. For unusual accommodations while soaking in the sights of "Thermop," try *Out West* (call 864–2700 for specifics) or *Faye's B&B* (864–5166). The latter, located at 1020 Arapahoe, features three rooms with a shared bath that go for $65, double occupancy.

The countryside spreading away from Thermopolis provides a variety of sightseeing options in virtually every direction. A drive south through the *Wind River Canyon,* for instance, offers up-close looks at the bowels of the earth that are rivaled in few places. As you motor along next to towering cliffs, the raging Wind River churns white, roiling and frothing along on its way to becoming the Big Horn River. Signs along the length of the canyon interpret the geological formations you're looking at. Rocks in the canyon span eons of geologic time, from sixty-six-million-year-old Cretaceous formations to Precambrian layers more than two billion years old. A number of turnouts offer fantastic photo and picnic ops. Don's miss the precariously placed train tracks on the side of the canyon opposite the highway. In 1995 a massive rock slide obliterated sections of the track. The Chicago, Burlington and Quincy Railroad first went through the canyon in 1911, followed by the state highway in 1925. It's approximately a 60-mile round-trip from Thermopolis to Boysen State Park (see p. 143) on Highway 20 via Wind River Canyon.

To experience the Wind River up close and wet, consider a trip with *Wind River Canyon White-water,* operating out of an office in Thermopolis at 907 Shoshone. The season runs approximately from Memorial Day to Labor Day. For information call 864–9343 or 486–2253 during the off-season.

Outlaw Trail, Inc., a nonprofit community group of Thermopolis, organizes a once-a-year 100-mile trail ride for a hundred riders. Reservations are on a first-come, first-served basis. The trip caters primarily to experienced riders because each participant is responsible for caring for his or her own horse and tack. You'll follow the legendary Outlaw Trail of Butch Cassidy to Hole in the Wall country; no doubt you'll hear yarns both historic and modern as you sit around the campfire with your companions. For information on the historian-guided trip, call 864–2287 or write Outlaw Trail, Inc., Box 1046, Thermopolis 82443. Internet users can visit www.trib.com/~outlaw or E-mail the organizers at outlaw@trib.com.

> **Northern Wyoming Trivia**
>
> *Nomadic Indian tribes living at least part-time in Wyoming in historic times included the Arapaho, Arikara, Bannock, Blackfeet, Cheyenne, Crow, Gros Ventre, Kiowa, Nez Perce, Sioux, Shoshone, and Ute.*

Washakie County

The Big Horn Basin, stretching out from the west slope of the Big Horn Mountains, is blessed with fertile soils and a long growing season. Worland, population 5,742, is situated on the banks of the Big Horn River and is an agricultural community, with sugar beets the primary cash crop. The Holly Sugar plant here provides a strong base for the area's economy. Worland was founded in 1903, rather late for a Wyoming town, and named after one of the first pioneers to homestead in the area. Charlie "Dad" Worland ran a makeshift saloon and stage station. In 1906, the Chicago, Burlington and Quincy Railroad arrived, and a year later the 50-mile-plus Big Horn Irrigation Canal was completed, bringing water to the desiccated desert and transforming Worland into an agricultural and trade center.

Northern Wyoming Trivia

Between 1897 and 1908 bounties were paid on 10,819 gray wolves in Wyoming.

The rare black-footed ferret dines almost exclusively on prairie dogs.

Peter Toth chose Worland as the Wyoming location for his *Trail of the Whispering Giants* monument. Toth spent nearly two decades traveling the country and carving towering wooden Native American sculptures in each of the fifty states. He finished the Worland statue in September 1980. The massive carvings were made as a gift to each state; Toth accepted no payments. The only requirements for a state to receive its statue were the donation of a permanent pedestal and a commitment to maintain the sculpture. The Hungarian refugee began his unusual quest in February 1972 in La Jolla, California, where he built his first Indian monument, and finished his final work in May 1988 in Haleiwa, Hawaii. Wyoming's *Trail of the Whispering Giants* monument sits on the southwest corner of the Washakie County Courthouse lawn.

The *Washakie County Museum and Cultural Center* operates out of an old LDS church, 1115 Obie Sue Avenue. Inside you will find a recreation of the A. G. Rupp General Store, the Soapy Dale Peak Lodge (a Sheepeater Indian mountain shelter), and an exhibit of early 1900s black-and-white photographs by Rico Stine, which depict the town and surrounding areas. The museum sponsors an annual symposium in July for paleontologists working in the Big Horn Basin and Big Horn Mountains. It is open May through October, Monday through Friday, 9:00 A.M. to 5:00 P.M., and Sunday, noon to 5:00 P.M. During the rest of the year, hours are Monday through Friday, 10:00 A.M. to 4:00 P.M. For information call 347–4102.

Antone's Supper Club (347–9924), 3 miles east of town on Highway 16, and the dining room of the *Deer Haven Lodge* (366–2449), 7 miles east on Highway 16, are popular eating places for Worland residents and visitors alike.

By heading north from Worland on Highway 433, you'll trace a portion of the historic *Bridger Trail*. Frequent conflicts with Native Americans along the Bozeman Trail in the 1860s created the need for an alternative route to the southwestern Montana goldfields. Scout and explorer Jim Bridger blazed a new trail for the miners, crossing the Big Horn Basin near present-day Worland. East of Worland, 25 miles on the other side of some of the baddest badlands you'll ever lay eyes on, is the quaint cowtown of Ten Sleep. If you go there, on the eastern outskirts of Worland, you'll find a marker commemorating the *Colby Site,* where Dr. George Frison of the University of Wyoming unearthed the remains of a woolly mammoth and Paleo Indian stone tools.

The name of the town of Ten Sleep, population 330, is said to have come from the Sioux Indians, who had a large camp along the North Platte River near present-day Casper. They measured distances by the number of days, or "sleeps," it took to get from one place to another. It was ten sleeps from the North Platte River camp to the present-day site of Ten Sleep; likewise it was another ten sleeps from there to a certain area of Yellowstone.

The *Ten Sleep Pioneer Museum* is located on the east edge of town in the Ten Sleep Public Park, a pleasant place for a picnic on a hot summer Big Horn Basin day. The museum is open Memorial Day through Labor Day from noon to 6:00 P.M. The Pioneer Museum highlights history and memorabilia from the Spring Creek Raid, one of many battles that blew up between cattlemen and sheep ranchers in the West.

To preserve "their" range, cattlemen set up boundaries, or "dead lines" (so-called because if sheep crossed the line they and their owners could soon be dead), beyond which sheep were forbidden. In late March 1909, a French sheepman named Joe Allemand—in the company of his nephew Jules Lazier and Joe Emge, a cattleman turned sheepman—departed Worland with 5,000 head of sheep and headed toward Spring Creek, southeast of Ten Sleep. On April 2, 1909, seven masked men raided the sheepherders' camp, killing all three men and a number of their sheep. Five of the raiders were sent to prison for their deeds, while the other two plea-bargained for their freedom. The killings created a public uproar and virtually ended the range war between cattlemen and sheepmen. A monument marking the site of the tragedy is located on the east side of Highway 434 about 6½ miles southeast of Ten Sleep.

A bit hard to find but well worth the search is the Nature Conservancy's *Tensleep Preserve,* set aside to protect a unique medley of canyon, upland, meadow, and forest environments. More than hundred bird species are at home on the preserve, as are mountain lion, elk, black bear, beaver, and the rare spotted bat. Fishing and hiking are among the recreational pursuits possible at the preserve, which is open to visitors from May through mid-October. Accommodations are in tent cabins, with common indoor kitchen and shower areas. The Wyoming chapter of the Nature Conservancy owns and manages this preserve, as well as two others in the state, for the purpose of conserving rare plants and animals and the lands and water they need for survival. For information on supporting the Wyoming chapter, or to make reservations to stay at the Tensleep Preserve and to obtain directions for finding it, call 366–2671.

Leaving Ten Sleep via U.S. Highway 16 East puts you on one segment of the *Big Horn Scenic Byways.* The road climbs through stunning Ten Sleep Canyon, one of the scenic marvels of the West, before crossing the crest of the Big Horns at Powder River Pass, elevation 9,666 feet. Numerous Forest Service campgrounds line the road. The Cloud Peak Wilderness to the north offers trips for hikers and horseback riders, while certain nonwilderness trails of the surrounding Bighorn National Forest are great for mountain biking. The highway eventually drops out of the Big Horns and into the town of Buffalo—but we'll get to that town later, after traveling in a longer, roundabout manner to get there.

Big Horn County

From Ten Sleep drive north on a primitive dirt road for 18 miles to Hyattville. (Inquire at the Ten Sleep Mercantile for directions to the turn.) The fascinating *Medicine Lodge State Archaeological Site,* one of the most significant prehistoric sites in the United States, is found 6 miles northeast of Hyattville off Cold Springs Road. Medicine Lodge Creek runs through the lush meadows and groves of tall cottonwoods, offering outstanding picnicking, camping, and fishing opportunities. The site's plentiful food, shelter, and water have attracted humans for some ten thousand years.

The excavations have been filled in for preservation and safety reasons, but prehistoric petroglyphs and pictographs remain on the walls of brilliantly colored sandstone. Interpretive displays at the cliffs and in the nearby log cabin visitor center provide glimpses of the sixty cultures that camped at the site through the centuries. Stretching away from the archaeological site is the 12,100-acre Medicine Lodge Wildlife Habitat Management Area, a refuge for an extensive elk herd and numerous other types of wildlife. A self-guiding pamphlet leads to various petroglyphs along the cliff walls, while the *Medicine Lodge Nature Trail* brochure highlights the area's natural history. The Medicine Lodge State Archaeological Site grounds are open from May 1 through early November, and the visitor center is open from May 1 to Labor Day. For information call 469–2234.

There's a wonderful backcountry scenic byway that will bring you out around Shell; it's recommended if you have the four-wheel-drive vehicle that it demands. Inquire about road conditions and directions at the archaeological site visitor center. Once you reach Shell, you'll see the **Shell Stone Schoolhouse,** which is listed on the National Register of Historic Places. Built in 1903 it was the first nonlog community building. It was in use until the early 1950s. One of the world's largest allosauruses ("Big Al") was excavated near Shell, and since 1934 paleontologists have unearthed twelve large sauropods in the area. The dinosaur beds, located 10 miles north of Shell on Bureau of Land Management lands, are open to the public.

From Shell head east for another segment of the **Big Horn Scenic Byways,** this one leading through the gorge of Shell Canyon. Watch for the statuesque red Chimney Rock near the west entrance to Shell Canyon. You'll travel briefly into Sheridan County, but a left at Burgess

The Medicine Lodge Creek Site

*T*he summer after graduating from the University of Wyoming in 1973, I was fortunate to be hired by Dr. George Frison as a member of the crew that would excavate the Medicine Lodge Creek archaeological site. The site, nestled in the sandstone Big Horn foothills outside Hyattville, proved to be one of the most productive and important archaeological finds ever located in the Rocky Mountains. Today, the site—and what we unearthed there— provide the centerpiece of a stellar Wyoming state park.

Most people associate archaeological excavations with exacting equipment like fine-mesh wire screens, whisk brooms, trowels, and even dental picks. Indeed all of those tools were employed at Medicine Lodge Creek. However, as I recall, the lion's share of our work that summer involved far cruder methods of excavation— shovels, iron bars, backhoes, even

dynamite—because often we had to break through thick sandstone slabs that over the years had fallen off the overhanging cliffs. By the time excavations were completed in the mid-1970s, crews had identified some five dozen levels of occupation going down more than twenty feet below the ground surface. The age of the cultures ranged from historic Crow (1800s) to Paleo Indians of more than nine thousand years ago.

Several crew members that summer, including me, holed up in the rustic old farm house adjacent to the site, which has since been renovated and turned into the park manager's residence. Today's park, where top-notch camping, fishing, and canyon hiking can also be enjoyed, would be a beautiful place to visit even if it didn't encompass such fascinating and important archaeological findings. But that it does.

Junction onto Highway 14A heading west will take you back into Big Horn County.

Alternatively, from Hyattville follow paved roads west to Manderson, then take U.S. Highway 20/16 north to Greybull, population 1,789. Greybull, too, is home to some of the world's most productive dinosaur beds. The town is located at the confluence of the Big Horn and Greybull Rivers and Shell and Dry Creeks. It was established in 1909 as a stop along the Chicago, Burlington and Quincy Railroad and derives its name from a legendary albino bison that was sacred to Native Americans.

Area sites include Sheep Mountain, a thousand-foot-high ridge extending for some 15 miles northeast of Greybull. According to geologists it's a textbook example of a *doubly plunging anticline*. Signs depicting a red devil will lead you to Devil's Kitchen, where fossils and other unusual rock finds are common. Ask for directions at the Greybull Chamber of Commerce on Highway 16, or call 765–2100.

Fossils, petrified wood, Native American relics, and semiprecious stones form the nucleus of the excellent **Greybull Museum,** found at 325 Greybull Avenue. The museum is open daily except Sunday the year

An Unlikely Dessert

*D*uring the summer I worked at the Medicine Lodge Creek Site outside Hyattville, I was befriended by a gregarious Big Horn Basin cattleman (whose name I won't divulge here). I recall walking with him early one warm August evening in one of his pastures after enjoying supper with him and his family. That's when my typically carefree buddy got all fired up and began ranting about "them *%!&* environmentalists."

His soliloquy centered on the fact that certain individuals were lodging complaints about the grazing of private cattle on the public lands of the Bighorn National Forest. He uttered many choice words en route to the lecture's

culmination, when my friend, red-faced and waving his arms wildly in the dry air, yelled, "They even complain about my cows crapping in the streams . . . why, look," he bellowed, bending down to pick up large chunk of a dried cowpie, which he proceeded to stuff into his mouth. Then he started chewing like a madman. What he said next, with his mouth crammed full, sounded like, "It annuthn brt!," but I think he meant, "It ain't nothin' but dirt!"

After calming down and realizing what he'd done in his moment of raging indignation, my friend spent the next five minutes spitting and sputtering and looking more than a little bit sheepish.

around. From June 1 through Labor Day, it's open from 10:00 A.M. to 8:00 P.M.; Labor Day to November 1 from 2:00 to 5:00 P.M.; and the rest of the year from 2:00 to 4:00 P.M. For more information call 765–2444.

At the Greybull Airport examples of World War II's mighty bombers and transport aircraft make up the *Museum of Flight and Aerial Fire-fighting.* You'll learn, among other things, about the first aerial fire reconnaissance, which took place in 1919 in California. Before the advent of the radio, messages were relayed to ground by notes dropped by parachute or transported by carrier pigeon. You'll also see five of the remaining flying P84Y-2s used against the Japanese in the South Pacific theater during World War II.

Surrounded by mountains on three sides—the high Absaroka and Beartooth Ranges to the west, the rugged Pryor Mountains to the north, and the Big Horns to the east—Lovell, population 2,131, began life as the area's largest ranch. The ML Ranch, founded by Anthony L. Mason and Henry Clay Lovell in 1880, ran some twenty-five thousand head of cattle. Lovell the town got going 1890 and was incorporated in 1906, with ranching and the sugar beet industry providing economic stability.

Lovell is known as the Rose City of Wyoming; rose-filled planters and gardens grace the streets, parks, and private yards. The 120,000-acre *Bighorn Canyon National Recreation Area* encompasses a variety of empty landscapes, from badlands and steep-sided gorges to high prairie laced with trails. The Yellowtail Dam in Montana, dedicated in 1968, created 71-mile-long Bighorn Lake, now a prime boating and camping area. Stop at the solar-heated Bighorn Canyon NRA Visitor Center at the east edge of Lovell for maps of the area and directions to various and varied attractions. The visitor center regularly runs an orientation film on Bighorn Canyon's history, natural features, and available activities. For information call 548–2251.

North of Lovell on Highway 37, you can discover the nation's first wild horse preserve in the form of the remote, 47,000-acre *Pryor Mountain Wild Horse Range.* The mustangs running the range here possess the distinctive dun color and dorsal and zebra stripes typical of horses with Spanish ancestry—genetic features not commonly found among wild horse bands in this country. (You can even, if you're interested, look into adopting a horse through the Bureau of Land Management's wild horse management program.)

A short loop tour out of Lovell takes you through the small towns of Byron, Deaver, Frannie, and Cowley, which have a combined population of fewer than 1,300. Five miles east of Lovell on Highway 14A, there's an information marker describing the 37-mile *Sidon Irrigation Canal,* completed by Mormon pioneers in 1895. Work on the project was halted by a large boulder that was in the way. According to legend prayer and divine intervention caused the rock to split, allowing the canal work to proceed. The split rock became known as Prayer Rock. Three miles east of there is the oilfield community of Byron, which contains a number of attractive old log structures. The area has produced more than 117 million barrels of oil and 13 million cubic feet of gas since 1918.

The Medicine Chest

*N*ative Americans in the Rockies have traditionally traveled to mountain peaks to pray and seek divine intervention from the powerful spirits there. The **Medicine Wheel,** a National Historic Landmark, is a sacred aboriginal site where Indians still perform religious ceremonies. Located at the top of Medicine Mountain at an elevation of nearly 10,000 feet, the wheel consists of twenty-eight spokes radiating from a central hub. The wheel is 80 feet in diameter, and hub and spokes are made from unhewed rock pieces. Six additional mounds, or cairns, are spaced unevenly around the rim. Each mound has an opening that faces a different direction, and the wheel rim has a break in its eastern edge.

The origin and meaning of the wheel are matters of debate. Some archaeologists maintain that it resembles the Mexican calendar stone, while others believe it was used for astrological purposes other than marking the passage of time. In any event meditating on the Medicine Wheel can be a powerful and mystical experience. Although they had no direct connection to the creation of Medicine Wheel, Chief Joseph of the Nez Perce fasted at

the site, and Shoshone chief Washakie visited the spot to seek guidance in leading his nation. The Medicine Wheel reflects a symbol that is at the very heart of Native American being: the circle. Consider these words from the Lakota Sioux Black Elk, in his book Black Elk Speaks: "Everything the power of the world does is done in a circle. The sky is round, the earth is round, and so are all the stars. . . . The life of a man is in a circle from childhood to childhood, and so it is in everything where power moves."

Medicine Wheel National Historic Landmark is administered by the U.S. Forest Service. The site provides breathtaking vistas of the Big Horn Basin, the Wind River Range, and the Absaroka and Pryor Ranges. The site is located off Highway 14A, 3 miles north on Forest Service Road 12. The turn is found about 30 miles west of Burgess Junction, or 27 miles east of Lovell. Vehicles pulling trailers are not recommended on the narrow dirt road leading to the parking area. From the parking area it's about a 1¹/₂-mile walk to the Medicine Wheel. Please respect the site and do not disturb any of the cultural artifacts while in the area. For information call 548–6541.

Taking Highway 114 north you next arrive at Deaver and the **Deaver Reservoir,** which teems with bluegills and crappies. Six miles north on Highway 310/789, just 2 miles south of the Montana state line, is Frannie, population 148, "The Biggest Little Town in Wyoming." If you've nothing better to do, you can stand in the middle of Frannie and have one foot in Big Horn County and the other in Park County. The town of Cowley, several miles east of Deaver, holds a host of historic sandstone buildings worthy of a look. It's also home to a number of artesian wells, with 98 percent pure water. Stop for a refreshing sip before heading back east.

Sheridan County

The Big Horn Scenic Byways are especially stunning when decked out in their colorful autumn foliage. Travel on Highway 14 is open year-round, with occasional closures due to weather in winter. Highway 14A is open from approximately mid-May through mid-November. Elevations on the three byways range from 4,800 feet to over 9,600 feet. On a clear day you'll be able to see Devils Tower rising beyond the Sheridan Valley. The switchbacks on Highway 14 lead you past signed geologic formations, including the Amsden, Chugwater, Gros Ventre, and Tensleep formations. Up high you're guaranteed to see an abundance of wildflowers and wildlife in summer: More than 265 species of birds make the Big Horns their home, and bighorn sheep, mule deer, elk, and moose often make their presence known along the byways.

Highway 14 drops eastward out of the Big Horns into Dayton and nearby Ranchester. Near Dayton you'll pass the **Sawyer Battlefield.** Here Col. J. A. Sawyer's men battled Indians for thirteen straight days before General Connor's troops came to the rescue. On Main Street you'll see the **cabin of Hans Kleiber,** a famous artist/naturalist. (A number of his paintings are located at the Bradford Brinton Memorial, which we'll visit in Big Horn later.) Another interesting site is the **Dayton Bell Tower,** located in the city park. It was built in 1910 and used by residents as an observation point during World War II. In 1911 Dayton became the first community in Wyoming to elect a woman mayor. Mayor Susan Wissler was the first woman mayor in America to serve two consecutive terms. She also operated a millinery and dry goods store and taught in the local school. In Ranchester you'll find the **Connor Battlefield** in the city park, which is located along the Tongue River bottomlands. The site marks a major military engagement of the Powder River Expedition in 1865, when Gen. Patrick E. Connor's forces attacked and destroyed Arapahoe Chief Black Bear's village of 250 lodges. Today the battlefield is an unsettlingly peaceful place to picnic or take a hike. (Cross over the river on the cable footbridge to find additional hiking paths.)

The Big Horn Mountains and their Bighorn National Forest rule the western horizon as you travel through the Sheridan area. John D. Loucks plotted Sheridan in 1882, naming it after his Civil War commanding officer, Gen. Philip Sheridan. The Burlington and Missouri River Railroad came to town ten years later. To the credit of its citizens, Sheridan has managed to keep most of its downtown buildings intact, and the entire Main Street district has been designated a National Historic Landmark. It boasts the largest collection of original buildings from the late 1800s and early 1900s in all of Wyoming.

The mansion of senator, governor, and rancher John B. Kendrick, known as the "Sagebrush Senator," offers a great diversion where you can while away several hours. Kendrick served as governor of Wyoming from 1914 to 1916 and as a U.S. senator from 1916 until his death in 1933. The Kendrick ranches of northern Wyoming and southern Montana encompassed more than 200,000 acres. Now called the *Trail End Historic Center,* Kendrick's 1913 Sheridan home, an example of Flemish-Revival architecture, which was a rarity in the West. The house contained a number of devices that were innovative for the time, including an intercom system that functioned throughout the house, a dumbwaiter that moved between floors, and a stationary vacuum system with a motor in the basement, which helped ease the staff's workload.

A self-guided tour booklet leads you through the mansion, where you'll see beautiful stained-glass windows, a white Italian marble fireplace, French silk damask wall coverings, and sprawling Oriental rugs. Machine-tooled woodwork and a hand-painted ceiling embellish the grand foyer. Also noteworthy is a log cabin at the site that served as the first post office, store, law office, and bank in the city of Sheridan. The grounds are beautifully bedecked with flower beds, and a plant identification list is available. The Trail End Historic Center, located at 400 East Clarendon Avenue, is open to the public for self-guided tours from April through mid-December. From June through August, the facility is open from 9:00 A.M. to 6:00 P.M. During the rest of its months of operation, it's open from 1:00 to 4:00 P.M., except Memorial Day and Labor Day weekends, when reduced hours are observed. Guided tours for groups may be arranged by calling 674–4589.

Don King (not the one with the big hair), founder of *King's Ropes and*

Saddlery, started handcrafting saddles and tooling saddle leather more than fifty years ago. He passed along the operation to the next generation, but Don's handiwork is still much in evidence in the combination store-museum at 184 North Main Street in Sheridan. Some of the younger fellas have picked up a thing or two from the old pro over the years, and their creations are displayed, too. Whether you need only to outfit yourself in a King's cap—the unofficial Wyoming state hat (the official one being the cowboy hat, of course)—or are looking to saddle up, King's is the place for quality ropes, saddles, and accessories. The museum collection includes an interesting array of spurs, chaps, and saddles. Hours are 8:00 A.M. to 5:00 P.M., Monday through Saturday. For information call 672–2702.

For delectable Italian food served in an intimate atmosphere, chow down at *Ciao Bistro.* The prices are moderate to expensive at the bistro,

The Sheridan Inn

*B*uilt in 1893, the **Sheridan Inn** was financed by the Burlington and Missouri River Railroad. William F. Cody led the Grand March from the dining room at the inn's opening on June 23 of that year. The W. F. Cody Hotel Company, of which Buffalo Bill was part owner, managed the inn from 1894 to 1902. When in town, Buffalo Bill was known to sit on the porch of the Sheridan Inn and audition acts for the upcoming season of his Wild West Show. The show premiered in 1870 and later starred such noteables as Annie Oakley and Sitting Bull.

Hand-hewn beams span the entire dining area. The ornate bar in the inn's Buffalo Bill Saloon came from England by boat, by rail to Gillette, and by ox-drawn wagon the rest of the way to Sheridan. The lobby's counter, stone fireplace, and cigar case are all original. The inn had electric lights when it opened and was touted as the finest

establishment between Chicago and San Francisco. Its two rooms with bathtubs were the first of their kind in the area. Room and board could be had for the pricey sum of $2.50 per day. Famous visitors at the hotel have included Calamity Jane, Ernest Hemingway, General John Pershing, Will Rogers, Charlie Russell, and Presidents Hoover, Taft, and Teddy Roosevelt.

Architect Thomas Kimball modeled the inn after a hunting lodge he had visited in Scotland. The Sheridan Inn, featuring 14-foot-wide porches encircling the entire building, was highlighted in Ripley's Believe It or Not as "The House of 69 Gables." The inn was designated a National Historic Landmark in 1964. It ceased to operate as a hotel in 1965; it is now in the process of being restored under the direction of the Sheridan Heritage Center Board. The inn is located at Fifth Street and Broadway.

located at 120 North Main Street. For reservations call 672–2838. For flavor a bit more local in nature, visit *The Mint,* 151 North Main Street. This famous watering hole provides an authentic taste of the West, with plenty of Charles Belden photographs, stuffed critters, cattle brands, and working cowboys wetting their whistles after a day on the range. Call 674–9696.

Sheridan Inn

Traveling south from Sheridan, forsake I–90 for the more picturesque U.S. Highway 87, and then take Highway 335 to Big Horn. This area is home to one of the oldest polo clubs in the United States: the Big Horn Equestrian Center, located on Bird Farm Road south of Big Horn. The center schedules polo matches every Sunday afternoon from May to September. It also sponsors steeplechase races, dressage competitions, steer-roping events, and soccer tournaments. Not surprisingly there's a strong British influence in the area; many of the early ranches here were begun by titled English families.

The *Big Horn Store* is a general mercantile that will bring to mind a simpler time. Built in 1882 it's one of the oldest businesses in northern Wyoming. The *Bradford Brinton Memorial,* located at 239 Brinton Road in Big Horn, is also an informative and worthwhile stop. The property, listed on the National Register of Historic Places, lies on the internationally recognized Quarter Circle A Ranch. William and Malcolm Moncreiffe established the original homestead in 1892, and Bradford Brinton purchased the property in 1923. Brinton raised Thoroughbred horses on the ranch. He also enlarged the house to its present size of twenty rooms. Tours are available of the two-story, white neo-Colonial ranch house.

Brinton loved the West, and it shows in his significant collection of more than 600 original oils, watercolors, and sketches by American artists. Many well-known Western artists were among his friends and ranch visitors. The collection of art displayed includes works by John J. Audubon, Edward M. Borein, E. W. Gollings, Will James, Hans Kleiber, Frederic Remington, Charles M. Russell, and others. Artwork can be found in both the gallery and the ranch homestead.

In addition to paintings the gallery showcases an excellent array of Native American crafts and clothing items, such as a painted steerhide dance shield, baby cradleboards, a Cree saddle cushion, Sioux ceremonial dress, and a Nez Perce buckskin shirt. Other attractions include a Jefferson Peace Medal dated 1861, which was a gift to a Native American chief from Lewis and Clark, and an Abraham Lincoln letter dated 1848.

Original art found in the homestead includes a Charles M. Russell bronze sculpture, *The Bucker and the Buckeroo,* Frederic Remington's watercolor *Harnessing the Mules,* and a hallway frieze created by Brinton's friend Ed Borein, one of the most prolific Western artists of all time. The Bradford Brinton Memorial collection holds more than 175 pieces by this master alone.

Among the memorial's distinguished visitors have been Queen Elizabeth II, Prince Philip, and James Michener. Brinton died in 1936 and left the house and ranch to his sister, Helen, whose will created the Bradford Brinton Memorial, which opened in 1961. The memorial is open daily from 9:30 A.M. to 5:00 P.M., May 15 through Labor Day. Each year the memorial sponsors a special Christmas holiday art exhibit featuring a single artist. For information on regular and special exhibits, call 672–3173 or E-mail: qca@cyberhighway.net.

Spahn's Big Horn Bed & Breakfast is found 6 miles beyond Big Horn on Highway 335. Drive until the pavement ends, then proceed another 1/2 mile on gravel to the sign marking the B&B. Turn left there and follow the road as it winds 3/4 mile into the timber. Ron and Bobbie Spahn built the log home from scratch using little modern equipment; the result is one beautiful home and bed and breakfast, with a gorgeous view of the valley and surrounding mountains to boot. It's a hypnotic setting, with the breeze blowing through the surrounding pines and, season permitting, snow settling softly on the ground outside. Ron also has groomed a number of cross-country skiing and hiking trails through the surrounding woods. Your hosts know the area well and can direct you to any number of scenic attractions. Rates range from $75 to $125 per night, depending on accommodations and season. For information and reservations call 674–8150.

Return to Highway 87 through Big Horn and head south through a region teeming with the haunting history of the Indian Wars. The first site you'll encounter, located about 13 miles down the road, is Massacre Hill, which marks the site of the 1866 Fetterman Fight. The impressive, 20-foot high *Fetterman Massacre Monument* sits atop the hill, overlooking the battlefield.

Capt. William J. Fetterman, who cut his battle teeth during the Civil War, knew little about the strategy of fighting Indians. The skirmish here was precipitated by the government's construction of Fort Phil Kearny, which was in direct violation of a treaty with the Sioux Nation. Led by Red Cloud and Crazy Horse, a band of Arapahoe, Cheyenne, and Sioux retaliated on December 21, 1866, ambushing Captain Fetterman and his troops, who had been sent to rescue a wagon train under attack. More than eighty soldiers and civilians were killed during the battle. Evidence indicates that Captain Fetterman and one of his officers chose to die by their own hands. There were no white survivors at the fight the Indians called the "battle of one-hundred-in-the-hands."

The shooting started about noon and ended about a half hour later. The massacre created fears that the Indians would subsequently attack Fort Phil Kearny, so John "Portugee" Phillips's was sent on a 236-mile, blizzard-hampered ride to seek reinforcements at Fort Laramie. Phillips' horse collapsed and died on their arrival at Fort Laramie on Christmas night. Despite outnumbering the soldiers at Fort Phil Kearny by several thousand, the Indians never did attack.

A number of interpretive plaques at the battlefield bring the bloody scene back to life and lead you to ponder the decisions Fetterman made during the conflict. Fetterman imprudently ignored the basic rules of Indian fighting, and his was the worst loss suffered by the army in western battles until Custer's Last Stand, which exploded not far from here on the Little Big Horn River a decade later.

The August following the Fetterman Massacre, in 1867, Indians again staged an attack, this time on a detail of twenty-eight soldiers and four civilians on a woodcutting mission under the command of Capt. James Powell. The **Wagon Box Fight** owes its name to the fact that soldiers defended themselves from attack for more than three hours by removing the wheels from their wagons and arranging the fourteen wagon boxes into a circular barricade. With their improvised fort and their newly issued Springfield breech-loading rifles—which could fire up to twenty rounds per minute—the soldiers staved off the Indians, even though the natives far outnumbered the soldiers. Three white men were killed and two wounded, while Indian casualty estimates ranged from a few dozen to several hundred.

The Wagon Box Monument is located near the town of Story. Directional signs lead you to the battle site.

Johnson County

N ow we turn to Fort Phil Kearny, where the bloodiest of the Indian battles took place. The fort was established in July 1866 as a command post for the 18th Infantry, whose job it was to protect travelers tackling the Bozeman Trail. Named after a popular Union general killed in the Civil War, the fort was constructed of logs cut in and hauled from the Big Horn Mountains. More than four thousand logs were used to erect the stockade, one of the few palisade fortifications in the West.

After the Union Pacific Railroad laid its tracks far enough west to allow travelers to avoid the Bozeman Trail, the forts built to protect Bozeman Trail travelers were no longer necessary. Gen. Ulysses S. Grant ordered the closing of Fort Phil Kearny after the Treaty of 1868 was concluded. As a result of the treaty, the area belonged exclusively to the Indians (until the conclusion of the Indian Wars), a fact the Indians underscored by burning the fort to the ground not long after its abandonment.

The *Fort Phil Kearny Museum and Visitor Center* is open April 1 through May 14 and October 1 through November 30 from noon to 4:00 P.M. on Wednesday through Sunday. From May 15 to September 30, it's open from 8:00 A.M. to 6:00 P.M. daily. It is closed December through March. There is a $1.00 gate fee for those 18 and older. The fort grounds, which contain a number of historic interpretive signs and markers, are open year-round from dawn to dusk. Taking place in mid-June at the fort are Bozeman Trail Days, with activities that include both white and Native American interpretations of the Wagon Box Fight and Fetterman Massacre, archaeological tours, and living-history programs. To find Fort Phil Kearney, from Story take Highway 193 southeast about 5 miles to the road leading to the post. For further information call 684–7629.

Father Pierre Jean DeSmet (known as "Black Robe" to Native Americans) left his mark on Wyoming as the first Catholic missionary in the territory. DeSmet passed Independence Rock, and near Daniel in 1840 he celebrated the first Roman Catholic mass in the region. In 1851 he also discovered *Lake DeSmet,* which is located 8 miles northeast of Buffalo off Highway 87. (Ask a local about the dragon of Lake DeSmet, which reportedly devours young maidens.) You can take advantage of picnic and camping sites at the lake, and you'll also find an 18-foot high Father DeSmet Monument overlooking it at a turnout along Highway 87.

Buffalo, population 3,358, is an attractive town perched on the west slope foothills of the Big Horn Range. The community surrounds a historic Main Street that's worth a few hours' browsing time. Ask for a self-guided

Main Street Walking Tour brochure at the Chamber of Commerce, found at 55 North Main Street. The tour includes a rundown of more than twenty buildings, many of which feature historic self-portraits in their front windows or on mounted plaques. For information call 684–5544 or (800) 277–5122.

The Johnson County War

*J*ohnson County was not only the scene of some of the most vicious fighting between whites and Indians in the West, but it also hosted the infamous 1892 Johnson County War. The fight—during which men were killed, cattle rustled, and homesteads burned—pitted owners of large ranches against homesteaders (also called nesters) and small-scale ranchers.

Absentee cattle barons from Cheyenne put out the word in Texas that they were hiring gunslingers at $5.00 per day, with a $50 bonus for every man killed in Johnson County. On April 6, 1892, a train carrying twenty-six hired guns from Texas and another couple of dozen Wyoming men departed from Cheyenne. They were led by Maj. Frank Wolcott, a former Union army officer now in the employ of the Wyoming Stock Growers Association, which was ruled by the big cattle outfits.

Carrying a "dead list" of seventy known and suspected rustlers and sympathizers, including Johnson County sheriff Red Angus, the "Invaders" first stopped at the KC Ranch near present Kaycee and ambushed two men on their list, Nick Ray and Nate Champion. The battle lasted hours. Ray died early on in the battle, but Champion fought on until the gunmen torched the cabin and shot him as he fled the conflagration.

Wolcott and his army then moved 30 miles north to the TA Ranch, where they holed up and awaited the arrival of Sheriff Angus. An informant had told them that Angus had gathered an armed force and was moving in their direction. At daylight the Cheyenne Invaders found themselves surrounded by two hundred well-armed and enraged Buffalo-area ranchers and nesters. A running three-day gun battle ensued, costing two of the Texas men their lives.

Peace was finally restored after Governor Barber cabled President Harrison for federal assistance. The president sent troops from nearby Fort McKinney to quell the uprising, and the cavalry arrived as Sheriff Angus and his "Defenders" were preparing to attack the ranch house with dynamite. The cavalry escorted the invading gunmen and their leaders to Fort McKinley and later returned them to Cheyenne. None of the perpetrators was prosecuted; rather, the men were set free on the pretense that Johnson County could not afford to pay for the trials.

Although the cattle barons' hired guns got off without so much as a day in jail, the Johnson County War marked the end of the reign of the cattle barons.

A good place to start your tour is at the old *Occidental Hotel.* Located at 10 North Main Street, the hotel no longer lets rooms, but it is listed on the National Register of Historic Places. The original 1880 hotel was a log structure, but that was replaced in 1910 by the current brick building. At one time the hotel occupied the entire block. Today various businesses occupy parts of the big structure—including a barbershop operating in the original barbershop location, still using the original barber chairs. *Deerfield at the Occidental Saloon,* a boutique and espresso bar, resides in the hotel's former saloon and includes the original tin ceiling and back bar with stained-glass canopy. Ask to see the bullet hole in the bar drawer. There's also a 1944 wall mural of the Hole in the Wall, where Butch Cassidy's gang hid out, reportedly painted by a down-and-out saloon customer to pay off his bar tab.

Look for the *Johnson County Cattle War Commemorative Bronzes* on South Main Street near its intersection with Angus Street. The three-quarters life-size sculptures by artist D. Michael Thomas, *Ridin' for the Brand* and *Living on the Edge,* depict the deadly face-offs between the cattle barons' men and their attackees.

The *Johnson County–Jim Gatchell Museum,* located at the corner of Main and Fort Streets in Buffalo, is a rare find. Pioneer druggist Jim Gatchell's Western and Native American collections form the nucleus of the museum's holdings. The displays of prehistoric artifacts constitutes one of the major collections in Wyoming. The Johnson County War exhibit offers a detailed description of the fighting and events leading up to it; a ring belonging to the slain Nate Champion is among the cattle war memorabilia. Particularly interesting are the Cattle War, Wagon Box Fight, and 1880s Buffalo Main Street dioramas. Bugler Adolph Metzger's crushed bugle testifies to the final moments of the Fetterman Massacre. The museum is located in the 1909 Carnegie Library Building, not to be overlooked itself. Check out its Neoclassical architectural features. The museum is open May 1 through October 31, 9:00 A.M. to 8:00 P.M. daily in summer, and 9:00 A.M. to 5:00 P.M., Monday through Friday, May, September, and October. It's open by appointment only from November through April; call 684–9331 to make one.

Northern Wyoming Trivia

In 1890, Mayoworth, now a discontinued post office in Johnson County, was named by the first post mistress after her daughter May and May's husband William Worthington.

At Two North Main Street try out the *Busy Bee Lunch.* The site first housed a popcorn stand, but the Busy Bee took over in 1928, and it's been going strong since. The Bee is *the* regular spot for locals, so you're bound to catch up with gossip about folks you've never met. Try the homemade pie, it's mouth watering. Don't look for any tables—it's strictly a stools and counter kind of place. As you relish your pie, you can watch and listen to Clear Creek, which flows past just outside the window.

If you've any room left after lunch, stroll down to **Seney's Drugs,** located at 38 South Main Street, and belly up to the soda fountain, a favorite Buffalo gathering spot for generations. Seney's malted milks and milk shakes were once recommended by Duncan Hines in his newspaper column. The 1895 building at 84–89 South Main Street features an unusual white cast-iron facade on the second floor.

Take a look at the mural on the side of the building at 51 South Main Street. It proclaims Buffalo as more than a one-horse town. A variety of businesses have operated out of this structure through the decades, including a butcher shop, grocery store, jewelry store, and city electric building. Today it houses the **Hitching Post Art Gallery,** representing the work of local and other Wyoming artists, with an array of unique wildlife and Western limited editions, woodcarvings, pottery, baskets, beadwork, sterling silver jewelry, and bronzes. For information call 684–9473.

Spend an hour or two at **Buffalo's Washington Park** pitching horseshoes, enjoying a walk, picnicking, or cooling off in Wyoming's largest free outdoor swimming pool. The park is located at the intersection of Burritt Avenue and Angus Street. Also located on Burritt Avenue, at 590 North Burritt, is the **Cloud Peak Inn,** a bed-and-breakfast establishment occupying a grand turn-of-the-century house (once the in-town home of a wealthy rancher). Lavish oak paneling, a fireplace incorporating fossils, and plentiful servings of gourmet breakfast creations are

The Clear Creek Trail System

*T*he Clear Creek Trail System, a project still under development, stretches through the heart of downtown Buffalo, then runs along the south side of Clear Creek through the city park. After joining the Green Belt, the trail traverses the lands of the Wyoming State Veterans' Home for 2.65 miles. Another stretch reaches from Clear Creek up toward the Big Horn Mountains. Some portions of the trail, 8 miles-plus and growing, are hard surfaced, while others are graveled or unsurfaced. Points of interest for walkers, cyclists, and others using the trail include the old **Occidental Hotel,** which played a role in Owen Wister's novel, The Virginian, and the **Johnson County–Jim Gatchell Museum.** Following the Clear Creek Trail is a great way to get acquainted with this historic, quintessentially Western town. To find the way just watch for the historic buffalo some of the attractions. You can unwind on the porch, on the balcony, or in the Jacuzzi. Prices are in the $50-to-$100-per-night range. For information or reservations call 684–5794 or (800) 715–5794.

Day trips out of Buffalo provide a range of activities and sights. You can pick up a copy of the *Scenic Tours of Johnson County* brochure at the Chamber of Commerce for a comprehensive listing with descriptions, but here are some to consider for starters: Begin with a half-day tour of **Crazy Woman Canyon** on Highway 16, directly west toward the Big Horn Mountains. Crazy Woman Canyon Road is well signed where it branches off to the left about 25 miles out of town. On the drive you'll encounter rugged mountainous terrain, so make sure your brakes are working and leave your travel trailer behind. You'll drive through the resplendent canyon, viewing high cliffs and giant boulders that have tumbled down from above. A Sioux legend says the creek was the haunt of an old insane squaw who could be seen shooting the rapids in her canoe and leaping from village to village on moonlit nights. Other stories offer different explanations for the name of the canyon and creek. To return to Buffalo continue along the gravel road that took you through the canyon until you reach Highway 196. Turn left and you'll be back in town after 10 miles.

You can go back millions of years in just a few hours by driving to the **Dry Creek Petrified Tree.** Proceed east on I–90 until the Red Hills exit. Take the gravel road north for 5 miles, then turn left and follow that road to the petrified tree and surrounding stumps. The self-guided tour includes a series of eight information stations. The cypress trees, when they were composed of wood rather than mineral, grew when the climate was not unlike that of today's Okefenokee Swamp in Georgia.

Meet up with Butch Cassidy at the **Outlaw Cave,** which requires a rugged full day's journey to find. The cave is located on public land with access via Bureau of Land Management roads. First drive south to Kaycee on I–25, then head about 0.9 mile west on Highway 190 to the Barnum Road junction. Follow Barnum Road 17 miles to a sign for the Middle Fork Management Area of the Powder River. Take a left at this sign onto the gravel-and-dirt road designated as the Bar C Road. Most of the road is hard surfaced in dry weather; however, the upper portion requires a vehicle with high clearance and preferably four-wheel drive—or you can mountain bike the final section of the trip. After traveling $8^1/2$ miles from the Middle Fork sign, you will encounter the Outlaw Cave turnoff. From this point it's approximately 2 miles to the cave. The scenery is arresting, with panoramas encompassing brilliant red canyon walls. You're also within walking distance of the **Indian Rock Art Cave,** which contains seventeen carvings, including one of a large warrior figure. The infamous Hole in the Wall is located nearby on private property. (For information on visiting the Hole in the Wall country by another means—namely, horseback—see the information on Outlaw Trail, Inc., listed under Thermopolis, p. 89.)

In Kaycee visit **Hoofprints of the Past,** as the Southern Johnson County Museum is officially known. Indian artifacts on display, along with the old Mayoworth Post Office, the old Kaycee jailhouse, and information on the Johnson County War. The museum (738–2381) is open daily from Memorial Day through October.

Before leaving the Kaycee area, you'll want to study the KILLING OF CHAMPION AND RAY information sign located just south of town on the east side of old Highway 89. The story details the Johnson County Cattle War battle at the KC Ranch.

To continue on to Campbell County, you can drive east from Buffalo on I–90 or take the longer but more intriguing backroad route along U.S. Highway 14/16. On the latter, between Clearmont and Leiter, you'll have an opportunity to see, up close and personal, bison grazing on the **RBL Bison Ranch.** Tours of the ranch are $5.00 per person and take place daily at 2:00 P.M. from May through September. The ranch has raised some prize bison, including T.J., a gold-medal winner at the National Western Livestock Show in Denver, and Tiny, T.J.'s father, the largest domestic bison ever known to be weighed in the United States or Canada. Tiny stood 6 feet, 6 inches tall and weighed 2,700 pounds. The bison ranch also features a restaurant serving buffalo meat, and a gift shop hawking buffalo-related items. The ranch's rental cabins go for $48 per night for a double, while bed-and-breakfast accommodations are available for $78 per night. For information call 758–4387 or (800) 597–0109.

Campbell County

Stop for a photo shoot at **Spotted Horse,** which was named after a Cheyenne chief. The whole town is wrapped up in a combination bar, cafe, and gas station. It's located on Highway 14/16 not long after you leave Sheridan County and enter Campbell County.

With the photo op taken advantage of, it's time to continue through the wide-open spaces toward Gillette. The drive leads through some of the most productive and scenic ranch country in Wyoming. A few miles east of Spotted Horse is the northerly turn to Recluse, established in

1918 as a post office; in fact, the town earned its name owing to the great distance between area ranches and the post office. The **Recluse Branch Library** of the Campbell County Public Library system is most interesting. Located in the Recluse Community Hall, it consists of a wall cupboard that is opened on request to permit patrons to peruse the collection. The library was first organized in 1927 as The Pleasant Hour Club, then in 1934 moved into the Community Hall, a log building constructed with logs cut and hauled by area residents.

Northern Wyoming Trivia
The odd "haystack" terrain outside Gillette results from layers of erosion-resistant clinker (burned coal and clay) that cap individual haystacks.

On to Gillette, namesake of railroad surveyor Edward Gillette, who laid out the track for the Burlington and Missouri River Railroad between Gillette and Sheridan (from which point it continues north to Montana). Edward Gillette was credited with saving the railroad 5 miles of track and thirty bridges in the Campbell County area by routing the railroad through the spot where the town of Gillette grew up. The town was incorporated in 1891, a year after the track was laid.

Gillette's economic well-being centers around the coal industry. The boom in coal production has made Gillette the state's fifth largest city, with a population of nearly 18,000—representing more than half of Campbell County's 30,000 people. The wealth deriving from coal has bought the city some impressive cultural facilities. The **Campbell County Public Library**, for instance, houses an extensive collection of books on Wyoming and an impressive array of art by name artists. You can also visit the city's planetarium, a 960-seat theater, and the Cam-Plex Heritage Center Gallery. Call 682–0552 for more information on these and other area attractions.

The Campbell County Public Library, at 2102 4-J Road, features the **Sheepherders' Monument,** with its beautiful bronze sculpture and an original "stone johnny" (sheepherder's stone marker) brought in from a nearby ranch. The Campbell County Public Library is open Monday through Thursday, 9:00 A.M. to 9:00 P.M., and Friday, and Saturday, 9:00 A.M. to 5:00 P.M.

A real treat in town is the **Campbell County Rockpile Museum,** located at 900 West Second Street. Here you'll find a fine collection of pioneer vehicles, including a chuck wagon, sheep wagon, and horse-drawn hearse. Black horses pulling the hearse signaled that a man was to be buried, while gray horses indicated that a woman or child had died. Also on display are hand-tooled saddlery, branding irons, barbed wire, and prehistoric Native American artifacts. Outside there's a one-room schoolhouse, where in winter students were warmed by a woodstove—and by running as fast as possible to the outhouse when necessary. You'll also learn yet more about railroading and coal mining. The museum is open June 1 through August 31 on Monday through Saturday, 9:00 A.M. to 8:00 P.M., and on Sunday, 12:30 to 6:30 P.M. During the rest of the year, the hours are 9:00 A.M. to 5:00 P.M., Monday through Saturday. For additional details call 682–5723.

If you're interested in touring a local mine, call the Gillette Convention and Visitors Bureau at 686–0040 or (800) 544–6136 to make arrangements. Alternatively drive out to the **Wyodak Overlook** to earn an impressive overview of a coal mine in operation. To reach the overlook take Highway 14/16 about 5 miles east from town. The Wyodak Mine, which opened in 1922, is the oldest operating coal mine in the Powder River Basin; it still produces nearly three million tons of coal annually. Approximately half of that is burned at the adjacent **Wyodak Power Plant.** You can tour the 330-megawatt power plant, which burns coal to generate steam that, in turn, is used to produce electricity. Power plant tours are conducted on Monday through Friday between 9:00 A.M. and 3:00 P.M. Again, for more information visit the Gillette Convention and Visitors Bureau, 314 South Gillette Avenue, or call them.

Northern Wyoming Trivia

The town of Banner was named for the flaglike brand of a local rancher out of whose dining room the town's first post office was run.

A variety of dining experiences await you back in town. For Chinese-American cooking try the **Hong Kong Restaurant** (682–5829), 1612 West Second Street; for homemade specialties try **Bailey's Bar & Grill** (686–7678), 301 South Gillette Avenue; and for Mexican food visit **Casa Del Re** (682–4738), 409 West Second Street. Food prices are moderate at all three restaurants.

Nature lovers shouldn't miss **McManamen Park,** with its excellent birding opportunities. The park is designed to attract waterfowl, and benches and viewing blinds are available for up-close bird-watching. McManamen Park is located between Brooks and Gurley Streets along Warlow Drive on the north side of Gillette.

As evidenced aplenty in and around Gillette, Campbell County is coal country. The Powder River Coal Basin contains an estimated one trillion short tons of coal reserves. Behemoth draglines load 240-ton trucks with coal from the Black Thunder Coal Mine near Wyoming's newest community, Wright, population 1,236. Wright lies at the northwest corner of the massive **Thunder Basin National Grassland.** In all the grasslands cover some two million acres that were set aside by the federal government for soil conservation and plant and wildlife preservation. To reach this, the heart of the nation's largest deposit of low-sulphur coal, drive 40 miles south from Gillette on Highway 59. There are seventeen coal mines in the area, some of which provide tours. For information call the Thunder Basin Coal Company at 939–1300, extension 294.

Although the town was founded only in 1976 and incorporated in 1985, it has already assembled a decent museum. The **Wright Centennial Museum** boasts an interesting collection covering not only coal mining, but also incorporating World War I memorabilia and pioneer farm implements. Outside the museum sits a seventy-ton truck that was retired in 1990. The museum, located at 104 Ranch Court, is open May 15 to October 20, Monday through Friday, 10:00 A.M. to 5:00 P.M. For information call 939–1261.

Tours are also in the offing at the **Durham Buffalo Ranch.** With more than 3,000 head, it's one of the largest private buffalo herds existing. The buffalo (*Bison bison*), or American bison, is a favorite of Wyomingites; the beast is prominently featured on the state flag and serves as the official state mammal. Weighing up to two tons, the bison is the largest North American land mammal. At one time more than seventy-five million of the big critters roamed the prairies and high plains. In a sad saga familiar to most Americans, millions were slaughtered for food and sport in the late 1800s. Hunters like Buffalo Bill Cody earned their reputations shooting hundreds of bison to supply railroad crews with meat and hides. By the time Congress passed the first federal protection legislation for buffalo in 1894, their numbers had dwindled to less than one thousand individuals in all of North America. The disappearance of the buffalo helped to destroy the traditional life ways of Native Americans on the Great Plains, who had relied on buffalo to provide food, clothing, shelter, cooking utensils, tools, weapons, and fuel.

Today the buffalo is enjoying a resurrection, with more than 70,000 of them scattered across the country in herds ranging in size from several hundred to several thousand. The animal is no longer endangered, so don't hesitate to sample a buffalo steak or burger if your curiosity is piqued. Buffalo meat is lean, healthy, and downright tasty. (To have some cut and wrapped by the pound to take some home, you can call Marion Scott at 682–3994.) The Durham Buffalo Ranch, located on Highway 59 about 8 miles north of Wright, encompasses more than 55,000 acres. Group tours can be arranged by making advance reservations; call 939–1271.

Crook County

Proceed easterly from Gillette to Moorcroft, population 768, located on the banks of the Belle Fourche (pronounced *bell foosh*) River. Drovers on the Texas Cattle Trail moved thousands of cattle through the Moorcroft area in the 1880s and 1890s, and the town also served as a major railhead for cattle shipped from the large ranch spreads in this region. In fact, in 1891 Moorcroft ranked as the leading cattle shipping point in the country. *The Western Texas Trail Museum* in downtown Moorcroft captures the essence of those cattle-driving days and the rich legacy of the area's ranching past. The museum is located at 220 South Big Horn. It is open daily from 1:00 to 4:00 P.M., May through September.

As you drive from Moorcroft toward Devils Tower on U.S. Highway 14, you'll notice Keyhole Reservoir on your right. From *Keyhole State Park* you can peer at the astounding formation of Devils Tower, rising beyond your crackling campfire. Keyhole State Park's fourteen thousand acres of water provide plenty of boating, fishing, and swimming opportunities. The reservoir and surrounding wetlands are also a mecca for more than two hundred species of birds. Be on the lookout for bald eagles, common yellow-throat, osprey, wild turkeys, and white pelicans. At park headquarters you can obtain a complete bird list.

The Legend of Devils Tower

Geologists still argue whether Devils Tower is the result of a volcanic core exposed after millions of years of erosion, or molten rock forced upward from the bowels of the earth through existing rock layers. The rocks and boulders at its base are broken pieces of columns shed from the core.

One way or another, though, the geologist's outlook is a pragmatic one. The area's Native Americans have their own ideas. The most popular of the Mateo Tipi, or Bear Lodge Indian legends, involves the story of a bear chasing seven Indian girls. To escape, the girls jumped up on a rock several feet high and prayed, "Rock, save us." Hearing the pleas of the girls, the rock began to elongate itself upward, pushing them higher and higher into the air, out of the clutches of the bear. The bear clawed at the sides of the rock, which continued to grow until it reached the sky, and the claw marks are there to this day. As for the Indian girls, they became the seven stars making up the constellation Pleiades. (In Greek mythology these seven stars are the daughters of Atlas.)

The park was named after the "keyhole brand" used by the nearby McKean Ranch. The park entrance is situated on the south side of the reservoir and is accessible from Highway 113. From Memorial Day through Labor Day, you can walk the park's 6.2-mile official Volksmarch trail. A full-service marina, motel, and cafe are located on Headquarters Road, adjacent to the lakeshore. For information call 756–3596.

Continue winding along U.S. Highway 14 to reach Devils Tower Junction. Turn north there onto State Highway 24, and soon you'll arrive at the

Close Encounters of the Gravitational Kind

*A*fter sitting in the entrance station of Devils Tower National Monument for most of the summer of 1978, patiently accepting fees and orienting visitors, I'd heard it asked way too often, "What's it like on top?" (The only more common query was, "Where are the aliens parked?"—because the summer I spent working as a ranger at Devils Tower happened to be the one immediately after the release of the wildly popular movie Close Encounters of the Third Kind.)

"Oh, it's grassy, flat, a couple hundred feet across," I'd respond time and again. "Birds and small mammals and even some snakes live up there." But I felt slightly deceitful every time I recited the description because I'd never seen the top of Devils Tower with my own eyes. By late in the summer, I decided it was time to change that.

Fellow ranger Hollis Marriott, an expert rock climber, offered to lead me and another neophyte climber to the top of the tower. Until then I'd done absolutely no technical climbing. I'd never tried rappelling, either, even off a modest cliff, but Hollis assured me I'd do fine. She proposed to lead us up the Durrance route, the easiest of several-

dozen routes to the top of the tower. But easiest is a relative term, as I was reminded on that day.

I was in pretty respectable aerobic shape from running that summer, but my lack of specific climbing strength and skills required me to use far more energy than necessary. Climbing Devils Tower ended up being one of the toughest things I'd ever done, and also the scariest. My legs and arms shook almost uncontrollably at times from a combination of fear and fatigue. From the top—which indeed was grassy, flat, and a couple of hundred feet across—in order to get back down I had to step off into a void, seeing nothing below me but air for some 500 feet (that's the approximate height of a fifty-story building). The nothingness ended harshly in a jumble of rocks and boulders. I had to place great faith in the climbing rope, the carabiners, and my climb leader to do their jobs properly, which they all did.

To say I was happy to get back to horizontal ground is a world-class understatement. But after that I spoke with a new authority—and with a knowing twinkle in my eye, I'm sure—when asked, "What's it like on top?"

Devils Tower

access road leading to ***Devils Tower National Monument.*** The first documented white men to take in the stunning view of the tower were members of Capt. W. F. Raynold's 1859 Yellowstone expedition. Col. Richard I. Dodge led a U.S. Geologic Survey expedition to the unique formation in 1875. Appreciating its unique attributes, President Theodore Roosevelt designated Devils Tower as the nation's first national monument in 1906.

Devils Tower is a magnificent sight, rising an abrupt 865 feet. The top spreads out to a 180-by-300-foot oval. A paved 1¹/₄-mile walking path surrounds the base of the big rock's perimeter. Nearby a large prairie dog town will keep you and the kids occupied, as the furry critters vie for your attention with a variety of amusing antics.

The unique geological phenomenon of Devils Tower made it to the big screen in Hollywood's production of *Close Encounters of the Third Kind.* Devils Tower has also drawn a lot of attention due to the large number of rock climbers scaling its sheer sides. (Recently climbing limitations and bans have been enacted by the National Park Service, following complaints from Native Americans who consider the tower sacred.) Wyoming rancher William Rogers was the first to reach the top of the formation on July 4, 1893, using wooden pegs that he pounded into crevices in the rock face. More modern rock-climbing techniques were not employed to climb the tower until 1936, when Fritz Wiessner and other members of the American Alpine Club made the ascent.

Try to be at the tower around sunset for a spectacular sight; one that resists description. It simply must be seen to be believed.

Devils Tower National Monument is open year-round; however, the campground, restaurants, and gift shops operate on a seasonal basis. There is a minimal entrance fee per vehicle. Inquire at the visitor center about special programs and interpretive presentations. The center, open daily from 8:00 A.M. to 7:45 P.M., is located 10 miles south of Hulett on Highway 24, then west 3 miles on a paved park road. For information call 467–5283.

Crook County was named after the famous Indian fighter, Gen. George Crook. Another, less-skilled and less-fortunate Indian fighter, Gen. George A. Custer, traveled through Crook County as he led the first government expedition searching for gold in the Black Hills of South Dakota and Wyoming. You can still make out remnants of Custer's exploratory trail, which was carved in July 1874 by a hundred wagons and a force of one thousand troops, engineers, geologists, and miners crossing the terrain. For the most part the 1876 Black Hills gold rush was confined to the South Dakota side of the border, but a few abandoned glory holes are located in the Aladdin area. A Custer Expedition interpretive sign is found about 3 miles west of Aladdin on the south side of Highway 24.

The Black Hills of Wyoming deliver a treasure of a sort other than gold. The route along the Bear Lodge Mountains, as you wend between Devils Tower and Alladin on Highway 24, dishes up a veritable mother lode of lofty sandstone cliffs, red hills, wildflower-filled meadows, creeks and ponds, and clusters of ponderosa pine, cedar, and oak. Along the way you can picnic at the Bearlodge campground west of Aladdin or at any of the other campgrounds in the Black Hills National Forest.

The name of the town of Alladin was taken from the character in *Arabian Nights* who rubbed the lamp and released two genies. The name was chosen by the California capitalist who laid out the town as a rail stop for the Wyoming and Missouri Valley Railroad.

Although there may or may not be any genie here, Alladin will cast a small-town spell on any visitor who bothers to spend an hour or two at the *Aladdin General Store.* In addition to serving the local area with groceries and hardware, the store operates as the post office and community center. Here issues of the day are discussed. The general store also encompasses a little museum. The structure housing the Aladdin General Store was built by Bill Robinson in 1896 as a saloon, and today the building is listed on the National Register of Historic Places—as is a mine tipple from the late 1880s that's located 2^1/$_2$ miles east of town. It is one of the few remaining tipples in Wyoming.

In Aladdin's Antique Attic, which is part of the general store, you'll discover antique furniture, blankets, rugs, books, and Western art. So grab a book and a refreshment and kick back on the front porch. The Aladdin General Store is open daily Monday through Saturday from

8:00 A.M. until 6:00 P.M. in the winter, and until 7:00 P.M. in the summer, and on Sunday from 10:00 A.M. to 5:00 P.M. in the winter, and 9:00 A.M. to 6:00 P.M. during the summer. For information call 896–2226.

The largest community in Crook County, and our last stop there, is Sundance, population 1,139. You can get to Sundance from Alladin by following State Highway 111 south, then I-90 southwest; or, alternatively, by returning to Devils Tower Junction and driving southeast on U.S. Highway 114. The town boasts a number of attractions, including the *Crook County Museum and Art Gallery,* where you can see the original furniture from the courtroom where the Sundance Kid was tried and convicted of horse thieving. He had made the terrible mistake of stealing a slow horse. The misadventure cost Cassidy, then known as Harry Longbaugh, eighteen months in jail.

Other museum displays include cowboy gear, branding irons, a re-creation of a prehistoric buffalo jump, and Native American artifacts. The art gallery displays works by Crook County artists and photographers. Summer hours are 8:00 A.M. to 8:00 P.M., Monday through Friday, and 9:00 A.M. to 4:00 P.M. on Saturday. Off-season hours are 8:00 A.M. to 5:00 P.M., Monday through Friday. The museum and art gallery are located on the lower level of the Crook County Courthouse, located on Cleveland Street. For information call 283–3666.

The town sits below Sundance Mountain—whose Sioux name is *Wi Wacippi Paha,* meaning "Temple of the Sioux"—where Sioux Indians once performed sacred sun dances. The religious ceremony represented the triumph of good over evil and marked the beginning of life. The sun dance ritual lasted from several days to weeks, and many Native Americans traveled to *Wi Wacippi Paha* to observe the ceremony.

Weston County

Newcastle, population 3,003, lies along the Cheyenne–Black Hills Stage Route, only 10 miles from the South Dakota border. The town, founded as a coal-mining and -shipping center, named after the better-known Newcastle-upon-Tyne, the great English coal port. (Burlington Northern trains coming from the massive coal mines in the Thunder Basin rumble through Wyoming's version, demonstrating that you can at least haul coal through, if not to, Newcastle.)

One attraction in town is actually outside of town, at the ghost town site of *Cambria.* Cambria once was a thriving Burlington and Missouri River Railroad coal town, with a population of 1,500 people comprising some two dozen nationalities. From the 1880s through 1928, Cambria supplied the nation with thirteen million tons of coal. There's a *Cambria Mining Camp Marker* located approximately 5 miles north of Newcastle on the west side of Highway 85. The ghost town site is roughly 5 miles west of the sign, located on private property. Inquire at the Newcastle Chamber of Commerce (800–835–0157) about obtaining permission from the property owner to view the Cambria site.

Three miles farther north on Highway 85, you arrive at the *Flying V Cambria Inn.* Cambria's Flying V Casino opened in 1928, just months before the mines closed for good. It now houses a bed and breakfast and a restaurant in a beautiful, hilly setting. The Tudor castle-like structure is listed on the National Register of Historic Places. The restaurant specializes in Italian food, fish, and steaks, and serves dinner only. It's open from May through December. Prices are moderate. For information or reservations call 746–2096.

Back in Newcastle the *Anna Miller Museum* features an abundant collection of material about, and artifacts from, the international melting pot of Cambria. The museum is housed in one of the last-constructed Army National Guard cavalry stables, built in the 1930s and now listed on the National Register of Historic Places. Browse through collections of fossils, 1890 firefighting equipment, and various means of horse-drawn transportation, as well as through the country store and pioneer doctor's office. Outside you can visit the 1890–1930 Green Mountain Schoolhouse and the early 1900s Novak Miller Cabin. The museum is open the year-round, Monday through Friday from 9:00 A.M. to 5:00 P.M., and 9:00 A.M. to noon on Saturday in the summer only. It's located at Delaware and Washington Park, off Highway 16. For information call 746–4188.

On the north side of Main Street, east of the railroad tracks, there's a sign marking, THE HANGING OF DIAMOND L. SLIM CLIFTON. Clifton was lynched in 1903 after the murder of his neighbors, Louella and John Church. An angry mob stormed the jail and took Clifton from the sheriff at gunpoint. He was hanged from the railroad bridge, which has since been removed.

For a bite to eat before leaving Weston County for Niobrara County, consider stopping at the *Old Mill Inn,* found at 500 West Main Street. As its name indicates, the structure once operated as the town flour mill. Hours are 5:00 A.M. to 11:00 P.M. daily. For information call 746–2711.

**PLACES TO STAY IN
DEVILS TOWER–
BUFFALO BILL COUNTRY**

BIG HORN
Bozeman Trail Bed
& Breakfast,
304 Highway 335;
(307) 672-2381 or
(877) 672-2381

BUFFALO
Blue Gables Motel,
662 North Main Street;
(307) 684-2574 or
(800) 684-2574

Comfort Inn,
65 Highway 16 East;
(307) 684-9564 or
(800) 228-5150

EconoLodge,
333 Hart;
(307) 684-2219 or
(800) 55-ECONO

Wyoming Motel,
610 East Hart;
(307) 684-5505 or
(800) 666-5505

CODY
Buffalo Bill Village
(seasonal),
1701 Sheridan Avenue;
(307) 587-5544 or
(800) 527-5544

The Burl Inn,
1213 17th Street;
(307) 587-2084 or
(800) 388-2084

Elk Valley Inn (seasonal),
3256 North Fork Highway;
(307) 587-4149

Holiday Inn,
1701 Sheridan;
(307) 587-5555 or
(800) 527-5544

Skyline Motor Inn,
1919 17th Street;
(307) 587-4201 or
(800) 843-8809

GILLETTE
Arrowhead Motel,
202 Emerson;
(307) 686-0909

Holiday Inn,
2009 South Douglas
Highway;
(307) 686-3000 or
(800) HOLIDAY

Quality Inn,
1004 East Highway 14/16;
(307) 682-2616

GREYBULL
Greybull Motel,
300 North 6th Street;
(307) 765-2628

Yellowstone Motel,
247 Greybull Avenue;
(307) 765-4456

HYATTVILLE
Paintrock Inn (seasonal);
(307) 469-2335

KAYCEE
Cassidy Inn Motel,
346 Nolan Avenue;
(307) 738-2250

LOVELL
Super 8 Motel,
595 East Main;
(307) 548-2725

Western Motel (seasonal),
180 West Main;
(307) 548-2781

MEETEETSE
Oasis Motel,
1702 State Street;
(307) 868-2551

Vision Quest Motel,
2207 State Street;
(307) 868-2512 or
(888) 281-9866

MOORCROFT
Cozy Motel,
219 West Converse;
(307) 756-3486

Moorcourt Motel,
Highway 14 &
Devils Tower Road;
(307) 756-3411

NEWCASTLE
Flying V Cambria Inn
(seasonal),
23726 Highway 85;
(307) 746-2096

Fountain Motor Inn,
2 Fountain Plaza;
(307) 746-4426 or
(800) 882-8858

Sundowner Inn,
451 West Main;
(307) 746-2796

POWELL
Best Western Kings Inn,
777 East 2nd Street;
(307) 754-5117

Park Motel,
737 East 2nd Street;
(307) 754-2233 or
(800) 506-7378

SHERIDAN
Guest House Motel,
2007 North Main;
(307) 674-7496 or
(800) 226-9405

Mill Inn Motel,
2161 Coffeen Avenue;
(307) 672–6401

Best Western Sheridan
Center Motor Inn,
612 North Main;
(307) 674–7421 or
(800) 528–1234

SUNDANCE
Bear Lodge Motel,
218 Cleveland;
(307) 283–1611 or
(800) 341–8000

Sundance Mountain Inn,
26 Highway 585;
(307) 283–3737

TEN SLEEP
Log Cabin Motel;
(307) 366–2320

Flagstaff Motel (seasonal);
(307) 366–2745

THERMOPOLIS
Coachman Inn,
112 Highway 20 South;
(307) 864–3141

Holiday Inn,
Hot Springs State Park;
(307) 864–3131 or
(800) HOLIDAY

Super 8 Hot Springs Motel,
Lane 5 Highway 20 South;
(307) 864–5515

WORLAND
Town House Motor Inn,
119 North 10th;
(307) 347–2426

**PLACES TO EAT IN
DEVILS TOWER–
BUFFALO BILL COUNTRY**

BUFFALO
Colonel Bozeman's Family
Restaurant,
675 East Hart;
(307) 684–5555

The Busy Bee,
2 North Main;
(307) 684–7544

RBL Bison Ranch,
4355 Highway 14/16 East
(in Clearmont);
(307) 758–4387

CODY
Franca's Italian Dining
(3-star AAA),
1421 Rumsey Avenue;
(307) 587–5354

Irma Hotel & Restaurant,
1192 Sheridan Avenue;
(307) 587–4221

Royal Palace Restaurant,
103 Yellowstone Avenue;
(307) 587–5751

Sarsaparillas Saloon–
Buffalo Bill Village,
1701 Sheridan Avenue;
(307) 587–5544

Olive Glenn Golf & Country
Club (must golf to eat),
802 Meadow Lane;
(307) 587–5688

GILLETTE
Granny's Kitchen,
1414 West 2nd Street;
(307) 687–1200

Peking House Restaurant,
2701 South Douglas
Highway;
(307) 682–7868

Mona's Cafe,
403 El Camino Drive;
(307) 686–6506

Bailey's Bar and Grill,
301 South Gillette Avenue;
(307) 686–7678\

GREYBULL
MJ's Cafe,
333 North Second Street;
(307) 765–9228

Lisa's Restaurant,
200 Greybull Avenue;
(307) 765–4765

HYATTVILLE
Paintrock Inn;
(307) 469–2335

KAYCEE
The Invasion;
(307) 738–2211

LOVELL
Rose Bowl Cafe,
483 Shoshone Avenue;
(307) 548–7121

Big Horn Restaurant,
605 East Main;
(307) 548–6811

MEETEETSE
Lucille's Cafe,
1906 State Street;
(307) 868–9909

The Broken Spoke,
1947 State Street;
(307) 868–2362

MOORCROFT
Donna's Diner,
203 West Converse;
(307) 756–3422

NEWCASTLE
Flying V Cambria Inn,
23726 Highway 85;
(307) 746-2096

Old Mill Inn,
500 West Main;
(307) 746-2711

POWELL
Skyline Cafe,
141 East Coulter;
(307) 754-8052

Powell Drug
(soda fountain),
140 North Bent;
(307) 754-2031

SHERIDAN
Ciao Bistro,
120 North Main Street;
(307) 672-2838

Sanford's Grub,
Pub & Brewery,
1 East Alger;
(307) 674-1722

Silver Spur Cafe,
832 North Main Street;
(307) 672-2749

SUNDANCE
Higbee's Cafe,
101 North Third;
(307) 283-2165

Log Cabin Cafe,
1620 Cleveland;
(307) 283-3393

Aro Restaurant,
203 Cleveland;
(307) 283-2000

TENSLEEP
Flagstaff Cafe;
(307) 366-2745

Mountain Man Cafe;
(307) 366-2660

THERMOPOLIS
Holiday Inn,
Hot Springs State Park;
(307) 864-3131 or
(800) HOLIDAY

Pumpernick's,
512 Broadway;
(307) 864-5151

WORLAND
Antone's Supper Club,
973 Highway 16 East;
(307) 347-9924

Coffee & Cakes,
7th Street and
Big Horn Avenue;
(307) 347-6488

Central Wyoming: Oregon Trail—Rendezvous Country

The North Platte River and the towns lining its banks help define the eastern half of this region, where history was made by the tens of thousands of people who, often possessing little more than a dream of a better life, migrated west along the Oregon and Mormon Trails. A slightly later regional history involved the forts, fights, and treaties—and treaties broken—of the Indian wars.

From Lusk, U.S. Highway 18/20 will take you to I-25 and the North Platte River corridor. From the city of Casper, you'll head west through a relatively bleak countryside inhabited by pronghorn antelope and oil wells pumping overtime, and little else. The wide open begins closing in some west of Riverton, where Lander and Dubois serve as major staging points for adventures in the mountains of the Shoshone and Bridger-Teton National Forests, where you can explore some of the wildest and most spectacular country the contiguous 48 states have to offer.

Niobrara County

Lusk, population 1,504, boomed after the cry of "Gold!" was heard in the nearby Black Hills in the late 1800s. A much later upward turn in the area economy was related to the post–World War II oil boom, which eventually went bust after the wells dried up. The town lies at the intersection of U.S. Highway 20, coming out of the east from Nebraska, and U.S. Highway 85, which more or less follows the historic route of the Cheyenne–Black Hills Stage and Express Line. A trip on this line covered

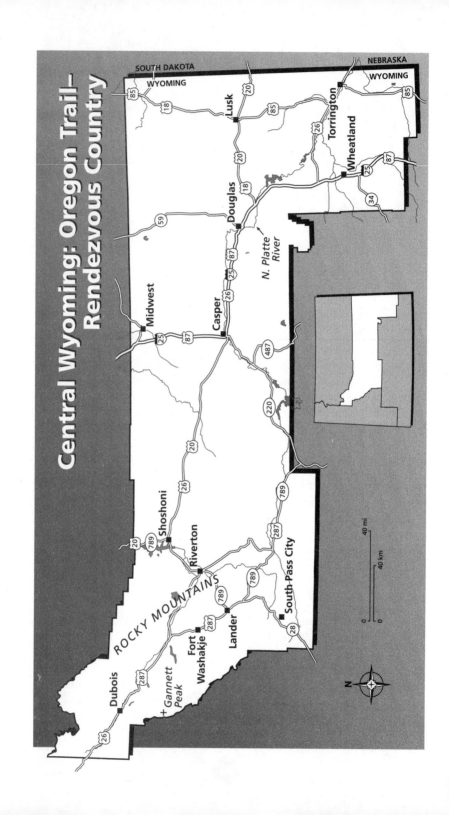

Central Wyoming: Oregon Trail–Rendezvous Country

BEST ANNUAL EVENTS IN OREGON TRAIL–
RENDEZVOUS COUNTRY

Wild West Winter Carnival,
Riverton; late January/early February;
(307) 856–4801

Wyoming State Winter Fair,
Lander; February; (307) 332–3892

Summer Solstice at the Crimson Dawn,
Casper; June; (307) 235–1303

Parade and Antique Fire Engine Muster,
Torrington; June; (307) 532–3879 and
(800) 577–3555

**Jackalope Days & Western
Fine Arts Show,**
Douglas; June; (307) 358–2950

Popo Agie Mountain Man Rendezvous,
Lander; June; (307) 332–3892

**Homestead Heritage Day
Dutch Oven Cook-off,**
Wheatland; June; (307) 322–2322

**South Pass City
Fourth of July Celebration,**
South Pass City; (307) 332–3684

Fort Fetterman Days,
Douglas; July; (307) 358–2864

The Legend of Rawhide,
Lusk; July; (800) 223–LUSK (5875)

Frontier Fourth of July,
Fort Laramie; (307) 837–2221

Deer Creek Days,
Glenrock; July; (307) 358–9288

Wyoming State Fair,
Douglas; August; (307) 358–9288

**Whiskey Mountain Buckskinners
Rendezvous,** Dubois; August;
(307) 455–2556

Fur Trade Living History Weekend,
Fort Laramie; September; (307) 837–2221

Cowboy Poets Roundup,
Riverton; October; (800) 325–2732.

---

some 300 miles of rough roads and treacherous river crossings through Indian territory.

What better location, then, than Lusk to find the *Stagecoach Museum*? The museum occupies the former National Guard Armory, 322 South Main Street. The transportation section houses more than merely stagecoaches: a fine collection of covered wagons, for instance, including a dray wagon, Lusk's old street sprinkler, and early fire-fighting wagons. The centerpiece is a stagecoach used on the Cheyenne–Black Hills line. Built by Abbott & Downing of Concord, New Hampshire, in the 1860s, the coach features a leather brace suspension system that eliminated the need for metal springs. A similar stagecoach is exhibited at the Smithsonian Institution in Washington, D.C.

You can explore four pioneer rooms and an early doctor's office, stare at the always-popular two-headed calf mount, and inspect the front of an old store moved in from the Silver Cliff townsite. The volunteer-staffed museum is open May through October from 10:00 A.M. to 7:00 P.M., Monday through Friday, and weekends from 1:00 to 7:00 P.M. For information call 334-3444.

Several miles east of Lusk on Highway 20, you'll find a restored *Redwood*

Water Tower, one of few still standing in the country. The Fremont Elkhorn/Missouri Valley Railroad built the tower in 1886 to supply water for its steam engines. When the railroad tracks reached Lusk on July 13, 1886, a gold spike was driven with a silver hammer to commemorate the occasion. A little farther east from the water tower, you can locate a *Texas Trails Marker,* honoring the cowboys who drove thousands of head of cattle from Texas to Montana between 1876 and 1897.

Approximately 13 miles north of Lusk on Highway 18/85, the *Fort Hat Creek* interpretive sign marks the 1875 establishment of an outpost by soldiers from Fort Laramie. Ironically the soldiers weren't where they thought they were: They located the fort on Sage Creek in Wyoming rather than Hat Creek in Nebraska. The *Hat Creek Monument* and the old fort site are located on private land 2 miles east on a county road, then southwest 1 mile on gravel. (The marker and log building used as a stage station can readily be seen from the road, so please respect the rights of the property owner.)

Fort Hat Creek played a prominent role in the surrender of Chief Crazy Horse. The Sioux chief sent a messenger to Hat Creek on May 1, 1877, announcing his intention to surrender. The message was then telegraphed to Camp Robinson. On May 6, Chief Crazy Horse rode up to the Red Cloud Agency, shook hands with General Crook's emissary, and smoked the peace pipe, thus concluding the Great Sioux War.

For a decidedly Western experience, drive 50 miles north of Lusk on U.S. Highway 85 and then 2½ miles north of Mule Creek Junction to the *Sage and Cactus Village.* Here you can sleep in a tipi situated on a bluff overlooking the Cheyenne River. You'll awaken to the powerful aroma of cowboy coffee brewing over a campfire, then enjoy a hearty breakfast. The Sage and Cactus Village is open daily Memorial Day to Labor Day (sometimes earlier or later, weather conditions dictating). Rates run $50 for two people per night. For information and reservations call 663–7653.

A unique Western character, *Mother Featherlegs Shepard,* earned her name and reputation by riding herd on her cattle with her red pantaloons flapping in the breeze like feathers. The roadhouse madam on the Cheyenne–Black Hills Stage Line was murdered by "Dangerous" Dick Davis in 1879. A monument to Mother Featherlegs is located 10 miles southwest of Lusk. Access to the site is by way of a dirt road located just south of the rest area on U.S. Highway 85.

Two architecturally notable buildings that you can't miss in Lusk are the 1919 *Niobrara County Courthouse* and the 1919 Renaissance/Italianate

Niobrara County Library, the last Carnegie Library in Wyoming still serving its intended purpose. The dilapidated *Yellow Hotel* south of the Chicago Northwestern Railroad Depot has known better days, like when owner Madame Del Burke ran a successful brothel at the hotel. Lusk reportedly owes its early water and electrical systems to her generosity (she apparently financed many of the city bonds for those services).

The annual *Legend of Rawhide* pageant takes place in Lusk in early July. This celebration of Wyoming's Wild West has been continually polished and perfected for nearly half a century. The grisly sounding story revolves around a white man who kills a Indian maiden and is subsequently skinned alive by vengeful Indians. Festivities include two live performances, with a cast of two hundred, as well as a country-western music concert and barbecue, an art show, a parade, and outdoor pancake breakfasts. For information and dates call (800) 223–LUSK (5875).

Goshen County

The Oregon, Mormon, and California Trails all played roles in the early history of Goshen County. Fort Laramie, a resting and replenishing place for weary emigrants, was also an important stop on the Pony Express route and the Cheyenne–Black Hills Stage Line. But before visiting Fort Laramie, let's stop in at Torrington, located 57 miles southeast of Lusk on U.S. Highway 85, only 8 miles from the Nebraska border.

Torrington's *Homesteader's Museum* features a Cheyenne–Black Hills stagecoach that was cheered by thousands attending Buffalo Bill's Wild West Show after the turn of the century. The museum is located in the 1926 Union Pacific Depot just south of town, across the road from Torrington's largest employer, the Holly Sugar factory. The depot is a rather ornate structure designed by the noted architectural firm of Gilbert Stanley Underwood. Inside you'll find materials from the 4A Ranch, historic photographs of the area, and information and artifacts relating

---

BEST ATTRACTIONS IN OREGON TRAIL–RENDEZVOUS COUNTRY

Legend of Rawhide,
Lusk; (800) 223–LUSK
(5875)

Oregon Trail Ruts,
Guernsey; (307) 777–6323

Fort Fetterman,
outside Douglas;
(307) 358–2864

Ayres Natural Bridge,
outside Douglas;
(307) 358–3532

Hell's Half Acre,
west of Casper;
(307) 472–0018

Club El Toro and Svilar's Bar & Dining Room,
Hudson; (307) 332–4627
and 332–4516

Sinks Canyon State Park,
Lander; (307) 332–6333

South Pass City State Historic Site;
(307) 332–3684

Willie Handcart Company site,
south of Atlantic City;
(307) 775–6256

National Bighorn Sheep Interpretive Center,
Dubois; (307) 455–3429

---

to Wyoming homesteaders. The museum is open from 10:00 A.M. to 5:00 P.M., Monday through Saturday, and 1:00 to 4:00 P.M. on Sunday, during the summer. Call 532–3879 for information and winter hours.

Twenty-two miles south of Torrington just off U.S. Highway 85, you'll find a pleasant park in the form of **Hawk Springs State Recreation Area.** The park provides excellent fishing and picnic facilities, but the real draw is the blue heron rookery found at the site. With some time and patience you might spot blue herons, great horned owls, wood ducks, a variety of teal, and a host of other birds. Be sure to bring along a pair of binoculars. Camping fees are just a few dollars per vehicle per night. For information contact the Hawk Springs State Recreation Area at 836–2334.

Traveling west on Highway 26, you'll come to the town of Lingle, situated within 2 miles of the August 19, 1854, **Grattan Massacre.** It was the first major confrontation on the Great Plains between U.S. troops and Native Americans. The incident was touched off when Lt. John Grattan went to a Sioux village to arrest a tribal member for killing a steer. A shot was fired, panic ensued, and Grattan and his twenty-eight men were killed. The massacre led to the tragic Plains Indian Wars and the eventual removal of tribes to reservations in the late 1800s.

Fort Laramie National Historic Site is a premier reconstruction, with excellent interpretive programs and fort tours. Top-notch facilities notwithstanding, the site retains "off the beaten path" status owing to its location. Fort Laramie is open year-round, but it's in summer that the place really fires up, when park rangers dress in period costumes and transform themselves into the characters that made Fort Laramie such a vibrant and vital part of the story of western expansion from 1841 until the end of the Indian Wars in 1890.

Fort Laramie

It began in 1834 when William Sublette erected a trading post at a nearby site. Sublette sold his Fort William in 1836 to the American Fur Company, which later rebuilt the fort a mile up the Laramie River at the eventual site of Fort Laramie. The government purchased the fort in 1841.

There's plenty of history to be absorbed at Fort Laramie today, along with the possibility of encountering a ghost or two inhabiting certain post buildings. Ask your guide to elaborate. *Old Bedlam,* located within the fort near the west end of the parade grounds, is the oldest remaining structure in Wyoming. Built in 1849, through the years it served as post headquarters, officers' quarters, and living quarters for other post residents. Additional original structures worthy of touring include the bakery, cavalry barracks, commissary, guardhouse, officers' houses, powder magazine, and surgeon's quarters. The visitor center at Fort Laramie is open from 8:00 A.M. to 4:30 P.M. daily year-round, except for federal holidays between October and April. The fort grounds are open until dusk every day of the year. Fort Laramie National Historic Site is located 3 miles southwest of the town of Fort Laramie off Highway 26. For more information call 837–2221.

Fort Laramie

*W*ithout a doubt Fort Laramie is a must-see for anyone traveling through the region, just as it was for travelers in the mid- to late 1800s. The fort was a gathering spot for Native Americans, trappers, traders, gold seekers, Pony Express riders, and emigrants. By the time Oregon Trail travelers reached Fort Laramie, they had journeyed 650 miles since leaving Independence, Missouri, and they still had some 1,200 miles to go through the deserts and mountains stretching westward before them. Six-mule-team wagons were their preferred method of travel, but oxen were often substituted for mules because they were less expensive. A six-mule team commanded around $600, whereas eight oxen could be purchased for around $200. Emigrants typically spent between $800 to $1,200 to properly outfit themselves for the journey.

The dangers were many, such as those recorded by one emigrant:

"We passed Fort Laramie yesterday and obtained several little articles needed in camp. At this camp, an emigrant, who, with his wife, was travelling with another family, murdered the other man and his wife. He then took possession of the man's team and provisions and he and his wife started the return trip to the Missouri River, reporting that they had become discouraged and would go no further. Within a day, the dead bodies of the murdered couple were discovered and the officers at Fort Laramie notified. We heard that they were apprehended, tried at Fort Laramie at the charge of murder, convicted and hanged. We did not learn their names."

Platte County

ollowing U.S. Highway 26 west into Platte County, you'll cross the North Platte River at Guernsey, population 1,155. But first enjoy a pleasant side trip to the almost ghost towns of *Hartville* and *Sunrise* by turning north about 1 mile east of Guernsey onto State Highway 270. The road winds amid a series of red gorges, rolling rangelands, and pine- and juniper-studded hills. Four miles north along the way is picturesque Hartville, Wyoming's oldest incorporated town still going (even if not going strong). The Hartville Uplift contains one of Wyoming's richest mineral deposits, and prospectors searching for gold, silver, copper, and other minerals in the Eureka Canyon area settled Hartville in the 1870s. After the copper deposits played out in the late 1880s, an iron deposit discovered near the future site of Sunrise kept things moving along. Sunrise was incorporated in 1900, by which time it was a thriving "city" with a population of 750 and, among other amenities, an opera house.

Stop in at the *Old Miners' Bar,* the state's oldest house of libation, for a gander at one of the grander back bars ever to inhabit a Wyoming tavern. Crafted in Germany in 1864, it traveled the final miles of its long journey to Hartville by wagon in 1881. The old stone buildings (in particular, the town jail) with their false fronts provide great backdrops for photos. Ask a local for directions to the boothill cemetery, where you're bound to dig up some interesting tidbits of lore.

With a large Italian population in the area, it's not surprising to find Hartville's *Venice Bar,* nor to find that it serves excellent Italian dinners—unfortunately, however, only to parties of fifteen or more, so that counts out most lone traveling families. For more information and reservations, call 836–2881.

Sunrise, located a mile east of Hartville on Highway 318, possesses its own allure. The Colorado Fuel and Iron Corporation employed some seven hundred workers here at its Chicago Mine, known as Glory Hole. One of the nation's largest open-pit iron ore mines, it has been idle since 1980. Still you can garner an understanding of the scope of the mining activity that went on here for decades. A few brick houses and the YMCA remain standing in Sunrise.

The Guernsey area offers a lot to history buffs and to the outdoors oriented. A short drive from town leads to two vivid reminders of days gone by: the *Oregon Trail Ruts* and *Register Cliff.* The cumulative effect of thousands of wagons traversing relatively soft sandstone outcroppings resulted in wagon wheel ruts between 2 to 6 feet deep. The action of wheels rolling across sandstone was exacerbated by the ponderous hooves of countless mules and oxen, grinding away at the rock above the banks of the North Platte. Today the deep ruts serve as a profound connection to one of the largest human migrations the world has known. The ruts and associated interpretive signs are located ½ mile southeast of Guernsey, off Highway 26. Simply follow the signs.

Emigrants also carved their names into Register Cliff, located 2 miles southeast of Guernsey. The earliest names date back to 1829. For information on both the Oregon Trail Ruts and Register Cliff, contact Wyoming State Parks & Cultural Resources in Cheyenne, 777–6323.

Guernsey was named after Charles Guernsey, an area rancher, legislator, and early promoter of the Guernsey Dam and Reservoir. He also wrote the popular read *Wyoming Cowboy Days*. **Guernsey State Park** provides ample recreational opportunities and camping facilities. The park encompasses more than 6,200 acres of land and nearly 2,400 acres of water. It features 142 campsites and three day-use areas. The tall bluffs and warm waters make the park a favorite with day-trippers and overnight campers alike. The park also features a 6.2-mile **Volksmarch** route, which follows a scenic trail at an elevation of around 4,500 feet, overlooking the dam, reservoir, and down-slope countryside. The trail's difficulty is rated 4.0 on a 5.0-point scale, meaning it's a pretty darn demanding stroll. For more park information call 836–2334.

In the 1930s the Civilian Conservation Corps (CCC) had built a number of rock-and-log structures in the state park, and they also had constructed much of the park's road system. One section of road the young men affectionately dubbed "Mae West Drive" because of its beautiful curves. One of the most impressive rock buildings built by the CCC houses the **Guernsey State Park Museum.** Its large arched rock entrance, native flagstone floors, hand-hewn roof timbers, and wrought-iron

Oregon Trail ruts near Guernsey

Central Wyoming Trivia

Spanish Diggings is an area of roughly 10 miles by 40 miles southwest of Lusk. Here prehistoric Native Americans dug deep holes into high-quality quartzite to acquire the raw materials for fabricating stone tools. The site was named by a cowboy named A. A. Spaugh, who came across it in 1879 and incorrectly surmised that Spaniards had dug the holes while searching for gold.

fixtures reflect the quality craftsmanship typical of CCC works. The exhibits, which also were fashioned in the 1930s, illustrate the ways in which humans through the ages have adapted and related to the area's natural environment. Museum hours are from 10:00 A.M. to 6:00 P.M., seven days a week, May 1 through October 1. For information call 836–2900.

For an uncommonly pleasant drive, weather and time of year permitting, from Guernsey follow the paved road marked Greyrocks Road or Power Plant Road. En route to Wheatland the road traverses some captivating countryside and also wends past the *Greyrocks Reservoir.*

For a restful night make reservations at *The Blackbird Inn* in Wheatland, population 3,271. The 1910 Victorian B&B, operated by Alice and Scotty Anderson, displays many antique furnishings. Each room suggests a theme, from "Alaska" and "Whale" to "Wyoming" and "LaRamie." You'll have the opportunity to savor a sit on the inn's front porch, with its swing and wicker furniture, as the brilliant Wyoming sun sets. Don't think too much about the next morning's breakfast, or you might not get that much sleep after all: fried eggs and spuds, fresh fruit, bagels, muffins, juice, sausage and bacon, hot coffee . . . for openers. Overnight rates are in the $50 range at the inn, located at 1101 11th Street. For reservations call 322–4540.

According to legend the name of the town of Chugwater (population 192) derives from the racket stampeding buffalo made as they splashed into the water after being driven off nearby bluffs by Indians. The Swan Land and Cattle Company called Chugwater its headquarters, even though most of the company's stockholders called Scotland home. It was among the last and most famous of the great ranch spreads of the 1880s. At one time more than 113,000 head of cattle grazed on the cattle company's land. The brutal 1886–87 winter killed off many of the enterprise's cattle, but the company reorganized and managed to stay in business another fifty years. After the turn of the century, however, the legendary cattle company switched species and turned to raising sheep.

Chugwater is home to another well-known ranch—the *Diamond Guest Ranch, Inc.*—where weary travelers can spend a day or a week and experience ranch life as it was and is. The ranch was founded by horse breeder George R. Rainsford in 1880; four generations later, it continues as a working ranch, with many of the original buildings still in use. From the ranch proper you can head out on a trail ride, cast for fish while standing in the shade of a broad cottonwood, or just plain old relax . . . the Diamond Guest Ranch has it all—and good food, to boot. Additional activities and facilities include a Saturday night dance, hayrides, a swimming pool, breakfast cookouts, and horseshoe pits. The Diamond Guest Ranch is open to the public from Memorial Day to Labor Day. You can book a deluxe or ranch room in the historic 1878 ranch house, or camp at one of the many campsites with or without water and electrical hookups. Room rates start at $50 per night. The ranch is located 14 miles west of Chugwater on Diamond Road. For more information and reservations, call 422–3567 or (800) 932–4222.

On the way out of town, stop on Main Street and treat yourself at the *Chugwater Soda Fountain,* one of the oldest fountains in Wyoming, the purveyor of some truly outstanding ice-cream treats.

Unfortunately it's now time to tackle a stretch of I–25. Head north for the last stop in Platte County, the town of Glendo, which occupies the site of the 1861 Horseshoe Stage Station of the Hockaday-Ligget Stage Line. John "Portugee" Phillips stopped at the station in 1866 during his famous ride in blizzard conditions to Fort Laramie from Fort Phil Kearny, following the late-December Fetterman Massacre. A better known western personality, Buffalo Bill Cody, rode for the Pony Express out of the Horseshoe Stage Station.

The major attraction at Glendo today is the *Glendo State Park,* with its 12,500 acres of remarkably clear reservoir waters, offering fishing, waterskiing, sailing, and power boating. From a pine-shrouded campsite, you can watch the sunlight play off 10,272-foot Laramie Peak in the Medicine Bow National Forest to the southwest. A small buffalo herd grazes near the south side of the reservoir. For park and campsite information call 735–4433.

Converse County

There's no con in Converse County unless, of course, you consider the jackalope. Long a source of speculation and heated debate, the famous critter calls Converse County home. In fact Douglas is the self-proclaimed *Jackalope Capital of the World,* as evidenced by the giant statue of the beast in the middle of town at Jackalope Square. Obviously Douglas stands at least a hare above other would-be contenders for the honor.

The *Wyoming Pioneer Memorial Museum,* on the Wyoming State Fairgrounds in Douglas, has a great display of saddles. Also on exhibit are the original bar (crafted by Brunswick in England in 1914) from the LaBonte Inn, guns and memorabilia from the infamous Johnson County War, Native American clothing and decorative arts, and a collection of Western art. The museum is open year-round, Monday through Friday from 8:00 A.M. to 5:00 P.M. and, in summer only, on Saturday from 1:00 to 5:00 P.M. For information call 358–9288.

Thirty-two miles south of Douglas on Highway 94, you'll stumble on Esterbrook, a copper-mining town established in 1886 but soon thereafter relegated to has-been status. The main attraction remaining is a rustic log church, the *Esterbrook Chapel,* which is still used for weddings and other special events. Laramie Peak towers above the town, providing a truly inspirational backdrop for the betrothed.

Take Highway 93 for 11 miles northwest out of Douglas to reach *Fort Fetterman,* named after Lt. Col. William J. Fetterman, who was killed by Indians in 1866 near Fort Kearny at what became known as the Fetterman Massacre. Fort Fetterman was built in 1867 to supply troops

The Jackelope

*S*cientifically known as Pegirus lepuslopus ineptus, *the jackalope's lightning-like speed is partly to blame for the legions who doubt its existence. But for clear evidence, one has only to view the large ruts in the earthscape just south of Douglas to see where today's jackelope's ancient ancestors, the dynalopes and jack-asaurs, roamed.*

Today's jackelope, a direct descendent of those earlier models, is known after dark to sometimes mimic the singing and yodeling of lone cowboys. Contrary to myth, however, they do not sing in harmony with one another. Although you likely won't spot a jackelope, primarily because of their great speed and intense dislike of humans (unless you spend several days out on

the lonesome prairie), you will undoubtedly see their droppings in many places. The pellets appear much like those of a rabbit, only about half again as large.

A good jackelope mount is a trophy without equal. Many authorities have argued that the animal is misnamed, and that it should be known as the jackadeer. Its antlers are much more like the antlers of a deer than they are like the horns of a pronghorn antelope; moreoever, like a deer, they shed their antlers annually (pronghorns don't shed their horns).

When its comes down to it, you can say just about anything you want about the jackelope and dare others to prove you wrong.

engaged in subduing Indian uprisings. A major named Dye, who was assigned to build the fort, wrote that the post was "situated on a plateau . . . above the valley of the Platte, being neither so low as to be seriously affected by the rains or snow; nor so high and unprotected as to suffer from the winter winds."

Dye sorely underestimated the potency of Wyoming winds and winters. Difficult work under brutal weather conditions earned the fort the reputation as a "hardship post" by the men stationed there. After the Treaty of 1868, Forts Reno, Phil Kearny and C. F. Smith were abandoned, leaving Fort Fetterman as the lone army outpost in or near the disputed Indian territory. The fort was abandoned in 1882 after the Native Americans were moved to reservations and no longer posed a threat to travelers and settlers.

The restored Officer's Quarters houses a museum interpreting the fort's history. Living history programs are presented during the summer season, which runs from Memorial Day through Labor Day. Visitor center hours are from 9:00 A.M. to 5:00 P.M. daily, while the grounds are open from sunrise to sunset. Fort Fetterman Days is held in early July, with artillery, infantry, and cavalry demonstrations, as well as crafts, folklore, and frontier-flavored musical performances. For information call 358–2864.

Few people, it seems, other than in-the-know locals, find their way to the peaceful sanctuary of *Ayres Natural Bridge.* The cascading waters of LaPrele Creek flow under the 150-foot span formed by centuries of erosion. Be careful; the soothing sound of the flowing water can cast a hypnotic spell, and you may inadvertently spend hours at the site. Adding to the natural beauty, the bridge is framed by sheer red sandstone walls, lending the entire scene an amphitheater effect. Elm and cottonwood trees provide shade and put the finishing touches on the picturesque scene.

It all began, as they say, some 280 million years ago, during the Pennsylvanian Age, when the sandstone of the Casper Formation was laid down as sand deposited by water. During ensuing centuries runoff water from the Laramie Range gradually eroded away the soft sandstone base, leaving a natural bridge 50 feet high. While many other natural bridges exist around the world, Ayres Natural Bridge is one of few with water still flowing underneath.

To reach the retreat follow I–25 for 11 miles northwest of Douglas to exit 151. The bridge is located 4 miles south from there, at the end of County Road 13. The surrounding park is open April 1 through October 31 from 8:00 A.M. to 8:00 P.M. Overnight camping, not to exceed three consecutive nights, is permitted. Note: Pets aren't allowed, and there is no potable water at the site. For information call 358–3532.

With your arrival at Glenrock, population 2,153, you are in oil country, as evidenced by the pumpers on the outskirts of town. Oil was first discovered around 1916, whereupon the town quickly swelled to more than five thousand residents. A second major strike in 1949 brought another round of prosperity. Today the town's economic viability hinges on another energy source: the Dave Johnston Power Plant, located 6 miles east.

Kit Carson guided John C. Fremont's first expedition to the West past

Bridging the Past

*A*yres Natural Bridge is one of Wyoming's unspoiled treasures. It's no wonder that emigrant found the site so refreshing. One wrote about his visit:

"Today we camped near the natural bridge and laid by to wash and rest our cattle. We noticed it had become general for the stock to begin to suffer and lag with the increasing roughness of the country. It is more noticeable among the horses than with the cattle. We saw several bands of buffalo today but got no meat. Grass is scarce and seems to be getting more and more scarce the further we go, having been used up by those ahead of us."

Pioneer travelers to the bridge included Robert Stuart in 1812 and Capt. Benjamin Bonneville in 1832. Other early trappers and prospectors plied the lower LaPrele Creek area for fur and gold. A number of subsequent emigrants left a mark, carving their names or initials into the red sandstone cliff walls. By 1851 Mormons traversing the emigrant trails had established abundant gardens in the valley with the help

of irrigation ditches. Large storehouses preserved surpluses to be shared with other Saints on the westward march to Utah.

Not all area inhabitants found the natural bridge inviting. Ancient Native American stories tell of an evil spirit, the King of Beasts, who was thought to live beneath the bridge. According to legend a hunting party sought shelter under the arch of the bridge during a terrifying thunderstorm. A lightning bolt struck and killed one of the braves. The others fled in terror, later telling their chief how the hills had opened up and the King of Beasts emerged with long, daggerlike teeth and flashing eyes to swallow the life of the young brave.

In 1881 Alva Ayres, a freighter and bullwhacker, purchased the property encompassing the bridge and used it as headquarters for his shipping business. Two years after his death in 1918, his heirs donated the bridge and fifteen acres of land to Converse County for designation as Ayres Natural Bridge.

the site in 1842. The name Glenrock came about as a pragmatic reference to the large rock resting in the glen at the edge of the townsite. A few of the estimated 350,000 Oregon Trail emigrants who passed by carved their names and the dates into the *Rock in the Glen.* It's located in the park on the south side of U.S. Highway 20/87, at the west end of Glenrock. The *Deer Creek Station* was built in the 1850s and served as an important stop on the Overland Stage and Pony Express routes and the emigrant trails. Native Americans torched the station in 1866; today all you'll find is a Deer Creek Station historical marker at Fourth and Cedar Streets in Glenrock.

A narrow gorge located a few miles outside of present-day Casper forced emigrants traveling on the south bank of the North Platte River to cross to the other side. Often the sheer numbers of people and wagons necessitated a several-day wait to be ferried safely across the river. Some of the more impatient tried to swim across and didn't make it.

An entrepreneur named John Richard (pronounced *re shaw*), along with four other French traders, built the first bridge to span the North Platte River, just above the mouth of Deer Creek, northwest of Glenrock. Richard and his partners expected huge profits, but their dreams, along with the wooden toll bridge, were washed down the river during the spring floods of 1852.

Even plenty of Wyomingites don't know about the *Paisley Shawl/Hotel Higgins,* located at 416 West Birch Street in Glenrock. Reopened in 1980, the restaurant elegantly serves a select and scrumptious menu of four choices, such as ribs, shrimp scampi, chicken Dijon, and New York pepper steak. You can order the full meal with an appetizer, salad, soup, and dessert included, or opt to order a la carte. Prices are moderate to expensive, but worth it. (The restaurant's name relates to a circa 1865 family heirloom shawl made in Paisley, Scotland.) Hours are generally Monday through Saturday, 11:30 A.M. to 1:30 P.M. and 6:00 to 9:30 P.M. Call 436–9212 for seasonal hours and menu changes.

Hotel Higgins was built in 1916 and reputed to be the "Finest Hotel North of Denver." It is listed on the National Register of Historic Places. The original terrazzo tile remains throughout the hotel. In its early days the hotel hosted celebrated folks like William Jennings Bryan and Governor Robert Carey. The current owner, Beverly Doll, has restored the rooms to their 1900 appearance, and Hotel Higgins now operates as a bed-and-breakfast inn, serving a full champagne breakfast in the enclosed porch area. Each room is uniquely decorated and appointed with a brass, iron, or carved-wood bed. Adjoining rooms are available for families. Rates are $60 for a double and $70 for a suite. For hotel and restaurant information or reservations, call 436–9212.

Natrona County

Take the Old Glenrock Highway (U.S. Highway 20/26) west out of Glenrock, avoiding the humdrum and bustle of I–80, and soon you'll enter the *Edness Kimball Wilkins State Park* (located just east of Hat Six Road). Nestled alongside the North Platte River, the park's 315 cottonwood-filled acres provide a shady oasis perfect for an afternoon picnic. You can walk along the tree-lined trails or stave off the summer heat by wading in the swimming pond. Bring your binoculars; there's an abundance of birds and wildlife to observe along the North Platte. Rainbow, brown, and cutthroat trout and channel catfish can be fished for in the river here, also. (For more information on fishing in the Platte/Powder drainages, contact Wyoming Game and Fish, 2800 Pheasant Drive, Casper 82604, or call 234–9185.)

Continuing on Highway 20/26 you arrive at Wyoming's oil capital, the great city of Casper (according to a friend of the author's who lives there, the greatest city in all of Wyoming). Casper grew up along the banks of the North Platte River, and there it remains. Turn south on Wyoming Boulevard to find your way to *Fort Caspar,* situated at 4001 Fort Caspar Road. Originally begun as a trading post in 1859, a volunteer cavalry company guarded the bridge and Platte Bridge Station beginning in 1861. On July 26, 1865, Lt. Caspar Collins and a small detachment, sent to escort a military wagon train, were attacked while crossing the bridge. Collins and four of his twenty men were killed. The three-wagon military train that Caspar's detachment was sent to protect was also attacked and destroyed by a party of Arapahoe, Cheyenne, and Sioux warriors. After four hours of fighting, twenty-two soldiers lay dead at what become known as the Battle of Red Buttes. You'll see a *Red Buttes Battle Marker* located on the north side of Highway 220 at a paved turnout about ¹/₂ mile west of Robertson Road. In tribute to Caspar, the government officially changed the post's name from Platte Bridge Station to Fort Caspar. (His surname had already been employed to name Fort Collins, Colorado.) Two years later the government abandoned the fort.

In 1936 the Works Progress Administration (WPA) reconstructed a number of the log buildings, using sketches made by Collins in 1863. An interpretive center/museum opened in 1983. The fort's buildings are open mid-May through mid-September from 8:00 A.M. to 7:30 P.M., Monday through Friday; 9:00 A.M. to 5:00 P.M. on Saturday; and noon to

5:00 P.M. on Sunday. In addition, the interpretive center is open during the winter from 9:00 A.M. to 5:00 P.M., Monday through Friday, and 1:00 to 4:00 P.M. on Sunday. For information call 235–8462.

The *Crimson Dawn Museum* preserves the Casper Mountain homestead of Neal (that's a "she") Forsling. Elizabeth Paxton, as she was

Beyond Jackson Hole

*J*ust about any skier in the U.S. can tell you that the Jackson Hole Mountain Resort is located in Wyoming. The somewhat more informed will also know that Grand Targhee Ski & Summer Resort is likewise situated in the Cowboy State. Other than that pair of Teton Range ski areas, however, few out-of-staters can name even one additional Wyoming ski area.

Surprisingly, eight additional ski areas, most of them small and family oriented, lie hidden high in the hills and mountains of Wyoming. Here's a list of all ten, along with the vital stats.

Antelope Butte, *east of Lovell; 655–9530*	*Vertical Drop: 1,000'; December to April*
Grand Targhee, *Alta; 353–2300*	*Vertical Drop: 2,000'; mid-November to April*
Hogadon, *Casper Mountain; 235–8499*	*Vertical Drop: 600'; Thanksgiving to Easter (also has several kilometers of groomed cross-country trails, some lighted for night skiing)*
Jackson Hole, *Teton Village; 733–2292*	*Vertical Drop: 4,139'; December to April*
Pine Creek, *east of Cokeville; 279–3201*	*Vertical Drop: 1,200'; mid-December to April*
Powder Pass, *east of Tensleep; 366–2600*	*Vertical Drop: 800'; late November to April*
Sleeping Giant, *west of Cody; 587–4044*	*Vertical Drop: 1,200'; December to April*
Snow King, *Jackson; 733–5200*	*Vertical Drop 1,571'; December to April*
Snowshoe Hollow, *Afton; 886–9516*	*Small hill with rope tow only; Saturday/holidays*
Snowy Range, *Centennial; 745–5750*	*Vertical Drop 1,400'; December to April*

known in her maiden days, homesteaded in 1929 on Casper Mountain, having moved west from her childhood home of Independence, Missouri. She soon met and married Jim Forsling who, sadly, froze to death in 1942, while skiing home from town with eighty pounds of supplies on his back. Neal started traveling a lot after that, painting the scenes she saw around the world. She always returned to her beloved homestead, however. Before she died at age 88 in 1977, Neal donated her remaining land to Natrona County to use as a park. Her former log cabin now serves as a museum, containing memorabilia from the family's life on the mountain, as well as several of Mrs. Forsling's paintings. The address is 1620 Crimson Dawn Road. It's open Mid-June through mid-October from 11:00 A.M. to 7:00 P.M., Saturday through Thursday (closed Friday). Call 235–1303 for directions and further information. (Also on Casper Mountain: *Hogadon,* an "upside-down" ski area whose parking lot is on top of the mountain.)

Central Wyoming Trivia

U.S. Geological Survey topographic maps for the entire state can be found on the Internet at the Web site of the Wyoming Spatial Data Clearinghouse: wgiac.state.wy.us/wsdc/wsdc.html.

Casper was incorporated in 1889, and the almost simultaneous discovery of oil in the area cinched the settlement's future. Many of downtown Casper's buildings were built during the 1920s oil boom. A walking tour of downtown is a fine way to spend a few hours in Wyoming's version of the Windy City. You can pick up a self-guided walking tour brochure from the Casper Historic Preservation Commission at Fort Caspar or at the Casper Area Chamber of Commerce office, 500 North Center Street. A couple of the more unusual structures you can investigate include the 1940 *Courthouse,* at 200 North Center Street, built by the WPA, and featuring an intricate frieze depicting the heritage of Casper; and the 1921 *Rialto Theater,* located at 102 East Second Street, boasting decorative cornices and a classic marquee.

At 302 South David Street, you'll find a late-Gothic Revival *fire station* with CASPER FIRE STATION 1 spelled out on the frieze above the fire truck entrances. The date of construction, 1921, is listed prominently in the terra-cotta shield at the top of the building's front. The fire station was added to the National Register of Historic Places in November 1993. Mission/Spanish and Colonial Revival architectural styles combine to create an intriguing structure at *230 West Yellowstone,* which housed the Casper Auto Company from 1918 until 1970. A red-tiled roof cornice and white terra-cotta detailing lend the building a look of classic distinction. It claimed a spot on the National Register in February 1994. While still in the downtown area, also have a look at the statue, *Prometheus,* who stole fire from Mount Olympus and gave it to man. It's located in front of the Natrona County Library, 307 East Second Street.

Two blocks away, at 400 East Collins Drive, is the intriguing *Nicolaysen Art Museum and Discovery Center.* The structure containing the museum and center is the beautifully refurbished Old Casper Lumber Company building. "The Nic" is a great place to browse, view special exhibits, or purchase unique art items by regional artists. It celebrates art with invitational shows and other special events, while offering kids of all ages hands-on creative experiences with a variety of activities in the Discovery Center. The art museum is open from 10:00 A.M. to 5:00 P.M., Tuesday through Saturday, and noon to 4:00 P.M. on Sunday. Admission is $2.00 for adults and $1.00 for children (on Thursday admittance is free). For information on the exhibit schedules, call 235–5247.

For a somewhat funkier experience, stop in at *Dr. Spokes Cyclery & Bicycles & Pedal Car Museum,* 240 South Center Street. The unusual museum is open in the summer from 9:00 A.M. to 8:00 P.M. on weekdays, on Saturday from 9:00 A.M. to 5:00 P.M., and on Sunday from noon to 4:00 P.M. For information call 265–7740.

At the Natrona County Airport, you'll find the *Casper Centennial Mural.* In this 9½-by-28½-foot oil painting, artist Richard Jacobi has incorporated a variety of images from Casper's colorful past. In all the mural includes twenty-eight different scenes and is one of the largest paintings in the country done on a single piece of canvas.

Two side trips out of Casper are recommended. First, take Highway 220 southwest of town about 10 miles to the *Goose Egg Inn.* In-the-know locals regularly travel here for the fine steaks and other specialties served. Appropriately the address is 10580 Goose Egg Road. For hours and reservations call 473–8838.

Central Wyoming Trivia

Bill, Wyoming, north of Douglas on State Highway 59, was named for the four men sharing the first name of Bill, whose homesteads cornered at the location.

The surrounding area brims with history. Spreading out along the North Platte River, the renowned Goose Egg Ranch served as a setting for Owen Wister's *The Virginian.* It was founded by the Searight Brothers of Texas, and subsequently it was owned by generations of Governor Carey's family. Later it was renamed the CY Ranch. A portion of the ranch land was platted as part of Casper, and the original 1877 ranch house was torn down in the early 1950s.

From the Goose Egg Ranch make tracks for *Independence Rock,* located 42 miles southwest of Casper on State Highway 220. This, probably the best known of all of the Oregon Trail landmarks —and also the most poignant—is also known as the "Register of the Desert." The 190-foot-high outcropping contains an estimated fifty thousand names inscribed by wagon train emigrants. It earned the name Independence Rock when explorer William Sublette celebrated the Fourth of July at the rock in 1830. He wrote:

> Most of our company visited the summit of Independence Rock, which was reached with much difficulty but without accident. We found the rock literally covered with the names of emigrants. Some of these names were written with chalk, some were cut with a cold chisel, whilst ohters [sic] were written with tar.

Near Independence Rock, Ella Watson, also known as Cattle Kate, scored another first for Wyoming women, earning the dubious distinction of becoming the first woman hanged in Wyoming. Ella and bar owner Jim Averill pursued the annoying hobby of stamping their brand on other people's cattle, until they were finally strung up by their neighbors for doing so.

The second excursion from Casper before continuing westward involves following I–25 north 21 miles, then State Highway 259 north for 4½ miles. On the right-hand (east) side of the road, you will see the remnants of the landmark whose name is associated with one of the biggest political scandals to come out of Washington.

Teapot Rock is clearly visible from the dirt turnout (don't look for a teapot anymore—two tornadoes in the 1920s destroyed the handle and spout). Teapot Rock is located on private property, so please don't trespass for a better look.

The Teapot Dome scandal erupted when President Harding's Secretary of the Interior, Albert Fall, leased the Teapot Dome oil fields to the Mammoth Oil Company, owned by Harry F. Sinclair, without first going through the proper bidding process. Wyoming's Sen. John Kendrick called for a complete investigation in 1922, and, after a six-year investigation, Fall was convicted of accepting a $100,000 bribe. He spent a year in federal prison.

Continuing on you'll pass the famous Salt Creek Oilfields, one of Wyoming's largest and still pumping. Then you'll arrive at Midwest, population 495. Proceed to the Town Hall, 531 Peake Street, and inquire about the **Midwest Museum.** If the museum's not open, they'll give you the key and ask you to lock up when you're finished. It's a delightful and informative little museum that presents the history of the town, nearby ghost towns, and the Salt Creek Oilfields. You'll learn, for instance, that the first claim was issued in 1883, oil was first discovered in 1889, and the first oil well was drilled in 1908 at a depth of 1,050 feet. The area's population peaked at around 9,500 in 1929, when the company-owned hotel was capable of feeding 1,200 people per hour. To contact the Midwest Town Hall, open 10:00 A.M. to 4:00 P.M. weekdays, call 437–6513.

Another excursion out of Casper you might want to consider is one organized and led by the *Historic Trails Expeditions.* A number of outings are available, via horseback, Conestoga wagon, and river raft. The tours range from several hours to several days in duration, and food and sleeping equipment are provided. For expedition information and reservations, call 266–4868.

About 42 miles west of Casper on Highway 20/26, pull over to gaze out across *Hell's Half Acre,* a starkly beautiful stretch of badlands that

Little Wonder He Became a Legend

*B*y the time he reached his twenty-first birthday, years before beginning his celebrated Wild West Show, William F. Cody had done things that most men, even of his day, dare only dream about. Born near LeClaire in Scott County, Iowa, on February 26, 1846, young Cody moved to the Salt Creek Valley of Kansas with his family. At age eleven he began working as an ox-team driver. In 1859, when he was thirteen, Cody went west to Pikes Peak, Colorado, joining hundreds of older men in the search for gold. Then, in 1860 he became one of the youngest of the Pony Express riders, serving a stint during which he earned quite a reputation, exhausting twenty horses as he accomplished a stretch of 322 miles in twenty-one hours and forty minutes.

At fifteen years of age, still employed by Russell, Majors, and Waddell (proprietors of the short-lived Pony Express) as an assistant wagonmaster, Cody drove a bull train to the Wyoming Territory. After arriving at Fort Laramie, he briefly joined a group of trappers working in the Chugwater River country. During the Civil War he served the Union as a scout in Missouri and along the Santa Fe Trail. Then, in March 1866 Cody married Louisa Federici and tried his hand at domestic living, as together the couple managed the Golden Rule Boarding House in Salt Creek Valley.

In 1867, the year Cody turned twenty-one, he was hired by the Goddard brothers to kill buffalo to provide meat for workers on the Kansas Pacific Railroad. During one eight-month period, he reportedly killed 4,280 of the easy-to-shoot beasts, and acquired the nickname "Buffalo Bill" after winning a bison-killing contest with another Bill—Bill Comstock.

provide the raw materials for some unusual Wyoming landscape photos. Indians once drove herds of buffalo off the cliffs to their deaths here, and Captain Bonneville's exploratory expedition stopped by in 1833. Today there's a Hell's Half Acre restaurant/store, where you can stock up on Hell's Half Acre postcards.

Fremont County

If you're running short of funds and would like to try some prospecting, consider making a trip to the Lost Cabin area near Lysite. Turn north at the metropolis of Moneta, population 10, onto Highway 176, the Lysite-Moneta Road. The pavement ends about 8 miles later at Lysite, where you might want to swing into the country store for a

Miles and Miles of Wyoming

I, along with several companions, once accomplished a feat few others can claim: We walked a beeline nearly 200 miles long through the heart of Wyoming.

We'd been dispatched to look for evidence of prehistoric Indian camps along the route of a proposed natural-gas pipeline. From south-southeast to north-northwest we walked, beginning south of Sinclair and winding up near Lost Cabin. We were compelled to walk right up, down, over, or through whatever we came to. That included historic Whiskey Gap, where a Maj. Farrell once ordered a contraband barrel of whiskey smashed near the spring where his troops were camped. As the booze poured into the spring and over the ground, soldiers scurried up with cups to save what they could; some lay on the ground and stuck their faces right into the eighty-proof stream. One soldier claimed it was the best spring water he'd ever tasted, and Farrell recorded in his journal that it

was fortunate the Indians did not attack that night.

As for our small army, each night we would meet up with the Jeep that carried our mobile camp. At one point, at a crossing of Sage Hen Creek, the Jeep got stuck. Because I was training for marathons at the time, I was elected by the others to trot westward over ridges and through valleys and come-what-may to seek help at a nearby uranium mine we knew to be somewhere in the vicinity.

Along this 200-mile swath of remarkably wild country, we also saw prong-horns and coyotes, rattlesnakes and raptors; a couple of our party members even hooked into some monster trout at the point where we forded the Sweetwater River.

Though it might be hard to come up with an excuse to do something like this, I highly recommend it. It's a trip that not only will take you off the beaten path, but way off any kind of paths at all.

snack and to inquire about road conditions before continuing on to Lost Cabin, located 3 miles northeast.

As the story goes, a band of prospectors extracted thousands of dollars worth of gold from a rich lode in the vicinity before Indians attacked and killed all but one or two of the miners, who escaped to the nearest town. Despite repeated attempts after that, the Lost Cabin Mine was never rediscovered. The site of present Lost Cabin is home to *The Big Tipi,* as Native Americans called the mansion built in 1900 by Wyoming sheep magnate John B. Odie. Odie outfitted the mansion with elaborately carved fireplace mantles, lavish chandeliers, costly Oriental rugs, and intricate and colorful panels of stained glass. The mansion also incorporates an unusual octagonal tower. Outside Odie constructed a greenhouse, dance hall, and aviary to house his collection of exotic birds. The mansion is located on private property, but you can't miss seeing it from the road.

Returning to Moneta, take Garden City Road 459 for 21 miles south, then BLM Road 2107 east to *Castle Gardens,* one of Wyoming's finest collections of ancient rock carvings. (It's suggested that you inquire at Moneta about road conditions before attempting this journey.) Perhaps the best-known petroglyph is one no longer residing there: the Great Turtle petroglyph, which disappeared from Castle Gardens one day only to mysteriously pop up years later at the Wyoming State Museum. It's still periodically displayed at the museum in Cheyenne. Another mystery surrounding the Great Turtle is, why would a water-loving snapping turtle from the Mississippi or Missouri River country appear in a petroglyph in arid Wyoming?

After hours of exploring the dry wide-open and then driving the 21 miles from Moneta to Shoshoni (population 497), you'll no doubt be ready for a burger and shake at the *Yellowstone Drug Store,* 127 Main Street. Over an average summer, the Yellowstone churns some thirty-five thousand rich malts and milk shakes for travelers. Head south one block from the drugstore and take a right before the railroad tracks to see a jail that's over a century old. Imagine what it must have been like to spend hot summer or frigid winter nights behind those bars, especially considering all the hell-raising that must've been going on: Hard as it is to imagine, during Shoshoni's boom years the town supported nearly two dozen saloons, along with two banks, two mercantile establishments, and several livery and feed stables.

Boysen State Park stretches from the outskirts of Shoshoni into the Wind River Canyon, a singularly spectacular drive that is described

Petroglyphs, Castle Gardens

earlier in the book (see Thermopolis). The first white men in the area were those with the 1825 Ashley Fur Party. The original dam was built in 1908 by Asmus Boysen, for whom the reservoir and park are named. The Chicago, Burlington and Qunicy Railroad laid tracks through the Wind River Canyon in 1911 and ended up suing Boysen after the tracks were flooded due to the waters impounded by the dam. The railroad won the suit and had Boysen's dam dynamited. The present dam was constructed in 1951, and the state park was designated in 1956. You'll find plenty of day-use and overnight facilities on the 76 miles of often wind-blown shoreline. For information call 876–2796.

Twenty-two miles southwest of Shoshoni on Highway 26/789 is Riverton, home to the mid-October *Cowboy Poets Roundup,* featuring the region's top rhymin' wranglers. The event happens at Central Wyoming College. For ticket information call the Riverton Chamber of Commerce at (800) 325–2732.

Hudson, population 392, located 14 miles southwest of Riverton, holds a pair of surprises: two of the most celebrated restaurants in Wyoming. *Svilar's Bar & Dining Room* (332–4516), at 173 South Main Street, specializes in melt-in-your-mouth steaks. Across the way, at 132 South Main Street, is *Club El Toro* (332–4627), also featuring fine beef cuts. Prices at both establishments are moderate, and the pair of eateries have an interesting understanding: Svilar's is closed the second and fourth Monday of the month, while Club El Toro closes on the first and third Monday. (Guess you'd better call ahead if the month you visit happens to include a fifth Monday.) Svilar's is also closed on Sunday.

The Fremont County Pioneer Museum, 630 Lincoln Street in Lander, exhibits its eclectic collection of pioneer items both inside and out. You'll see a 1929 Model A, a wooden coal wagon, an antique printing press, a re-created general store, and a pioneer parlor and kitchen. The log cabin accessed by way of the museum's side door served as the original museum, built in 1935. The museum is open 9:00 A.M. to 5:00 P.M., Monday through Friday, year-round. For information call 332–4137.

Motor or walk along Lander's Main Street between Sixth and Seventh Streets to have a look at the enormous stack of antlers marking the Fort Augur Trading Post. For a snack try *The Magpie,* 159 North Second Street, where you can sip or slurp coffee or tea and enjoy delicious scones and muffins. Note the building's tall false front. The Magpie is open Monday through Saturday from 6:30 A.M. to 7:00 P.M. in the summer, and from 7:00 A.M. to 6:00 P.M. in the winter. Call 332–5565.

For great barbecued steak and ribs, pull up to the *The Ranch,* 148 Main Street. Recent renovations have transformed a dilapidated old building into a stunning setting in which to dine. During the renovations several unexpected treasures were uncovered, in the form of gorgeous leaded stained-glass windows and a well-preserved embossed tin ceiling that was buried under decades' worth of remodeling. For information call 332–7641.

Across the street near the Popo Agie (*po PO zhuh*) River stands a Lander landmark, the 1888 mill built by Eugene Amoretti and used to grind wheat and supply electricity for the town. It's been in continual use as a flour and feed mill since its construction.

Not surprisingly, considering the grand mountains backing the town, a number of outfitters operate out of the Lander area. *Allen's Diamond Four Ranch,* a licensed professional outfitter since 1973, offers guided horseback tours by the hour or day and pack trips exploring the Popo Agie Wilderness of the Wind River Range. Pack trips last from four days to two weeks. For information call 332–2995.

Lander Llama Company provides a full line of outfitting services and pack trips, employing these ungainly but sure-footed beasts to do the hard work. For information (including details on the company's rentable bunkhouse) and reservations, call 332–5624 or (800) 582–5262.

Lander is also home to the headquarters of the *National Outdoor Leadership School* (NOLS), the foremost school of its kind in the country. NOLS, which was started by legendary mountaineer Paul Petzoldt, offers adventure-travel and

Central Wyoming Trivia

Fifteen species of bats reside in Wyoming: the California, Small-footed, Yuma, Little Brown, Long-legged, Fringed, Keen's, and Long-eared Myotis ("myotis" are the mouse-eared bats); the Silver-haired, Big Brown, Red, Hoary, Spotted, Townsend's Big-eared, and Pallid Bats. Also, the Brazilian Free-tailed Bat has been spotted rarely, and only in extreme southeast Wyoming.

leadership-training trips in the nearby Wind Rivers, as well as far-off Baja California, Alaska, Africa, and elsewhere. For a catalog detailing the school's offerings, drop by the old Noble Hotel in downtown Lander.

Just outside of Lander, at 2343 Baldwin Creek Road, enjoy the best in Western hospitality at the *Piece of Cake Bed & Breakfast.* Nestled

South Pass City

The first white men to cross the Continental Divide at South Pass were the fur traders known as the Astorians, in 1812. The pass was "discovered" again in 1824 by fur trapper Henry Ashley; however, Lt. John Charles Fremont is credited with widely publicizing the South Pass route after his expedition crossed through it in 1842. During the next two and a half decades, more than 350,000 Oregon-Mormon Trail emigrants traveled up the gentle slopes as they headed west to surmount the Continental Divide. South Pass, at a relatively low and accessible elevation of 7,805 feet, was key to making it feasible for the wagon trails even to pass through the Rocky Mountain region.

Thousands of gold-hungry California-bound prospectors passed through in the late 1840s and 1850s. Had they known what lay hidden in the ground of the surrounding area—gold, that is—they may have found little reason to push on to California.

The first version of South Pass City was an 1850s stage stop and telegraph station, where the Oregon Trail made its final crossing of the Sweetwater River. South Pass City at its present site was built in 1867 after the discovery of gold brought a flood of prospectors to the Sweetwater Mining District. The mining town soon flourished, becom-

ing the site of some three hundred buildings. The Carissa Mine began producing gold in 1867; it was last worked in the 1950s.

This once-thriving, rough-and-tumble gold camp gave birth to a women's suffrage bill, introduced to the first Territorial Legislature Assembly in November 1869 by South Pass City representative William Bright. The suffrage bill passed both the council and the house on December 10, 1869, and the governor of Wyoming signed it into law. The territorial legislature voted to repeal the suffrage bill in 1871, but Governor Campbell vetoed the action. Soon after, on February 14, 1870, Esther Hobart Morris became the first woman in the United States to hold political office when she was sworn in as justice of the peace at South Pass City.

The entire town almost pulled up stakes and moved to California in the mid-1960s. Thankfully a group of concerned Cowboy Staters outbid Knott's Berry Farm, which was trying to buy the town, so South Pass City remains where it grew up a century earlier—in the barren high country at the tail end of the Wind River Range—rather than in the coastal lowlands of California. The state of Wyoming subsequently purchased the settlement from its saviors, and later designated it the South Pass State Historic Site.

against a protective bluff, the views from the Piece of Cake main house and bunkhouse cabins are outstanding. Each room is furnished in western decor, and the main house features guest quarters and a kitchen complete with plenty of snacks. The food served for breakfast is tasty and plentiful. Overnight rates are in the $80–$90 range. To inquire about weekly rates or to make reservations, call 332–7608.

See the scenes behind the creation of bronze carvings and foundry work at *Eagle Bronze, Inc., Foundry & Gallery,* located at 130 Poppy Street on the south edge of town (in the industrial park off U.S. Highway 287). Eagle Bronze performs casting work for many of the West's top artists, and several of the foundry's creations are featured in the on-site gallery and in other places throughout Lander. Eagle Bronze offers foundry tours ($2.00 per person) May through August, 9:30 A.M. and 12:30 P.M., Monday through Friday; and September through April at 10:00 A.M. on Tuesday and Thursday. Call 332–5436 for further details.

Sinks Canyon State Park features a magic act performed by the Popo Agie River: It crashes and disappears into a large cavern, known as the Sinks, in the side of a mountain . . . only to reappear ½ mile down canyon in a trout-filled pool called the Rise. A couple of interesting facts about Sinks Canyon: First, more water comes out at the Rise than flows into the Sinks; second, the water flowing out at the Rise is a few degrees warmer than water entering the Sinks. A visitor center near the Sinks presents information on this unusual rock-and-water phenomenon and on area wildlife. The park includes self-guided nature trails, picnic grounds, and camp-sites. All visitors should walk across the swinging bridge spanning the Popo Agie, and the more ambitious will want to hike the Popo Agie Falls Trail for 1½ miles to a spectacular vista point. The visitor center is open Memorial Day through Labor Day from 9:00 A.M. to 7:00 P.M. To reach Sinks Canyon State Park, take State Highway 131 southeast out of Lander for 6 miles. For information call 332–6333.

Central Wyoming Trivia

The first commercial ferry operation in the Rocky Mountain West was established in 1847 on the North Platte River near the future site of Casper by Mormon leader Brigham Young.

Time of year and road conditions permitting, continue south from the Sinks on Highway 131 to the historic mining areas of Atlantic City and South Pass City. Alternatively you can return to Lander and travel to the area entirely on paved roads. It's approximately 25 miles from Lander via U.S. Highway 287 and State Highway 28, and the roads are well signed. Be sure to stop at the marked viewpoint to look down on stunning Red Canyon as you climb above Lander's valley setting.

Today **South Pass City State Historic Site** is one of Wyoming's largest and best restored historic sites, with more than thirty structures distributed over thirty-nine acres. Yet South Pass City, where the past is palpable, remains relatively little-visited. Boardwalks and dirt streets lead you to buildings such as the 1890 schoolhouse, the South Pass Hotel (opened as the Idaho House in 1868), the 1890s Carissa Saloon, the Riniker Cabin, and the 1870 Sweetwater County Jail. As you wander in and around the buildings, you'll earn a real sense of what life in an 1890s gold-mining town was all about. For a truly grand old time, come for the South Pass City Fourth of July Celebration. South Pass City State Historic Site is open May 15 through September 30 from 9:00 A.M. to 6:00 P.M. The entrance fee is $1.00 for those 18 and older. For further information call 332–3684.

For a good view of the Oregon Trail as it approached South Pass, drive to the Oregon Trail–Lander Cutoff–South Pass Area interpretive sign located on the south side of Highway 28, approximately 39 miles from Lander. Here you can still see the wagon ruts crossing the desert.

Two-Wheeled Solitude

*T*he Great Divide Mountain Bike Route is a 2,465-mile off-pavement bicycle touring route stretching along the Continental Divide from Canada to Mexico. As the route's primary architect, I was extremely concerned about what I would and would not find between South Pass City and Rawlins, where the route would necessarily encounter miles of high, dry desert and a corner of the vast Great Divide Basin. Would there be water? Would people end up hating this stretch of the route? Or, like some emigrants traveling through here, perishing? I certainly hoped not.

However, with the invaluable assistance of Bureau of Land Management recreation planner Ray Hanson, an outstanding route (with at least a little water) using existing dirt roads was linked together. Here the Great Divide Route occasionally coincides with more famous, and far older, trails: the Oregon-Mormon, the California, and the Pony Express trails. For 135 miles self-supported cyclists riding through the area see no trees, but they do encounter wild horses, pronghorns, and a historically vital slice of American backcountry visited by very few folks. Some who have ridden the entire route from Canada to Mexico, in fact, swear that this empty stretch of Wyoming was their very favorite part of the entire Great Divide.

For information on mountain biking in the Great Divide Basin and along other parts of the Great Divide Route, you can contact the Montana-based Adventure Cycling Association at (406) 721-1776.

Atlantic City Mercantile

On the way back to Lander, stop at the *Atlantic City Mercantile*, located at 100 East Main Street in the semighost town of Atlantic City. The town is reached by driving a few miles northeast on dirt from South Pass City. You'll see the remains of the Duncan Gold Mine along the way. Atlantic City is a delightful place to grab a bite or spend a night. The 103-year-old false-fronted Merc includes a saloon and steak house, with all sorts of historic paraphernalia and photographs hanging from or nailed to the walls. Browse through the small museum and check out the ornate antique, still in-use, stove in the saloon, and the set of swinging doors attached to the wall of the backroom.

The Merc serves up barbecue on Sunday between noon and 2:00 P.M. from May 1 through November 1. There's also a Wednesday-night, seven-course Basque dinner served family style (reservations only) and, on most days, steaks prepared on an inside open-pit fire stoked with aspen logs. During the summer you can tap your toe to lively music on Friday and Saturday nights. In the winter make the Merc your après-outdoors stop after cross-country skiing in the Winds or snowmobiling on the Continental Divide Trail. For information call 332–5143.

For bunking down in historic surroundings, you can't do better than the *Miner's Delight B&B.* The old hotel lets five rooms, some with private and some with shared bath, and serves a full breakfast. Reservations are required; call proprietors Donna and Lester Ballard at 332–0348 or (888) 292–0248 to secure one.

A United States Steel taconite strip mine (taconite is a low-grade iron ore) rejuvenated the area's economy from 1962 to 1983, but the mined-out hills are all that remain of that boom. Times are quiet for now . . . just awaiting the next boom.

An 8-mile side trip south on gravel roads from Atlantic City leads to a haunting piece of evidence of why the Oregon-Mormon Trails have been called "the longest graveyard in America." That evidence is the site of the ***Willie Handcart Company tragedy,*** where in the mid-1850s an estimated sixty-seven Mormon pioneers died—having never laid eyes their promised land in Utah—after being trapped by an unusually fierce October snowstorm. To find the unsettling spot, turn south at the Miner's Delight Inn and climb the big hill out of town; after 4 miles make a left and proceed another 4 miles.

From South Pass City-Atlantic City, return to Lander. The area provides countless outdoor recreation opportunities. In addition to the pack trips already mentioned, there's rock climbing in the Wild Iris Canyon, with routes ranging from 5.7 to 5.14 in difficulty. In winter there are thousands of snow-covered acres of cross-country skiing terrain, and the Continental Divide Snowmobile Trail runs from near Lander all the way to Yellowstone, with hundreds of miles of groomed trails traversing some of the most spectacular country in the world. For information on the trail, call the Bureau of Land Management at 775–6256.

Moving northwest from Lander on U.S. Highway 287, you'll drive through lands of the Wind River Indian Reservation, home to the Eastern Shoshone and the Northern Arapahoe tribes. The reservation encompasses some two million acres. On the reservation are the graves of three great Native American leaders: Shoshone chief Washakie, Arapahoe chief Black Coal, and Sacajawea, the Shoshone woman who traveled with the Lewis and Clark Expedition.

As a child, Sacajawea was captured by a Minataree Indians and sold to French fur trader Toussaint Charbonneau, who fathered their son, Baptiste. Sacajawea's ability to speak and understand both the English and Shoshone languages proved invaluable to the expedition's leaders, particularly when it came to horse trading with the Shoshone in the Continental Divide country of Montana and Idaho. Sacajawea returned to the Shoshone people late in her life and died in 1884. ***Sacajawea's Grave*** is located in the southwest corner of the Shoshone Cemetery at Fort Washakie, approximately ½ mile north of the Shoshone-Episcopal Mission sign. (It should be mentioned that some accounts argue that Sacajawea died and was buried at Fort Manuel in South Dakota.)

Chief Washakie allied himself with the white people's government as an intermediary for the Shoshone people, in a successful attempt at peaceful coexistence. Washakie was widely recognized as an sage leader, and his strategy of joining the government's forces in battles against other tribes was eventually rewarded with the presentation of large tracts of land in Colorado, Idaho, Utah, and Wyoming. In the end, however, the original reservation lands assigned under the Fort Bridger Treaty of 1863 were whittled down and negotiated away from the Native Americans, until all that remained were the lands of the present Wind River Reservation.

Chief Washakie died in 1900 on the Wind River Reservation at around the age of 100. Mount Washakie and the Washakie Wilderness were named after the great Shoshone chief, as were Fort Washakie, which was renamed from Fort Brown in

1878, and Washakie Center at the University of Wyoming in Laramie. The post at Fort Washakie was abandoned in 1909, but the town bearing the chief's name remains. His grave is found in the old fort cemetery: Take South Fork Road west until you come to the *Chief Washakie Gravesite.*

The Arapahoes, historic enemies of the Shoshone, were admitted onto the Shoshone reservation in 1878, supposedly on a temporary basis. Today, however, Arapahoes living on the Wind River Reservation outnumber the Shoshone approximately 3,500 to 2,500. During summer months residents of the reservation display their rich and colorful traditions in a variety of ways. Powwows, sun dances, horseback relay races, and rodeos all are open to the public, as are Shoshone and Arapahoe cultural centers and certain historic sites. To fish on tribal land, you must first buy a recreation stamp issued by the Shoshone and Arapahoe Tribal Fish and Game Department at Fort Washakie. For information call the Lander Chamber of Commerce at 332–3892 or (800) 433–0662.

Eleven miles before arriving in Dubois, turn right (north) onto the gravel East Fork Road (Road 277) for a scenic, 11-mile trip to the *Lazy L & B Ranch.* A wonderful family vacation can be enjoyed at this hundred-year-old cattle and guest ranch now owned by Lee and Bob Naylon. The ranch abuts

Crowheart Butte

After traveling north from Fort Washakie 16 miles on U.S. Highway 287, then northwesterly on U.S. Highway 26/287 for another 10 miles, you'll spot a large butte to the northeast. Legend explains that the name, **Crowheart Butte,** *derives from an 1866 struggle to the death between Crow and Shoshone chiefs. Victorious, the Shoshone chief celebrated by eating the heart of his vanquished rival (or, say some accounts, by simply displaying the heart on his lance). The Shoshone chief in question was Washakie. Queried years later about the accuracy of the story, he had only this to say, "One cannot always remember what he did when he was young and in the heat of battle."*

both the Wind River Reservation and a large elk refuge. You can bed down in log cabins surrounding a central yard or nestled alongside a singing stream. Down-home cooking begins with a breakfast served buffet style and continues with lunch served by the pool or on the trail. Then there's dinner, a real treat after a day filled with hiking, horseback riding, and fly-fishing. The kids eat with the wranglers, while the older folks enjoy quiet dinners and evening entertainment back at the ranch. To close the day you can soak your weary bones in the outdoor heated pool and watch as the setting sun turns the surrounding slopes of the Absaroka Range a brilliant crimson red.

The Lazy L & B Ranch, homesteaded in the 1890s by Scottish emigrants, sits at an elevation of 7,200 feet. Anglers can fish in stocked ponds or try their luck in the East Fork of the Wind River. Entertainment options include the ranch's own cowboy poet or driving to Dubois for dancing at the Rustic Pine Tavern. For the kids there's a petting zoo with goats, chickens, rabbits, sheep, ducks, geese, and other animals. The corrals are filled with horses and donkeys, with one to match the skill of any rider. The main lodge has two cozy fireplaces, a library, and game tables. All-log guest cabins have private baths or showers, electric heat, and sittin' porches. The season runs from the end of May through mid-September. (September is reserved for adults only.) Weekly rates are about $875 per adult and $775 per child under age twelve. Discount rates are available for early- and late-season arrivals. For information or reservations call 455–2839 or (800) 453–9488.

Jakey's Fork Homestead, 4 miles east of Dubois off Forest Service Road 411 south of Highway 26/287, offers another unique overnight option. You can sleep in an original homestead, with the cold water of Jakey's Fork flowing just outside your bedroom window, or in the two-room suite of the main house. In the morning you are welcome to explore the homestead, with its sod-roofed buildings, and the surrounding mountains and redrock badlands. Sourdough flapjacks and elk sausage, along with plenty of fruit and biscuits or Scottish oat scones, highlight the breakfast menu. The century-old barn at the homestead houses owner Justin Bridges's knife workshop. A founding member of the Professional Knife Makers Association, Justin handcrafts high-end sporting knives and kitchen cutlery under his Wind River Knives label.

The surrounding area offers plenty of diversions, from white-water rafting on the Wind River to scenic drives through the badlands. Nearby Trail Road (Road 257) offers views of bighorn sheep, osprey, waterfalls, and petroglyphs. Rates at Jakey's Fork Homestead are $75 to $90 per couple for one-night stays ($65 to $80 for minimum three-night stays). For information and reservations, which are required (no drop-ins, please), call 455-2769.

Within walking distance of the bed and breakfast is the **Dubois Fish Hatchery,** which has been in operation since 1930. The Lake of the Woods brood stock, obtained about 30 miles southwest of Dubois, furnishes a major portion of the cutthroat eggs for the entire state. The hatchery also raises graylings and golden, brook, rainbow, and brown trout. Rainbow trout make up approximately 60 percent of the hatchery's annual production. The hatchery's three incubators are capable of handling up to six million eggs at one time. The informative hatchery tour takes you through the entire process, from egg fertilization through fish planting. The fish hatchery is located at Five Fish Hatchery Court. For information call 455-2431.

Dubois, population 895, has kept its Old West ambience well intact. Boardwalks and false-front stores abound. You'll also notice immediately that wild animals are highly regarded by the townspeople: Oversize likenesses of bears, elk, moose, rainbow trout, and other critters embellish store fronts and parking lots. Dubois grew up around a post office established on Horse Creek more than a century ago.

A much newer addition to the town is the **National Bighorn Sheep Interpretive Center,** completed in 1993. It contains fascinating exhibits on bighorn sheep biology, habitat protection, and herd management techniques employed at the Whiskey Mountain Wildlife Habitat Management Area (located several miles east of town). Dubois is a natural location for the interpretive center because the area is home to North America's largest population of Rocky Mountain bighorn sheep. The center came about through the cooperative efforts of the USDA Forest Service, Bureau of Land Management, Wyoming Game and Fish Department, Town of Dubois, and private individuals and nonprofit organizations.

The central exhibit, a 16-foot-tall "sheep mountain," displays full-size bighorns in a simulation of their natural environment. Interpretive scenes ringing the slopes of the mountain depict predator-prey relationships, lambing areas, and dominance battles. Children young and old will be fascinated by the center's great hands-on displays. A gift shop offers nature books, posters and cards, wildlife-theme clothing, prints, sculptures, and antler art crafted by local artisans. For fall and winter travelers, a special treat awaits: You can drive your own four-wheel-drive vehicle or sign up for a guided drive to view wildlife in the Whiskey Mountain area. November is the prime bighorn rutting month. The tour starts at 9:00 A.M. and lasts approximately five hours. Binoculars and sporting scopes are provided, but participants are responsible for bringing their own lunches. Dress warmly! The tours begin in mid-November and continue through March.

The National Bighorn Sheep Interpretive Center is located at 907 West Ramshorn, off Highway 26/287. Hours from Memorial Day weekend to Labor Day weekend are 9:00 A.M. to 8:00 P.M. daily, and during the winter on Thursday through Monday from 9:00 A.M. to 5:00 P.M. Entrance fees are $2.00 per adult, 75 cents per child age twelve and under, or $5.00 per family. For information on the center or the winter wildlife tours, call 455–3429.

Immediately next door, at 909 West Ramshorn, is the *Dubois Museum,* with exhibits focusing on the Sheepeater Indians, the area's ranch and frontier life, and the timber industry's historical importance to Dubois. (The town's sawmill shut down in 1987, after which community leaders began putting a greater emphasis on tourism—spawning, among other things, the fine bighorn sheep museum described earlier.) The museum is open daily from Memorial Day to Labor Day, 9:00 A.M. to 5:00 P.M. Admission is $1.00 for adults and $.50 for children twelve and under. For information call 455–2284.

For a gourmet tune-up, pull into the *Old Yellowstone Garage,* an excellent western/Italian ristorante located on the main drag. The owners came to Dubois from northern Italy. The restaurant's menu changes daily; some of the more common offerings include a grilled endive and eggplant appetizer, homemade pasta, grilled boneless trout, grilled double-cut pork chops, and charred stuffed chicken. Don't miss this place: It's one of the state's true epicurial gems. For information call 455–3666.

Not far away, at 120 East Ramshorn, *Stewart's Trapline Gallery and Indian Trading Post* stocks a fine collection of original paintings and bronze sculptures by coowner Mark R. Stewart. Kit and Mark Stewart also display an extensive collection of traditional Native American art, representing more than two dozen tribes. Choose a treasure for your home from a variety of art forms, including beadwork, pottery and basketry, sand paintings, Navajo rugs, kachina dolls, Zuni fetishes, and contemporary Native American silver jewelry. For information call 455–2800.

A number of self-guided driving tours out of Dubois are worth considering. You have your choice of investigating badlands or motoring past a series of three glacial lakes for great fishing, wildlife viewing, and wildflower sniffing. Native American petroglyphs are also easily accessible for photographing. Pick up the map pamphlet describing "Six Loop Tour Options" in the Wind River Country at the Dubois Chamber of Commerce office, located at 616 West Ramshorn, or call them at 455–2556.

Driving northwest from Dubois on U.S. Highway 26/287, you'll come upon the *Union Pass Monument* about 8 miles out. The monument marks the first road across the Absaroka/Wind River ranges. The 9,210-foot Union Pass is a geographic oddity in that rivers flow in three different directions from there. Union Pass also is considered the point where a trio of mountain ranges converge:

> **Central Wyoming Trivia**
>
> *The Wyoming State Flag, adopted by the fourteenth legislature in 1917, was designed by Mrs. A.C. Keyes of Casper.*

the Absarokas (heading into Montana), the Gros Ventres (trending southwesterly), and the Wind Rivers (taking aim at the southeast). You can follow the Union Pass Road for a incredible trip, earning long-range views of the Tetons and close-ups of the Wind Rivers. The road eventually drops out above Pinedale in the Green River drainage. Parts of the route are very rough and poorly signed, so obtain supplies and a good map before striking out on the adventure.

Back along the main highway, drive another 9 miles and you'll reach the impressive carved *Tie Hack Monument.* Near the site of the first tie camp on the Wind River, the monument commemorates the tie hackers who cut some 400,000 railroad ties annually between 1914 and 1946. The ties were transported downstream on the Wind River during the spring runoff. The lumberjacks precariously went along for the ride, too, during an annual operation that lasted several wet weeks. Many of the men suffered from an ailment called "squeak heel," caused by having continuously wet feet. Eventually their Achilles tendons would dry out and actually make a squeaking noise when they walked.

Tie hackers had to cut a tie to a precise 7 inches per side to pass close inspection. For this they earned 10 cents per tie, or up to $3.00 a day, at a time when their room and board cost $1.50 per day. Each tie hacker cared for his own equipment, which would cost him roughly ten days pay to acquire. It was said that the Scandinavian tie hackers could plane logs so smooth with their axes that you could run your hand over them and pick up nary a splinter.

Ahead of you lies the beginning of the Wyoming Centennial Scenic Byway, leading to Togwotee (*TOE guh tee*) Pass, elevation 9,658 feet, and the Bridger-Teton National Forest. The route provides yet another way to descend into the incomparable beauty of Jackson Hole. (That area is covered in "Western Wyoming.") The drive up Togwotee Pass alternates between mountain meadows, lodgepole forests, and jagged cliffs. Not long before reaching Togwotee Pass, a right-hand turn will lead roughly 5 miles to the **Brooks Lake Lodge** (455–2121), a traditional western lodge-with-cabins enterprise that has been accommodating Yellowstone-bound travelers since the early 1920s. A fitting and proper place, indeed, to wind up a tour of the great state of Wyoming.

PLACES TO STAY IN
OREGON TRAIL–
RENDEZVOUS COUNTRY

ATLANTIC CITY
Miner's Delight
Bed & Breakfast,
290 Atlantic Road;
(307) 332–0248 or
(888) 292–0248

CASPER
Best Western Casper,
2325 East Yellowstone
Highway;
(307) 234–3541 or
(800) 675–4242

Days Inn,
301 East E Street;
(307) 234–1159

The Royal Inn,
440 East A Street;
(307) 234–3501 or
(800) 96–ROYAL

Super 8 Lodge,
3838 CY Avenue;
(307) 266–3480 or
(800) 800–8000

DOUGLAS
Alpine Inn,
2310 East Richards;
(307) 358–4780

Best Western Douglas Inn,
1450 Riverbend Drive;
(307) 358–9790 or
(800) 528–1234

Super 8,
314 Russell Avenue;
(307) 358–6800 or
(800) 800–8000

DUBOIS
Bald Mountain Inn,
1349 West Ramshorn;
(307) 455–2844 or
(800) 682–9323

Branding Iron Inn,
401 West Ramshorn;
(307) 455–2893 or
(888) 651–9378

Lakes' Lodge, Inc.,
1 Fir Road;
(307) 455–2171 or
(888) 655–LAKE

GLENROCK
All American Inn,
500 West Aspen;
(307) 436–2772

Higgins Hotel,
416 West Birch;
(307) 436–9212 (don't let
the exterior scare you off!)

LANDER
Best Western Inn at Lander,
260 Grandview Drive;
(307) 332–2847

Holiday Lodge,
210 McFarlane Drive;
(307) 332–2511 or
(800) 624–1974

Rock Shop Inn,
4260 Highway 28;
(307) 332–7396

LUSK
Hospitality House,
201 South Main;
(307) 334–2120

Town House Motel,
525 South Main;
(307) 334–2376

RIVERTON
Days Inn,
909 West Main;
(307) 856–9677 or
(800) DAYS INN

Holiday Inn,
900 East Sunset Boulevard;
(307) 856–8100 or
(800) HOLIDAY

Sundowner Station,
1616 North Federal;
(307) 856–6503 or
(800) 874–1116

TORRINGTON
King's Inn,
1555 South Main;
(307) 532–4011

Oregon Trail Lodge,
710 East Valley Road;
(307) 532–2101

WHEATLAND
Best Western Torchlight,
1809 North 16th;
(307) 322–4070

Wyoming Motel,
1101 9th Street;
(307) 322–5383

**PLACES TO EAT IN
OREGON TRAIL–
RENDEZVOUS COUNTRY**

(ALL AREA CODES 307)

ATLANTIC CITY
Atlantic City Mercantile,
100 East Main;
332–5143

Sagebrush Saloon & Cafe,
290 Atlantic Road;
332–7404

CASPER
The Cottage,
116 South Lincoln;
234–1157

Sanfords Grub & Pub,
241 South Center;
234–4555

The Goose Egg,
5 miles southwest of
Casper on Highway 220;
473–8838

Boscos,
847 East A Street;
265–9658

First Street Bakers,
260 West First;
472–0255

DOUGLAS
La Bonte Inn,
206 Walnut Street;
358–9856

Clementine's,
1199 Mesa Drive;
358–5554

Country Inn,
2341 East Richards Road;
358–3575

DUBOIS
Cowboy Cafe,
115 East Ramshorn;
455–2595

Old Yellowstone Garage,
112 East Ramshorn;
455–3666

Sally's Dunloggin' Cafe,
305 South 1st Street;
455–2445

GLENROCK
The Paisley Shawl,
inside the Higgins Hotel;
436–9212

Classic Cafe & Pizza,
201 South Fourth;
436–2244

Four Aces,
316 West Birch;
436–9010

LANDER
The Magpie,
159 North 2nd Street;
332–5565

The Ranch,
148 Main Street;
332–7388

LUSK
Fireside Inn,
904 South Main;
334–3477

RIVERTON
China Panda,
302 North Federal;
856–7666

The Depot,
110 South First Street;
856–2221

TORRINGTON
The Bake Haus,
1915 Main Street;
532–2982

WHEATLAND
Breakfast Inn,
86 16th Street;
322–9302

Vimbo's Restaurant,
203 16th Street;
322–3725

General Index

INDEX

INDEX

INDEX

Bed-and-Breakfasts, Hotels, Inns, and Lodges

Restaurants

INDEX

About the Author

Cowboy State native Michael McCoy lives in Teton Valley, Idaho, ten miles from the Wyoming border. His outdoor and travel writing has appeared in *Mountain Sports & Living, Men's Journal, Bicycling, Montana,* and other national and regional publications. McCoy holds degrees in anthropology from the University of Wyoming and zoology from the University of Montana. His other Globe Pequot books are *Montana: Off the Beaten Path, The Wild West,* and *Journey to the Northern Rockies.* He also works part-time for the Montana-based Adventure Cycling Association.